Guide to Australian Battlefields of the Western Front 1916–1918

Tyne Cot Cemetery, Passendale. The Cross of Sacrifice is set above the German blockhouse captured by Australians in October 1917.

Guide to

Australian Battlefields of the Western Front 1916–1918

John Laffin

Kangaroo Press
and
Australian War Memorial

By the Same Author:

Military

Middle East Journey
Return to Glory
One Man's War
The Walking Wounded
Digger (The Story of the Australian Soldier)
Scotland the Brave (The Story of the Scottish Soldier)
Jackboot (The Story of the German Soldier)
Jack Tar (The Story of the English Seaman)
Swifter Than Eagles (Biography of Marshal of the Royal Air Force Sir John Salmond)
The Face of War
British Campaign Medals
Codes and Ciphers
Boys in Battle
Women in Battle
Anzacs at War
Links of Leadership (Thirty Centuries of Command)
Surgeons in the Field
Americans in Battle
Letters From the Front 1914–18
The French Foreign Legion
Damn the Dardanelles! (The Agony of Gallipoli)
The Australian Army at War 1899–1975
The Arab Armies of the Middle East Wars 1948–1973
The Israeli Army in the Middle East Wars 1948–1973
Fight for the Falklands!
The War of Desperation: Lebanon 1982–85
The Man the Nazis Couldn't Catch
On the Western Front
Brassey's Battles (3,500 Years of Conflict)
Holy War (Islam Fights)
Western Front 1916–17 – The Price of Honour
Western Front 1917–18 – The Cost of Victory
World War I in Postcards
Greece, Crete & Syria 1941 (The Australian Campaigns)
Secret and Special
British Butchers & Bunglers of WWI
The World in Conflict
War Annual 1
War Annual 2
War Annual 3
War Annual 4
War Annual 5
War Annual 6
Western Front Illustrated
Panorama of the Western Front
Digging Up the Diggers' War

General

The Hunger to Come (Food and Population Crises)
New Geography 1966–67
New Geography 1968–69
New Geography 1970–71
Anatomy of Captivity (Political Prisoners)
Devil's Goad
Fedayeen (The Arab-Israeli Dilemma)
The Arab Mind
The Israeli Mind
The Dagger of Islam
The Arabs as Master Slavers
The PLO Connections
Know the Middle East
Dictionary of Africa Since 1960

and other titles

Laffin, John, 1992–
Guide to Australian battlefields of the Western Front 1916–1918.

2nd ed.
Includes index.
ISBN 0 86417 620 1.

1. World War, 1914–1918 – Battlefields – France. 2. World War, 1914–1918 – Battlefields – Belgium. 3. World War, 1914–1918 – Australia. 4. World War, 1914–1918 – Battlefields – Guidebooks. I. Australian War Memorial. II. Title.

940.4144

First published in 1992 by Kangaroo Press Pty Ltd
This revised edition published in 1994
3 Whitehall Road Kenthurst NSW 2156 Australia
PO Box 6125 Dural Delivery Centre NSW 2158
Typeset by G.T. Setters Pty Limited
Printed in Singapore by Kyodo Printing Co (S'pore) Pte Ltd

Contents

Acknowledgments

Over many years, numerous people have helped me with battlefield research. Outstanding among them is my wife, Hazelle, who has assisted me in the field and in the library, as a camera assistant, map reader and battlefield companion. The collection of Diggers' epitaphs which appears in this book is largely her work. The only way to see these epitaphs is to make the trip to every military cemetery. Hazelle and I have visited all 758 cemeteries in France and Belgium where Australians are buried. Some we have been to many times.

Other people to whom I owe my thanks for *direct* help are listed here by nationality and without any attempt to gauge their 'importance'.

Australian: Keith Pearson, John Bullen, Peter Stanley, Joyce Bradley, Noel Flanagan, Peter Burness, Stephen Allen, Michael McKernan, of the Australian War Memorial. Don Taggart, Alan Heggen and the late Alf Clarke, Office of Australia War Graves.

British: Steve Grady, Jerry Gee, Carol Kirby, Max Westland, Gordon Cheater, Jackie Whyte, Roger Dalley, Bernard McGee, of the Commonwealth War Graves Commission. The cartographer Philip Halsey drew the maps from my roughs.

French: Andre Coilliot of Arras; Jean Letaille of Bullecourt; Martial Delebarre of Fromelles; Jean Baudelicque of Montbrehain; Jean Pierre Thierry of Villers-Bretonneux. Joëlle Scalbert and Colette Vandeville of CWGC, Arras; M. Van de Kerchoue of Allonville; M. Vanderdriessche of Pozières.

Belgian: Anny de Decker of Steenvoorde; Tony de Bruyne of Ieper; Wilfried Werbrouck of Dikkebus; Charlotte Cardoen-Descamps of Poelcapelle.

In the final stages of work on this book I was aided by a small grant from the Commonwealth War Memorial. It permitted us to spend an intensive ten weeks on the Australian battlefields during the summer of 1989 in order to complete a great deal of essential field research and photography. I am grateful to the Australian War Memorial for this financial assistance.

This book is an original work but it owes something to the AIF official histories of C. E. W. Bean. It is not possible for any military historian to write about the Western Front (or Gallipoli) without reference to Charles Bean's massively detailed accounts of the various Australian operations. He was on the spot and he laboured diligently to obtain information which might otherwise have been lost. His volumes 3,4,5 and 6 of *Australian Operations in France* are indispensable to modern researchers. It is strange, though, that he left Belgium out of the title. As battlefield visitors soon find out, Australians fought and died in great numbers in Belgian Flanders. While Bean's volumes are fundamental research tools, they are not suitable as travel guides. They are just too detailed for this purpose and, naturally, Bean was not attempting to conduct tourists around the battlefields. Those Australians interested in a particular battlefield should read Bean before they set out on their pilgrimage.

Note to second edition

I have received many grateful and often profoundly moving letters from readers of the first edition. Mrs Patricia Smith of Clareville Beach, NSW, wrote: 'Future generations of Australians will call your name blessed for the time and effort, and love, you have put into gathering and publishing information about the WWI soldiers.' This is the most sensitive compliment I have received in half a century of authorship.

With the encouragement of my publisher, David Rosenberg, I have added two chapters to the second edition. One describes further significant cemeteries where Diggers are buried. The second concerns the many Australian commemorative activities on the Western Front in 1993, the 75th anniversary of the end of the war.

I welcome letters and information from families of WWI Diggers.

John Laffin

These deeds
which should not pass away,
names that must not wither

Epitaph on the grave of Private W. N. Smith, 53rd Battalion. He was killed in action at Fromelles on 19 July 1916, aged 24, and is buried in Ration Farm Cemetery, la Chapelle d'Armentières.

I must go
I am ashamed to be seen
without a soldier's uniform

Epitaph on the grave of Private A. K. Mallyon, 48th Battalion. He was killed at Villers-Bretonneux on 3 May 1918 and is buried in Adelaide Cemetery.

Map 1. The Western Front 1914 – 1918

Explanation

This book is a labour of respect. It is the result of the thirty-five years which I have spent on the 1916–18 Western Front of France and Belgium. In that period, 1956–91, my wife and I have 'served' a total of sixty months actually on the battlefields and in the regions where the men of the Australian Imperial Force (AIF) had their training grounds, camps, billets and hospitals. In addition, we have visited every one of the several hundred cemeteries, military and civil, where Australian soldiers are buried.

The AIF was on active service in France and Belgium from March 1916 until the war ended on 11 November 1918. Even then, many Diggers remained in the war areas until well into 1919 before they could be shipped home. A large number of men died in this postwar period, generally from the influenza epidemic which raged at that time. In the thirty-one months of warfare which the Australians spent on the Western Front they established a remarkably high military and personal reputation.

The AIF's area of operations was from Nieuport in Belgium on the Allied left or northern flank, to east of St Quentin, in France, on the right or southern flank. Traced along the front line of mid-1917 this was a distance of about 250 kilometres. The Australians fought across a battlefield that ranged from a few kilometres to 70 kilometres wide. This was because the front fluctuated according to major offensives carried out by one side or the other. Sometimes the AIF captured ground at great cost only to see the Germans retake it, generally while it was being held by some other Allied army. The Diggers would then sometimes be called upon to fight a second campaign or battle to win the territory again.

The human costs were immense. A total of 313 814 men embarked from Australia, including about 6000 who had returned and been discharged, only to re-enlist and re-embark. Those who lost their lives number 59 330 in all theatres of war. Wounds received by Australians number 152 171 — many soldiers were wounded more than once. These casualties amount to a staggering 65 per cent, by far the majority being suffered on the Western Front, where 179 537 Australian men were killed or wounded.

In the most successful period of the Australian campaign, 27 March to 5 October 1918, the five divisions of the Australian Army Corps represented less than 10 per cent of the whole British forces on the Western Front. The Corps' achievements in this period were immense, even when measured only by statistics. The Australians captured 23 per cent of the prisoners, 23.5 per cent of the enemy guns and 21.5 per cent of the ground wrested from the Germans.

The AIF's spiritual presence in modern Flanders (both Belgian and French) and in northern France remains significant. The emblem of the rising sun on soldiers' graves can be seen in cemeteries over a vast area. The names of soldiers with no known grave, listed alphabetically within their units, cover the walls of famous memorials. Each of the five divisions left a monument at the place which seemed most significant to them in terms of battles fought and deeds achieved. In addition, there are plaques in churches and cathedrals and outside on the wall of town halls. In other places, smaller memorials mark particular exploits. In yet others, street names speak of the Australian presence, Rue des Australiens at Mont St Quentin for instance.

In the great majority of places where Australians fought or endured great suffering, or where they lived, trained and rested, there is no monument or plaque. There were just too many actions and too many places for all to be commemorated on site. In most cases, the graves of the Australians who stayed in France and Belgium are the only memorials. There is no more vivid and dramatic example of service, courage, endurance, suffering and sacrifice than the graves.

For a long time the recollections of the French and Belgian people who knew the Australians were a form of memorial, but few were still living in 1990. Fortunately, I was able to speak with many of them during the 1950s and 1960s and where relevant, I have quoted them in this book.

My first visit to an AIF battlefield on the Western Front was to Passchendaele. It so moved me that I knew at once that I must study in comprehensive detail — and in the field — the Australian contribution to the war. I had very personal reasons for wishing to do so. Both my parents served with the AIF on the Western Front, my father as an infantry officer, my mother as a nursing sister. Born in 1922, I grew up during the peak years of the Anzac commemoration era. Most of my parents' friends were veterans and much of their conversation concerned memories of the war. I was not banished from adult company, as so many other children were, and I had many opportunities to ask questions. The former soldiers answered readily. Also, I read voraciously about the war. *Smith's Weekly*, 'the soldiers' newspaper', was a great source of information with its pages of 'Unofficial History of the AIF'. This form of history consisted entirely of soldiers' anecdotes. By the time I joined the second AIF for the second great war I was well informed about the first AIF, but I now had a further opportunity for learning. Many former soldiers, still only in their 40s, joined the forces in 1939 and 1940. Few of them were sent abroad but many served as instructors in the various training camps all over Australia. I met hundreds of them in army schools and messes, and on the training fields, and drew them out about their experiences in the earlier war. It was interesting to see how they used their experience at Gallipoli and on the Western Front in their lessons to recruits of a new generation.

Not surprisingly, by the time I actually reached the Western Front in 1956, I felt a sense of fulfilment. Even more important, I recognised many of the places about which I already had so much knowledge. But there was still much more to learn, especially in applying to the sites the written words of C. E. W. Bean, the official war correspondent, and his contemporaries. Bean's descriptions are superbly detailed but inevitably his accounts lack adequate landmarks. Many of the battlefields which he knew, especially the Somme and Passchendaele, had been laid waste by artillery fire so that few landmarks existed. In any case, when Bean was making his notes it was dangerous to go looking for reference points.

I have found it particularly difficult to follow some Victoria Cross exploits on the ground where they occurred. Many citations are so general in their descriptions that they are no help in fixing where an act of heroism occurred. Battalion histories are little more specific. However, by using all possible sources of reference, including trench maps, and by applying my own military knowledge of terrain, I have been able to give directions to many VC sites with reasonable confidence. In some cases I am certain of the place.

Even after so many years on the Western Front I often find an Australian presence that surprises me, a lonely grave in an obscure hamlet's churchyard, for example. I say to myself, 'What on earth are *you* doing *here*?' The soldier may come from a unit which I know was serving nowhere near the place of burial. The search for the military service which led to his being in that place can produce interesting information.

This book is intended to be more than a mere guide to places which will interest Australians. It is a comprehensive record of AIF service. Many Australians of later generations may be surprised by the extent of that service. The book is also a tribute to the splendid men and their devoted nurses of the Australian Imperial Force. They had style.

A leap of the imagination is required when visiting the battlefields. They are so tranquil, so rural, and rich with crops of all kinds, that the very thought of war is incongruous. The many cemeteries, lovingly cared for by the Commonwealth War Graves Commission, are constant reminders of the conflict but in themselves they are beautiful places, in harmony with the surrounding countryside. The imagination has to supply the vileness, made up of ruin and devastation, the shell holes, trenches and craters, the smoke, flame and noise, the cold and heat, the fear and pain and the shattered bodies.

World War I Australian Soldiers' Service Records

As this edition of *Guide to Australian Battlefields of the Western Front* went to press, the service details of AIF soldiers, formerly held by Central Army Records Office, Melbourne, were transferred to Australian National Archives, Mitchell, Canberra. This is an important transfer as information contained in the files is now in the public domain and it is no longer necessary to prove next-of-kinship to obtain access to a WWI soldier's file. However, many records are too fragile for handling and Archives can supply only photocopies for examination. Inquirers should write to: the Officer in Charge, Australian National Archives, Canberra, Mitchell, ACT 2911.

Using this Book

Australians visiting Europe can give only a limited time to the Western Front. Ideally, they need three weeks and, subjectively, I could wish that all Australians might have a three-months study tour. Realistically, most tourists can devote a maximum of a week to the Western Front. Some allot only a few days, then find that the battlefields are much more interesting than they expected, and wish that they could reshape their arrangements.

The AIF's theatres of operation are divided into seven main areas. They are Belgian Flanders (the Ypres Salient), French Flanders and Northern France, Northern Somme, Southern Somme, East of Bapaume, Mont St Quentin–Peronne, East of Peronne. As certain places do not fit into any of these geographical regions they are described under other categories.

All cities, towns, villages, cemeteries, monuments and battlefields are listed in the general index. Where a settlement or site is known to the French or Belgians by another name or by a different spelling, that name appears in brackets after the wartime name used by the British and Dominion armies. In all travel directions I use the modern local spelling: trying to find Ypres could be difficult on the ground and on a map when the spelling in Flanders is Ieper. A list of place-names appears on page 12.

Since the great majority of AIF actions were carried out in conjunction with British, Canadian, New Zealand and French allies it is neither possible nor desirable in this book to treat the AIF as if it fought and served in isolation. The Diggers would not wish it that way. Sometimes, though, in the writings of British and French historians it is possible to get the idea that Australians and other Dominion troops were not present, since all are lumped under the appellation 'British'. I concentrate on the AIF and if, in so doing, I sometimes give the impression that the Australians (like the New Zealanders) did more than their share, then so be it. The impression reflects the historical truth.

Abbreviations

ADS	Advanced Dressing Station
AFA	Australian Field Artillery
AIF	Australian Imperial Force
CCS	Casualty Clearing Station
CO	Commanding Officer (of a battalion)
CSM	Company Sergeant-Major
CWGC	Commonwealth War Graves Commission
DCM	Distinguished Conduct Medal
DSO	Distinguished Service Order
GHQ	General Head Quarters (the Army HQ)
GOC	General Officer Commanding
HQ	Head Quarters
KIA	Killed in Action
MID	Mention in Despatches
MDS	Main Dressing Station
MM	Military Medal
MC	Military Cross
MO	Medical Officer
NCO	Non-Commissioned Officer
OC	Officer Commanding (of a company)
RAP	Regimental Aid Post
RFA	Royal Field Artillery
RQMS	Regimental Quartermaster-Sergeant
RSM	Regimental Sergeant-Major
VC	Victoria Cross

A Bar to a decoration indicates that the decoration was awarded twice; a Bar is *not* a lesser award.

A Mention in Despatches was shown by a small bronze palm leaf worn on the campaign medal ribbon or, if no medal has been awarded, the palm was pinned to the tunic above the left pocket.

Changes in Place-names

Since 1918 a number of towns and villages have become known by names different from those familiar to soldiers on the Western Front and from those used in the AIF official histories. In most cases the change is the result of many towns in Belgian Flanders adopting Flemish spellings to replace the old French names. These are the main changes as they affect battlefield visitors:

French	*Flemish*
Comines	Komen
Courtrai	Kortrijk
Lille	Rijsel
Locre	Loker
Messines	Mesen
Mons	Bergen
Neuve Eglise	Nieuwkerke
Passchendaele	Passendale
St Ives	St Yvon
Warneton	Waasten
Ypres	Ieper
Yser (river)	Ijser

A few of the many cemetery signs in the Ypres Salient. These five cemeteries lie in Ploegsteert ('Plugstreet') Wood, one of which, Toronto Avenue Cemetery, is entirely composed of AIF graves. The photograph was taken in the mist which so often shrouds the Flanders battlefields.

Bailleul, in French Flanders, is sometimes signposted as Belle.

Priorities

For Australian travellers with little time to spare, I list the most significant sites on the Western Front. In terms of historical, emotional and spiritual importance, it is essential to see these places. They are the irreducible minimum.

Belgian Flanders
- The town of Ypres (Ieper) and Menin Gate.
- Polygon Wood and 5th Division Memorial.
- Messines Ridge and the Ploegsteert Memorial to the Missing.
- Broodseinde Ridge and Tyne Cot Cemetery, near Passchendaele.
- Talbot House in Poperinge and nearby Lijssenthoek Military Cemetery.

Northern France
- Fromelles battlefield and VC Corner Australian Cemetery.
- Anzac Cemetery, Sailly-sur-Lys, near Fromelles.
- Bullecourt battlefield and the AIF memorials there.
- Australian Cemetery, Noreuil, near Bullecourt.

North of the Somme River
- Pozières battlefield, with 1st and 2nd Division memorials; Mouquet Farm; Thiepval Memorial to the Missing; Thiepval Anglo-French Cemetery; AIF Burial Ground, Flers; Pozières British Cemetery. (All these sites are close to one another.)
- Bapaume Australian Cemetery in the town of Bapaume.
- 3rd Division Memorial at Sailly-le-Sec.

South of the Somme
- Villers-Bretonneux and the Australian National Memorial, together with the Anzac Museum at the primary school.
- Villers-Bretonneux Military Cemetery.
- Mont St Quentin and the 2nd Division Memorial.
- Peronne town, close to Mont St Quentin.
- Péronne Communal Cemetery Extension.

The Aisne (east of Péronne)
- 4th Division Memorial at Bellenglise.
- Montbrehain, the site of the AIF's last battle.

For the traveller in a hurry all these places can be visited in three days on the Western Front.

When to tour the battlefields

From November to March the weather is often wet, windy and bitterly cold. Many sites are snowbound or obscured by fog, while others are difficult to reach because of muddy roads and tracks. All the sites listed under **Priorities** are accessible at any time of the year. However, in winter, daylight hours are short and even the most beautiful garden cemetery is not as attractive then as in spring, summer and autumn. Tramping over battlefields — that is, farm fields — is difficult because of the mud. Paths in the many woods are also muddy. The best time to visit the battlefields is summer, effectively June to September, but May and October can be good months. It must be said that the Diggers were not able to choose their seasons for active service and a visit to the Somme in January will give the modern visitor some idea of what the soldiers had to endure.

Transport

By far the best way to see the battlefields is in your own rented car and it is preferable, in terms of convenience and economy, to hire it in Britain. Rent-a-car firms abound in Britain, the best-known being Hertz, Avis, Godfrey Davis and Kennings.

It is possible to travel to Ieper (Ypres) and Albert by train from London and hire a car there. An international licence is preferred to an Australian one. Rates vary enormously and the well-known firms generally turn out to be cheaper.

Driving on the right-hand side of the road is not difficult after the first five minutes at the wheel. Roads in the old battlefield areas are not crowded and the only really busy length of motorway within these areas is that between Lille and Arras. (See maps.)

It is possible to rent a bicycle in Ieper and visit the Salient battlefields and other sites in this way. Much of the countryside is flat and suitable for cycling. Even so, this form of transport is for the fit and younger visitor. Cycling is not recommended in France because the distances are much greater than in Belgium.

It is not possible to travel around by bus; bus services in the battlefield areas are infrequent and in many places non-existent. Even where they do exist, the stops are not arranged for the convenience of foreigners wishing to visit war memorials, cemeteries and battlefields.

General War Guidebook

For general British military history on the Western Front the one indispensable guidebook is *Before Endeavours Fade* by Rose Coombs (Battle of Britain Prints International, London, 1977). Miss Coombs, a former Imperial War Museum official, spent years amassing material for her book, which is profusely illustrated. She describes practically every spot worth visiting on the Western Front, if your interest is in United Kingdom involvement. Her book is very thin on sites of Australian interest but nevertheless, the Coombs book is a valuable tool for those Australian visitors who want to see more of the war than Australian areas of operations. Various itineraries are suggested and cover the entire Western Front.

Places to stay

Ypres (Ieper)

Old Tom, Grote Markt 8, 8900 Ieper, Belgium; Regina, Grote Markt 45, 8900 Ieper; Continental, R. Colaertplein 29, 8900 Ieper; Sultan, Grote Markt 33, 8900 Ieper. Prices (1991) for room and breakfast per night vary from 1000 Belgian francs to 2600; double room with bath, 1000 to 3500.

Poperinge

Poperinge, an interesting small town 13 kilometres west of Ieper, has four places where battlefield tourists might stay. They are: Amfora Hotel, Grote Markt 36, 8970 Poperinge, Belgium; Belfort Hotel, Grote Markt 29, 8970 Poperinge; Palace Hotel, Ieperstraat 34, 8970 Poperinge; Talbot House, Gasthuisstraat 43, 8970 Poperinge. Apart from Talbot House, prices range from 1150 Belgian francs for one person bed and breakfast to 1800 francs per person for full pension. Double and triple rooms are cheaper.

Talbot House is the Toc H hostel founded by Chaplain Tubby Clayton in 1915. Rooms are available to all, not merely to Toc H members, but no meals are provided. Instead, guests may prepare their own meals in the communal kitchen. As Talbot House is in the middle of town, groceries are easily available. Many people find it economical and convenient to get their own meals. The bedrooms have no ensuite facilities but showers are available. Prices are comparable to lower price hotel levels. We often stay at Talbot House, which is roughly the equivalent of a two-star hotel. It is a most evocative place but is not for travellers who want luxury and television.

Somme visits

Bavelincourt

Bavelincourt is a hamlet 10 kilometres west of Albert. The old chateau, in which Australian soldiers were at times billeted, is now a *gite* or guest house with five bedrooms, one of them ensuite. For one person the price, including continental breakfast, is 160 francs but as price is by the room two or three guests pay less. Madame Noel Valengin, Bavelincourt, 80260 Villers-Bocage, France.

Albert
Hotel de la Basilique, 4 Rue Gambetta, Albert 80300 France; Grand Hotel de la Paix, 3–5 Rue Victor Hugo, 80300 Albert; Le Relais Fleurie, 56 Avenue Faidherbe, 80300 Albert. The Basilique and Paix are in the centre of town and the Fleurie is on the edge of town. Room prices vary from 90 French francs per person per night to 260. In France, breakfast is generally charged separately and average price in Albert is 25 francs.

Pozières
Cafe des Routiers, 80300 Pozières, France. This travellers' restaurant has only eight bedrooms (16 beds) so advance booking is essential. 150–200 francs per room, not per person and 60 francs for dinner. Write to Mr Louis Mention and stress that you are Australian.

Ginchy
Mr & Mrs Roger Salmain run a 'Chambres d'Hôtes' establishment (a private hotel) in Rue de Flers, Ginchy, 80360 Combles, France. The hamlet of Ginchy was a centre of battle in 1916. Price of room with breakfast is 120 francs for one person per night, 160 for two people. Quiet, and recommended for Australians.

Grandcourt
The 'Chambres d'Hôtes' run by Mr and Mrs Louis Bellengez at Grandcourt, 80300 Albert, France, is part of their farmhouse. Situated 12 kilometres from Albert, it is very much in the old battlefield, though not in an AIF sector. Four bedrooms (12 beds). Recommended.

Neither of the Chambres d'Hôtes on the Pozières battlefield serve meals other than breakfast but they will provide a picnic lunch.

Peronne
Hostellerie des Ramparts, 21 Rue Beaubois, Peronne, 80200, France. This excellent hotel is in the middle of town. It has thirty-five rooms with prices up to 250 francs, half-pension. An even better hotel, also in the centre of town, is Hôtel St-Claude, 42 Place Louis-Daudre, Peronne 80200. It has thirty-seven rooms with prices rising to 300 francs, half-pension. The staff speak English better than those at the Ramparts. For a good, reasonably priced meal try Auberge 'La Quenouille', 4 Avenue des Australiens, Peronne 80200, on the edge of town on the way to Arras.

Amiens
This large city has many hotels. One of the cheapest is the one-star Central Anzac, 17 Rue Alexandre Patton, Amiens 80000, France. A good two-star hotel in the centre of town is Hôtel Ibis, Le Centrum, Rue du Mal-de Lattre de-Tassigny, Amiens 80000. English is spoken at both hotels and room prices range from 100 francs at Central Anzac to 250 at the Ibis.

Note
Many hotels in the provinces close for their annual holidays for a period during July and August so it is necessary to write for a reservation. Hôtel Ibis is open every day of the year.

General maps
Michelin publish five 1:200 000-scale road maps covering the main areas of the conflict. These are not historical maps and the roads shown are modern, but the maps are useful for visitors, whether driving or on a conducted tour.

Map 51: Boulogne-Lille, covers Lille, Ypres (Ieper), Loos, Passchendaele, Messines, Vimy, Mons, Calais, Bethune and the region north of Arras.

Map 52: Le Havre-Amiens, covers Amiens and district, south of Arras and the battlefields of the Somme.

Map 53: Arras-Charleville, covers the more eastern part of the Somme as well as Arras, Cambrai, St Quentin, Albert, Mons, Valenciennes.

Map 56: Paris-Reims, covers the German advance on Paris in 1914 and important battle areas.

Map 57: Verdun–Wissembourg covers one of the bloodiest battlefields of the war but the AIF was not involved in this sector.

Copies of Maps 51, 52 and 53 have a Commonwealth War Graves Commission overprint to show the position of the CWGC cemeteries, though not the smaller communal cemeteries where soldiers are buried. Each cemetery is indicated by a mauve dot. In effect, the great rash of dots produce a map of death which has a strong emotional effect on everybody who sees it. Some of the CWGC offices have mounted all the maps on their entrance wall in one grand map. While these maps emphasise the scale of casualties in the First World War, they are too small in scale for accurate navigation and no height contours are shown. They may be purchased from the CWGC.

Detailed maps: When visiting the Ypres Salient, Australian visitors should buy Map 28 of the National Geographic Institute (Nationaal geografisch instituut). It is to a scale of 1:50 000 or 1 cm to 500 m. While not a battle map, this map has comprehensive and clear detail. It is easily followed by anybody using this book. Published in Paris, it is available at the larger bookshops in Belgium. For postal inquiries, write in English to NGI, Verkoopdienst, Louizalaan 306-310, B-1050 Brussels, Belgium.

Another useful map for the Salient is the Westhoek-Flanders Touring Map on a scale of 1:132 000. With colours indicating heights and woods, it is bold and clear and provides an excellent picture of the Salient. Copies may be purchased from the tourist office in Ieper.

When touring the battlefields of France, the best maps are those of the National Geographic Institute, 1:25 000 (1 cm to 250 m). They are available in stationers and bookshops *(libraries)* and are generally displayed on racks. Ask for *serie bleu* (blue series) maps which cost between 33 and 39 francs each. They have a code number and on the cover is printed, for map identification, the name of a major town in the area.

For Australians travelling in AIF areas, the vital maps are:

- West Somme—*Map 2408 Ouest Albert.* Covers an entire area of AIF activity: Warloy-Baillon, Millencourt, Heilly, Mericourt-l'Abbe, Ribemont-sur-Ancre, Ville-sur-Ancre, Morlancourt, Hamel, Albert, Villers-Bretonneux and other places.
- East Somme—*Map 2408 Est/Bray-sur-Somme.* Covers another list of virtual Australian placenames: Fricourt, Montauban, part of Pozières, Maricourt, Proyart, Chuignolles, Cappy, Herbecourt, Hem-Monacu.
- From Pozières to Bapaume—*Map 2407 Est/Bapaume.* Covers the most important AIF battlefield of 1916-17, including Pozières, Flers, Gueudecourt, Ligny-Thilloy, Lesboeufs and Bapaume.
- East of Bapaume to Hindenberg Line—*Map 2507 Ouest/Croisilles.* Covers another major AIF area, including Bullecourt, Cagnicourt, Noreuil, Boursies, Hermies, Lagnicourt, Beugny, Vaulx-Vraucourt, Hendecourt.
- French Flanders and south-west Belgian Flanders—*Map 2402 Est/Armentières.* Covers Fromelles, Ploegsteert, Nieuwkerke, Nieppe, Warneton, River Lys.
- Hazebrouck area—*Map 2404 Ouest/Hazebrouck.* Covers many places associated with AIF operations, including Bailleul, Meteren, Merville, Estaires, Vieux-Berquin, Neuf-Berquin.
- Mont St Quentin and Peronne—*Map 2508 Ouest/Peronne Ouest.* Covers the famous 1918 battlefields of Mont St Quentin and Peronne, as well as Bouchavesnes, Clery, Doingt, Allaines and Haut-Allaines.
- Aisne battlefields of 1918—*Map 2508 East/Peronne Est.* Covers the AIF's advance from Peronne through Hancourt, Ste-Emilie, Ronssoy, Templeux-le-Guérard, Hargicourt, Villaret, le Verguier to Bellicourt.
- Final AIF campaign—*Map 2608 Ouest/Villers-Outreaux.* Covers Bellenglise and the St Quentin Canal, Estrees, Joncourt, Jeancourt, Ramicourt, Beaurevoir and Montbrehain.
- Southern Somme—*Map 2409 Est/Roye.* Covers many of the battlefields east and south-east of Villers-Bretonneux, including Rosières, Vermandovillers, Lihons, Vauvillers. This is not an essential map but it is useful to complete the set.

Battlefield Tours

Your first inquiry should be to the Returned Services League in your capital city. The RSL runs annual tours and knows of the private organisers who arrange tours.

In Britain, France and Belgium no organisation or tour operator offers standard tours to places of exclusively Australian interest. In fact, some of the operators have little knowledge of Australian involvement in Western Front operations. Understandably, this always comes as a shock to Australians. However, several British firms offer excellent general-interest Western Front battlefield tours. Australian visitors who do not wish to drive themselves around the Western Front may find these coach tours adequate. Remember, however, that they operate to an hour-by-hour programme. There is no time for visitors with particular interests to wander off on their own.

The battlefield tour operators include:

- Flanders Tours, 4 Spencer House, 45a Crystal Palace Rd, London SE22 9EX. This group, headed by Lieutenant-Colonel Graham Parker, operates tours from the Continent and Britain. In 1989 it was appointed tour operator for the Western Front Association.
- Major and Mrs Holt's Tours, 15 Market St, Sandwich, Kent. With vast experience in the

field, the Holts offer excellently run tours, if you don't mind being tightly organised.

- Martin Middlebrook, 48 Linden Way, Boston, Lincolnshire OE21 9DS. Mr Middlebrook is a military historian and is well informed. His tours are more informal than those of the Holts.
- No Man's Land Tours, 155 Bedfont Close, Bedfont, Feltham, Middlesex, TW14 8LQ.

Autralians with a real interest in the Western Front should consider membership of the Western Front Association. Founded in 1980 the WFA produces an excellent quarterly magazine and sells copies of trench maps and other useful aids to battlefield search and travel. Membership secretary: Paul Cobb, 50 Wealden Way, Tilehurst, Berkshire, RC3 6DA, Great Britian.

Office of Australian War Graves

Australians planning visits to Western Front cemeteries and battlefields should make their first inquiries to the Office of Australian War Graves, which is part of the Department of Veterans Affairs. The Office provides a service in advising on the location of memorials to the missing and burial places of Australian servicemen. It can supply grave and cemetery details and, in most cases, it can suggest whom to contact for further information. The address is: Office of Australian War Graves, P.O. Box 21, Woden, ACT 2606; telephone (06) 289 1111 and ask for War Graves.

When writing to the Office of Australian War Graves or to the Commonwealth War Graves Commission to seek information about a casualty's place of burial, provide as much information as possible. This could be not only the full name but service number, rank and unit. Also supply the date of death if known. A common name, such as Smith or Jones, can present difficulties without additional information.

Commonwealth War Graves Commission

As the Imperial War Graves Commission, this institution was established in 1917. Its function is to maintain the graves of the Commonwealth forces killed in the two world wars and to keep records and registers. Cost of the work is shared by the governments of Britain, Canada, Australia, New Zealand, India, Pakistan and South Africa.

Any Australian visiting the Western Front and wishing to trace a particular grave or cemetery may contact the Commission in Britain, France or Belgium. At the offices of the CWGC in France and Belgium the principal officers are British. Those handling visitors' inquiries are local people but all are fluent in English.

The addresses are: Commonwealth War Graves Commission, No. 2 Marlow Rd, Maidenhead, Berkshire SL6 7DX, UK; telephone 0628 34221. Commonwealth War Graves Commission, Rue Angele Richard, 062217 Beaurains, France; telephone 21 710324 (Beaurains is a suburb of Arras). Commonwealth War Graves Commission, Elverdingestraat 82, B-8900 Ieper, Belgium; telephone 057 200118.

The Commission does not arrange battlefield tours but visitors should not be hesitant about approaching the cemetery gardeners. Many of them speak English and are very ready to speak about their work. Most know little about the campaigns and battles which produced the cemeteries but a few are knowledgeable.

Using the register at a military cemetery

Most cemeteries have a register of graves, which is kept in a brass box either in the shelter near the gate or in a recess in the wall near the gateway. The book has a simple sketch map showing the location of other cemeteries nearby and a plan showing the layout of the cemetery. Each cemetery is divided into plots and rows and each headstone has a number carved into its shoulder. In the register, the number of a plot is indicated by a Roman numeral, the row by a capital letter and the grave by a number. For instance, in Adelaide Cemetery, Villers-Bretonneux, the grave of Sergeant David Allan MM, 52nd Battalion, is III.E.8. Even in a large cemetery any grave can be located in a few minutes. Occasionally, the CWGC departs from this system and uses Arabic numerals for the plot number. The inconsistency has been cited in this book. Some cemeteries are too small for the graves to be set out in plots, hence the graves appear in the register without Roman numerals. This also applies to a few larger cemeteries.

The particulars given in the register were compiled from information supplied by Record Offices and next-of-kin. In all cases, the relatives were asked to furnish the personal information they wished to appear in the register and where possible this was reproduced in their actual words. Where little information appears this is as the next-of-kin wished. For instance, in some entries no home address is given, in others the soldier's age was omitted.

At cemeteries where a register is provided there is also a visitors' book. It is often signed by French and Belgian visitors who, understandably, outnumber the British and Dominion visitors. Australian names and addresses are appearing more and more frequently.

General tourism in wartime areas

In this book I have necessarily concentrated on Flanders and the Somme as battlefields but they have other attractions for visitors. In Belgium, the town of Ieper is particularly interesting and the centre of numerous festivals. It is a good base for visiting the whole of West Flanders. Bruges and Ghent attract many visitors. Poperinge, 10 kilometres from Ieper, is a hop-growing centre and every three years the town holds a hop festival. In the *département* of the Somme, the city of Amiens is worth a visit. After all, the great cathedral possesses many treasures other than the memorial plaque to the AIF. Here are some addresses for general tourism inquiries:

- Ieper: Tourist Information Office, Stadhuis, Grote Markt, Ieper 8900, Belgium.
- Amiens: Comite Departemental du Tourisme de la Somme, Rue Ernest Cauvin 21, 80000 Amiens, France.
- Albert: Tourist Office, 4 Rue Gambetta, 80300 Albert, France (closed October–April).
- Poperinge: Tourist Information Office, Stadhuis, Poperinge, 8970, Belgium.

These Anzac brothers-in-arms in Bailleul Communal Cemetery Extension, northern France, were killed during the Battle of Messines. Conjoined badges are rare and indicate that the remains of the men could not be separated.

Unknown Soldiers

Graves of unidentified soldiers abound. They are unknown because every scrap of identification was somehow lost. Some men were blown to pieces by shellbursts and their identity discs and other potential distinguishing information, such as personal possessions and unit identification, disappeared. Many soldiers were buried with an identity disc still around their neck, in the standard way, but their graves were destroyed in later bombardments. Their remains may have been later gathered but without the vital identity disc. Many bodies remained unburied because burial parties could not safely reach them. Finally, when the remains could be buried identification might not have been possible.

Graves of unknown soldiers may be engraved in one of several ways. The basic style is:

A Soldier of the Great War
Known Unto God

If the soldier's rank is known the inscription will be:

An Australian Soldier
of the Great War
a lieutenant

Another inscription:

An Australian Soldier of
an infantry regiment
(or an artillery or other regiment)

Visitors to the war cemeteries will notice that in the case of British unidentified soldiers the regiment is nevertheless often precisely stated. This is because each British unit had its own distinctive metal badge and shoulder title and these often survived the fighting, the mud and the rain. Australian soldiers' only identification was the large 'rising sun' badge on the hat and smaller ones on the collar. The unit was indicated only by a felt colour patch worn on the upper arm of each sleeve. The shape and colour combination indicated the unit but these patches did not survive the period between a soldier's first burial on the battlefield and his final reinterment in an organised cemetery, perhaps years later. Nevertheless, sometimes enough of a colour patch remained for war graves staff to be able to discern a dead man's unit.

About 18 450 Diggers have no *known* grave on the Western Front but many of them have an unidentified grave in the cemeteries.

Above: Thousands of Diggers killed in action could not be identified. One of these graves holds the remains of three men so badly mangled by a shellburst that they could not be separated.

Right: Two Australians and a soldier of the Royal Engineers lie in the grave at left while two Diggers and a Scottish soldier lie under the centre stone. Note the conjoined badges. These graves are in Bailleul Communal Cemetery Extension, northern France.

The battlefield of Flanders as the Diggers saw it in 1917. Shelling reduced the trees of Sanctuary Wood to mere stalks and the fields to bogs. Many wounded and helpless soldiers drowned in the mud.

The Road to the Western Front

The soldiers of the AIF who were in the Middle East during 1914–15 had only a rough idea of the conflict in Europe. Most of their attention and energy was devoted first to training in Egypt and then, in the case of the 1st and 2nd Divisions, to the campaign on the Gallipoli peninsula. They heard and read about the 'Western Front' and the fighting there and most of them expected to be sent there in due course.

The Gallipoli misadventure over, with its hardships and high glory, the Australians rested in Egypt while they absorbed their reinforcements from home. They were a talking point among British leaders. Early in 1916 the Chief of the Imperial General Staff, General W. R. Robertson, telegraphed the British commander in Egypt: 'Three Anzac Divisions in France in April might be worth six at a later date'. This was an indirect compliment about the prestige they had won at Gallipoli.

The British and French troops along the Western Front had suffered terribly since August 1914 and Robertson knew that they needed help. The losses in men had been enormous. For instance, the Battle of Loos in September 1915 had cost General Sir John French 61 280 casualties. The British regular army had ceased to exist long before Loos and the divisions of the New Army created by Lord Kitchener, the Secretary of State for War, were being rushed into the trenches as fast as possible. But many units were raw and as crisis succeeded crisis, well-trained and veteran soldiers were needed.

The Australians in Egypt, avid for news, read the British newspapers on sale in Cairo. The reports gave them a false impression of the events in France and Belgium, since they emphasised the heroism of the troops rather than the horrors of the Western Front. Correct figures about the heavy casualties were censored and some defeats were presented as honourable draws if they could not be painted as victories.

In Egypt the Australians came to accept that the Gallipoli campaign had been a sideshow and that the war would be decided in Europe. They were anxious to move on and most believed they would be sent direct to England, or 'Home' as they called it.

The order to move came in March and Lieutenant-General Sir William Birdwood, the English general who had commanded them at Gallipoli, visited each brigade and gave the men the news, often during a church parade. He explained that they would be going to France, whose young men were already fighting for their country. He appealed to the men's honour to uphold the good name of Australia among the British, Canadian, French and other allied soldiers with whom they would be working.

On the troop ships which ferried the AIF across the Mediterranean to France the men speculated about what lay in store for them. Many were puzzled as to why the Allied armies could not drive the German invaders back to their own country. The Western Front, as shown in diagrams in the British newspapers, was a very long one. Surely it was possible to break the Germans somewhere.

Lieutenant F. P. Bethune, a minister turned soldier of the 3rd Machine-Gun Company, expressed his comrades' sense of idealism during a sermon on the troop ship *Transylvania*.

We know what we have come for. We have all read of the things that happened in France. We came of our free wills, to say that this sort of thing shall not happen in the world so long as we are in it. And what if we die? If it were not for the dear ones whom he leaves behind, might not a man pray for a death like that? We know we are not heroes and we do not wish to be called heroes. Here we are on a great enterprise with no thought of gain or conquest but to help right a great wrong. With our dear ones behind, and God above, and our friends on each side, and only the enemy in front, what more do we wish than that?

Lieutenant Bethune did well as a soldier. He won the Military Cross and issued one of the most famous orders in AIF history (see **Buff Bank**).

On 19 March 1916 the troop ships carrying the 2nd Division reached Marseilles on the Mediterranean coast, where the reputation of Australians as wild men in Cairo had aroused fears of riots. But no trouble occurred and when the 2nd and then the 1st Divisions had passed through Marseilles, British transport officers reported that no troops had ever given them less trouble.

Rumbling French troop trains carried the excited Australians through the lovely countryside of southern France, which showed no sign of war. Then the trains reached the battle area of the north, still in the grip of the long winter. The weather was wet, cold and snowy when the AIF men reached their billets in barns and houses of the St Omer-Aire-Hazebrouck area of French Flanders. They knew from the explosions of shells in the distance and the gunflashes and flares that they had reached the 'real war'.

But they were not yet in combat, only in what the army knew as 'the Nursery'. This was a region where reinforcements were trained before being posted into the trenches. The training was intense, with lectures on preventing frostbite and how to relieve a trench garrison, on the vital need for bathing and disinfection, on map-reading and observation. Many company officers, NCOs and men were sent to schools to learn about trench mortars, which they had not previously seen, and about sniping and bombing in the Western Front type of warfare.

AIF reconnaissance parties entered the line for the first time on 1 April and on the night of 7 April the 2nd Division was considered skilled enough to take over a sector. By mid-April the two Australian divisions were in the line at Fleurbaix, just south of Armentières. The Australians were now really on the Western Front.

Western Front - background

The term Western Front was applied to the German Western Front to distinguish it from the Russian or Eastern Front. However, the French and British allies quickly picked it up and adopted it. It referred to the battle line which, by 1915, stretched in an unbroken line of 700 kilometres from the Belgian coast, near Nieuport, to the Swiss border near Belfort.

From Nieuport to about Noyon, the Western Front ran on a north-south line. From Noyon to Verdun it ran east-west, but at Verdun it veered towards the south-east until it ended at Belfort. The Belgian army (or sometimes the French) held the far left of the allied line from Nieuport to Dixmuide, in Belgium. The British and Dominion troops held the north-central sector from Dixmuide to the Aisne River, and the French guarded the remainder of the line, the greatest length. Strategic or tactical requirements sometimes brought variations of these sectors.

For much of their front, the Belgians kept the Germans at bay by simple if drastic military engineering. First, the engineers dammed the culverts along the embankment which carried the Nieuport-Dixmuide railway. Then they jammed open the lock gates on the Yser River and its associated canals and allowed water to flood the fields. That part of the front became impassable. The Belgians arranged a new defence line along the railway which had become, in effect, a dyke.

Elsewhere, because of the complex trench system and its associated broad fields of barbed wire, neither side could achieve a breakthrough. Capture of the frontline trenches could never mean victory because behind the front trench lay the support trench and

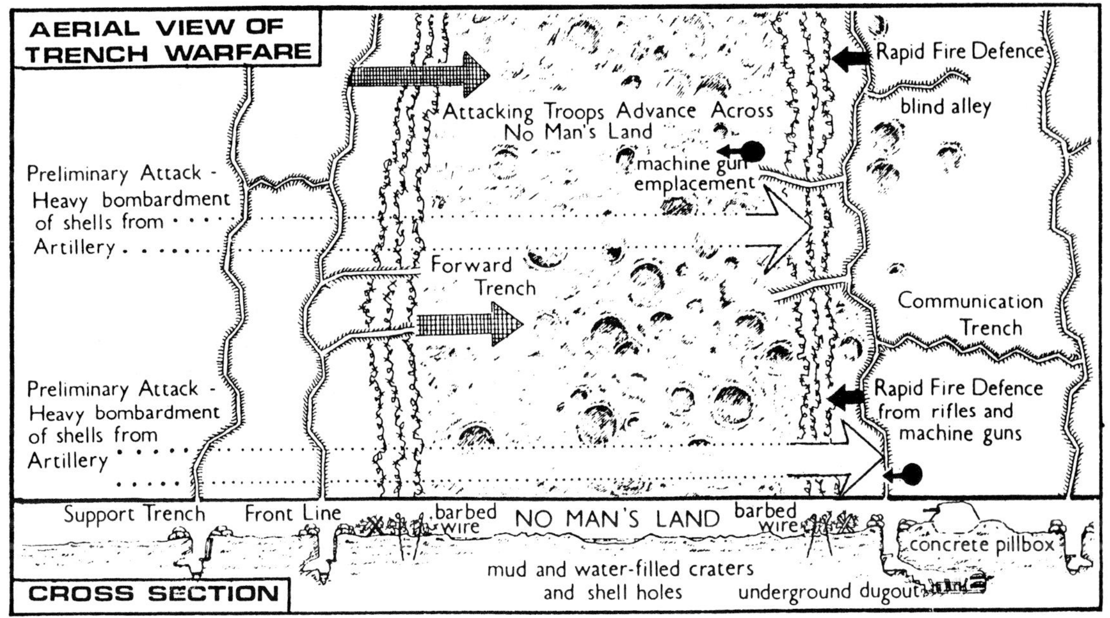

Sketch by David Simkin in *Contemporary Accounts of the First World War.*

then the reserve trench, both continuously manned. The Germans had several rows of trenches. First, the firing trench on their side of No Man's Land, then, about 20 metres to the rear, the 'cover' trench, followed by their support trench line, then the reserve trench line. Linking these well-made trenches with their deep protective shelters, were communication trenches. In key places switch trenches were prepared so that should the enemy break through the Germans still faced them in other trenches to which they had 'switched'. Within a single square kilometre there might be a mesh of trenches making a total length of 100 kilometres.

Life in the trenches, especially those of the front line, was sheer misery. The ever-present foul smell was a mixture of dead bodies, excrement, filthy men and the cordite from their rifles. Men reached the front lice-free but were soon infested. Rats, which gorged on the dead, were huge and aggressive. Trenches offered no shelter and uneasy sleep came only in snatches. For much of the year conditions were muddy, wet and unbearable; in summer they were stifling, hot and unbearable. All the time the soldiers faced the danger of death or maiming by bullet, grenade, high explosive shell or shrapnel shell. Thousands of men were blown to pieces. After a shellburst in a trench, dazed soldiers would look around to find that some of their mates had disappeared.

Against German defence in depth and massed machine-guns, the British and French generals could devise no better tactics than frontal assaults. Hundreds of battles, large and small, were fought along the Western Front. After 1915 the majority were initiated by the British or French and all resulted in shocking casualties. The principal offensives are shown below, with those involving the AIF printed in bold type.

1915

Allied offensive in Artois and Champagne, 1 January–30 March.

Battle of the Wöevre, 6–15 April. Repeated French assaults against the north side of the St Mihiel salient were repulsed with heavy losses.

Second Battle of Ypres, 22 April–25 May.

Battles of Festubert and Souchez (Second Battle of Artois), May–June.

Renewed offensives in Artois and Champagne, 25 September–6 November. The main battle was at Loos.

1916

Battle of Verdun, 21 February–18 December.

First Battle of the Somme, 1 July–13 November.

1917

Battle of Arras, 9–15 April. Capture of Vimy Ridge.

Battles of Bullecourt, April–May.

Nivelle Offensive (Second Battle of the Aisne, Third Battle of Champagne) 16–20 April.

British offensive in Flanders June–July. Messines captured.

Third Battle of Ypres (Passchendaele) 31 July–10 November.

Battle of Cambrai, 20 November–3 December.

1918

German Somme offensive, 21 March–5 April.

German Lys offensive, 9 April–8 May.

German Aisne offensive, 27–30 May.

First American offensive; Battle of Cantigny, 28 May.

Battles of Chateau Thierry and Belleau Wood, 30 May–17 June.

German Noyon-Montdidier offensive, 9–13 June.

German Champagne-Marne offensive and Second Battle of the Marne, 15–19 July.

Allied counter-offensive. Aisne-Marne, 18 July–5 August.

Allied Amiens offensive, 8–11 August; 21 August–4 September.

Second Battle of the Somme, 21 August–3 September.

Allied Meuse-Argonne offensive, 26 September–11 November.

Hindenberg Line offensive, 27 September–17 October.

British-Belgian final Flanders offensive, 28 September–14 October.

Allied Sambre-Scheldt offensive, 17 October–11 November.

Casualties on the Western Front: German and Austrian 1 500 000 killed, 3 500 000 wounded; French 1 250 000 killed, 4 000 000 wounded; British Empire 1 000 000 killed, 2 000 000 wounded; Belgian 13 745 killed, 44 686 wounded.

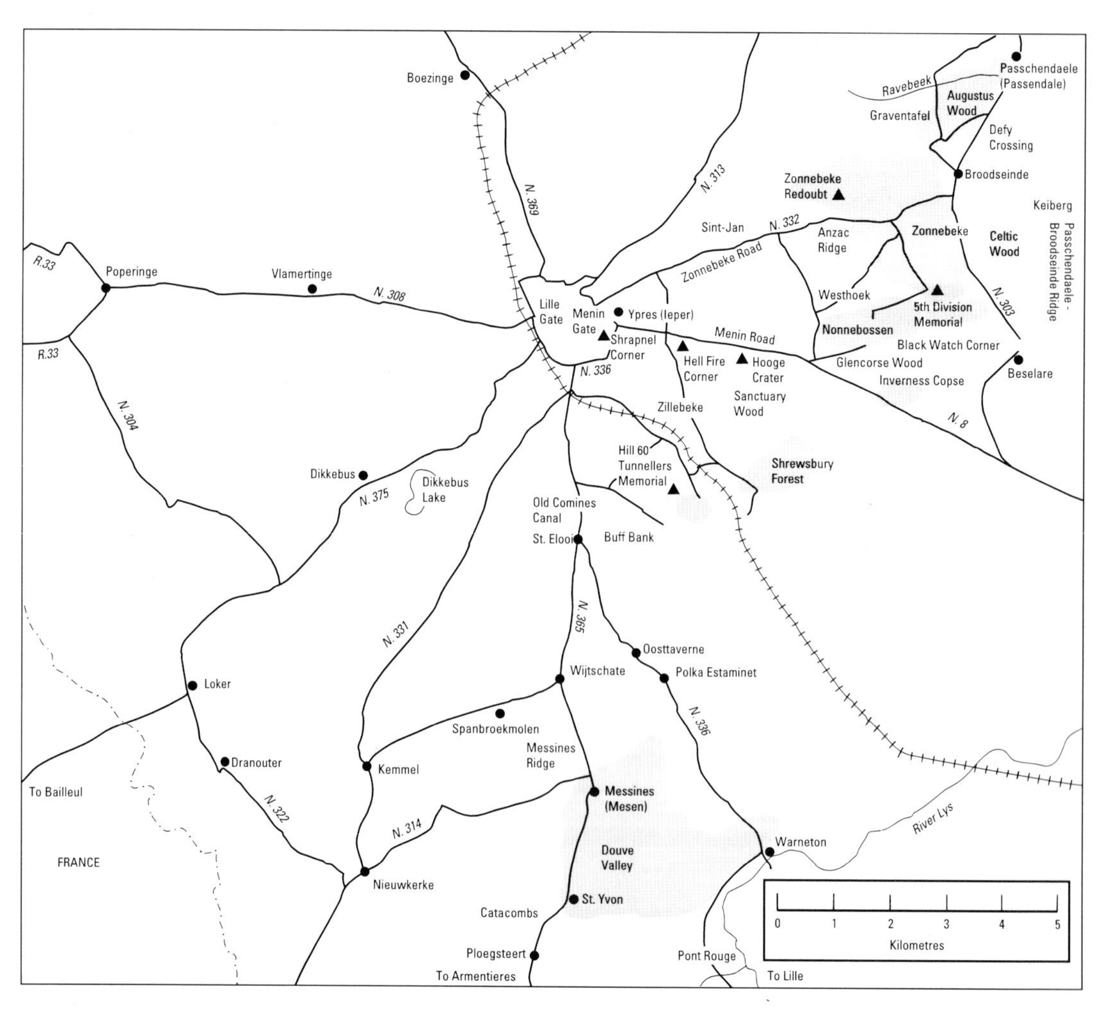

Map 2. Ypres Salient: AIF battlefields (Shaded)

Chapter 1

Ypres Salient - Belgian Flanders

A salient is a bulge driven into an enemy's front line. The Ypres Salient was the result of the first Battle of Ypres, 30 October–24 November 1914, when the British pressed a great dent into the straight German line. It ran from Boezinge in the north to Wytschaete, further south. A salient is deadly for the attackers, since the defenders can then fire into it from three sides. Thus, the British and Dominion troops were terribly vulnerable. In May 1917 the arc forming the bulge was no more than 20 kilometres long and at its furthest point east it was about 5 kilometres deep. This area, which was to become larger during the battles of the second half of 1917, was one of the most notorious killing fields of the Western Front.

General Haig launched eight offensives during the Third Battle of Ypres, or the Battle of Passchendaele as it became better known. By the time he settled on a winter front line in mid-November the British and Dominion armies had suffered 448 614 casualties since 31 July. Haig had captured no more than about 130 square kilometres of territory and his troops had inflicted 217 000 casualties on the German Army. In all, throughout the war the British and Dominion forces suffered more than one million casualties in the salient. All five AIF divisions were involved in fierce fighting there at one time or another between late 1916 and October 1917.

The tremendous bombardments by both sides tore the land to pieces, destroying the intricate drainage system of the flat land. Every ditch and stream was dammed with shell-torn earth so that when rain fell the entire battlefield turned into a morass and every shell hole and mine crater filled with water. Men could walk, though only with great effort. Guns, lorries and carts were bogged and supplies could not reach the infantry in the front trenches. At times nobody knew the position of the advancing units, so they went unsupplied and unfed.

In many large areas the only way across the fields of mud was by slatted footways known as duckboards. Should a man fall off a duckboard into the mud — or be blown off — he needed instant help to get out. Many wounded soldiers who toppled into the mud sank and were suffocated. Some of the worst stretches of morass were in the Australian and New Zealand sectors of October 1917. British rather than German artillery had created the quagmire. When a company went over the top in an advance it could not make a steady, uniform attack. The men had to find a path around the edge of shell holes, each man dragging one foot after the other from the sucking slime. Entire platoons, stuck in mud to the waist, were wiped out by machine-gun fire. The countless pools of water were full of stinking ooze and bodies or pieces of bodies. Fumes hung around the swamps for days after a gas attack.

Histories of Western Front warfare, including the official volumes by the incomparable Charles Bean, contain numerous references to the 'ridges' of the Ypres Salient — Broodseinde Ridge, Passchendaele Ridge and Messines Ridge, for instance. To understand the Ypres battlefield it is vital to realise that 'ridges' is a misleading term for people accustomed to thinking in terms of the Great Dividing Range and other mountains of Australia, or the precipitous ridges of Papua-New Guinea. In the Ypres Salient there is merely low ground and not-so-low ground. Broodseinde–Passchendaele Ridge, for instance, rises to a maximum of 60 metres over a distance of several kilometres and the gradient is barely perceptible. No definite ridge line exists and no vehicle need change from top gear. The entire country is flat but in certain areas it has a gentle slope. The nearest thing to the general notion of a ridge — or at least one that was fought over — is that on which stands the New Zealand memorial at Messines.

Advice and directions

For Australian visitors, the Ypres Salient is one of the most important sites on the Western Front. At least two full days are needed for a satisfactory Salient tour, since all the sites mentioned in this section of the book can then be visited. In particular, refer to Battle of Broodseinde, Battle of Menin Road, Battle of Passchendaele, Battle of Messines, Celtic Wood, Augustus Wood, Zonnebeke Redoubt, Tyne Cot Cemetery. For a good vantage point, go to Tyne Cot, climb on to one of the old German blockhouses and face the spires of Ieper. Ahead of you is a shallow basin stretching right and left. Behind you is Broodseinde Ridge. Within a few square kilometres of where you stand, thousands of Australian soldiers were killed or wounded. The remains of many hundreds who have no known grave lie there still. Their sacrifice was wasted. The final German onslaught of March — April 1918 swallowed up the gains made in the Salient by the Australians and others. At the end the British held an area that consisted of little more than Ypres itself and its outskirts.

Anzac Ridge or Spur, Zonnebeke

This length of higher ground ran north-south across the line of the British advance towards the Broodseinde Ridge. It was well-named considering the amount of Australian and New Zealand activity in the area. The spur was the 2nd Division's objective on 20 September 1917. Nothing distinctive remains but the ground is easily seen.

Directions
From Ieper, take the N332 Zonnebeke road 3.5 km to the great brickworks on the left. Here the road passes over the Hanebeke (a creek). Anzac Ridge is just beyond the creek and to its right. It runs north-south and is roughly parallel to the creek. Right of Anzac Ridge and 2 km distant is Polygon Wood.

Augustus Wood, Passchendaele

Augustus Wood, really only a large copse, was a feature on the Passchendaele-Beselare line, north of Tyne Cot and a little to the east of it. Despite atrocious weather and virtually uncrossable mud, General Haig ordered an attack on Passchendaele for 12 October 1917. It was made by the AIF 3rd Division and the New Zealand Division attacking side by side, with the AIF 4th Division in support. East of Augustus Wood the enemy machine-gunners, manning large blockhouses, stopped the advance. Captain Clarence Smith Jeffries of the 34th Battalion organised an assault party and rushed one the strongpoints, capturing four machine-guns and thirty-five prisoners. Under shellfire and machine-gun fire he ran his company forward at the double until another blockhouse stopped him. Again he planned an attack and was leading it when an enemy gunner swung his gun around and killed him. Sergeant J. Bruce completed the capture. Largely because of Jeffries' work some units reached the edge of Passchendaele. Jeffries, who was 23, was awarded the VC. Every officer of his battalion was killed or wounded that day.

Directions
Augustus Wood no longer exists but it is possible to find the site, as it was only 500 metres to the left of Tyne Cot Cemetery — that is, north of the cemetery. The Germans incorporated the wood into their defences of the Flanders I Line.

Captain Clarence Smith Jeffries VC is one of the 1368 Australians buried in Tyne Cot Cemetery on Broodseinde Ridge, near Passendale. In the background is a German blockhouse which the Diggers captured.

Broodseinde battlefield, near Passendale. On the far slope, 11 956 soldiers, including 1368 Australians, lie in Tyne Cot Cemetery. AIF units advanced from close to where this photograph was taken.

Battle of Broodseinde Ridge, Ypres 4 – 5 October 1917

This fight on 4 October 1917 was the AIF's third battle of the campaign to break out of the Ypres Salient. It was the most important of the Australians' actions of late 1917 and potentially the most decisive. After the Battle of Polygon Wood the 1st and 2nd Divisions replaced the 4th and 5th in the front line and were joined by the 3rd Division. On the 3rd's immediate left the New Zealand Division came into the line. This put four Anzac divisions side by side for the first time. They were the centre of a line of 12 divisions, the others being British, on a 13-kilometre front. The left, or northern boundary, was Graventafel Spur. Broodseinde was roughly in the middle and on the right was the village of Molenaarelshoek (Molenhoek on modern maps). Broodseinde Ridge was the Germans' main defensive line and from its greater height the German Staff viewed most of the Allied salient. The Australians reached their start positions during the night of 3 October and lay in shell holes under a steady drizzle.

Unknown to the British Command, the Germans had planned an attack for 4 October at precisely the same time as the British attack. At 5.20 a.m. the German guns opened, to be followed by a trench-mortar bombardment. About one Australian in seven was hit. The Australian barrage began at 6 a.m. and the surviving Diggers scrambled up and moved forward. At that moment 30 metres in front of them, infantry of the German 212th Regiment rose in front of them to begin their advance. The Australian Lewis gunners fired first, the enemy broke and few survived the Australian bayonet charge.

Sergeant Lewis McGee of the 40th Battalion, armed only with a revolver, dashed 50 metres across bullet-swept ground, shot some of a machine-gun crew who had caused many Australian casualties, captured the rest and seized the gun. McGee reorganised the advance at that part of the battlefield and showed outstanding leadership throughout a week's fighting. He was killed on 12 October, before he could learn of his award of the VC. On the same section of front Lance-Corporal Walter Peeler, of the 3rd Australian Pioneer Battalion, went into the attack with the 37th Battalion. Armed with a Lewis machine-gun, he attacked several enemy posts, killed thirty Germans and set such a fine example that the 37th Battalion captured 420 Germans, and twenty machine-guns, though it lost forty-seven of its own men killed and 152 wounded.

On the 40th Battalion's front, Captain H. J. Dumaresque with some men captured two blockhouses. As he reached one of these strongpoints, a German officer appeared, revolver in hand. Dumaresque knocked him unconscious with a blow to the jaw. Leaving the German, Dumaresque went on to help clear a second blockhouse. In the same

The Great Cross at Tyne Cot Cemetery was built over a blockhouse captured by the AIF in October 1917. In the foreground is one of the many blockhouses which defended the Broodseinde crest.

action Lieutenant C. H. Cane, also of the 40th, captured thirty-one prisoners from one blockhouse without firing a shot.

The Australians crossed the Passchendaele-Beselare road and reached trenches dug by British troops in the first months of the war, before Broodseinde Ridge was captured by the Germans. After capturing this strategic higher ground, the Australians, who had known nothing but mud for weeks, looked down on an amazing sight — green fields, hedgerows and farm houses still intact. This was German-held territory. British guns soon ranged on to the farms and demolished them. At the same time the Australians, triumphant on the crest, came under sniper fire and shellfire. The 41st Battalion was particularly badly hit. Despite its losses, the AIF counted the battle of Broodseinde one of its great successes.

Part of a German blockhouse shows through the large bronze wreath. The blockhouse forms the base for the Cross of Sacrifice at Tyne Cot Cemetery, Passendale.

Directions

The battle area is readily located. From Ieper, take the Zonnebeke road and pass through the village to the major T-junction. Turn left on to the Beselare-Passendale road, which runs north-south along the Broodseinde plateau. Follow the sign, on left, to Tyne Cot Cemetery. Tyne Cot is roughly in the middle of the AIF front of 4 October and to the right of middle of the 12 October attack. (See **Augustus Wood and Battle of Passchendaele**.) From Tyne Cot, drive north along the minor road towards

Passendale and it will take you across the old battlefield. Under fire, Diggers crossed your line of travel to attack German positions along the ridge on your right. You can reach Passendale from this road but its capture was never a direct AIF achievement. The exhausted and depleted AIF divisions were withdrawn and Canadian divisions were sent in to finish the job.

Buff Bank, Zillebeke

This position was close to the better-known Spoil Bank. However, Buff Bank is significant in AIF history as the site at which a famous order was issued. On 13 March 1918 Lieutenant F. P. Bethune, commanding No. 1 Section of the 3rd Machine-Gun Company, was instructed to post his guns at Spoil Bank. He considered the Spoil Bank position suicidally dangerous and demurred. Nevertheless, he led his men there. Before he could get into position a runner reached him with orders that he was now to establish his guns at Buff Bank. This was a good position but, without infantry nearby to cover them, the machine-guns were dangerously exposed. With the safety of that part of the line in his hands Bethune considered that his men should have written orders. He issued these instructions:

SPECIAL ORDERS No. 1 Section
13.3.18

1. This position will be held, and the Section will remain here until relieved.
2. The enemy cannot be allowed to interfere with this programme.
3. If the Section cannot remain here alive, it will remain here dead, but in any case it will remain here.
4. Should any man through shell-shock or other cause attempt to surrender, he will remain here dead.
5. Should all guns be blown out, the Section will use Mills grenades and other novelties.
6. Finally, the position, as stated, will be held.

F. P. Bethune, Lieut.
O.C. No. 1 Section.

Bethune and his squad survived their occupation of the post for eighteen days, and the position was held.

Directions
From Ieper, take the N336 Armentières-Lille road, passing the very large Bedford House cemetery on left. After a further 1.5 kilometres, just beyond a farm on the left, turn left onto a minor road. It runs parallel to the now disused Ieper-Comines canal. After 1 kilometre stop near Spoil Bank cemetery, on left. Across the road from the cemetery the long foliage-covered mounds are Spoil Bank. Buff Bank was a continuation of Spoil Bank, 200 metres further towards Hill 60.

Catacombs

The name given to a massive system of underground bivouacs dug by the 1st Australian Tunnelling Company in the spring of 1917. In a brief mention of the catacombs, C. E. W. Bean states that they were 'near Messines'. In fact, Hill 63, into which the shelter was dug, is closer to Ploegsteert (Plugstreet). Two battalions (about 1600 men) could shelter for short periods in these well-made underground barracks. Many Diggers found them a comfortable home for the winter of 1917-18. Hill 63 protected the broad entrance from all gunfire other than long-range howitzers, although there is no record of a howitzer shell being lobbed into the entrance. The catacombs have long since collapsed and there is nothing to indicate their entrance. However, older local people led me to the site in the 1960s.

Directions
From Ieper, take the Armentières road and pass through Messines towards Ploegsteert. As the two great stone lions marking the Memorial for the Missing come into sight, turn right. This minor road runs along the base of the old Hill 63. After about 100 metres there is a flight of steps up the hill to the summit. The entrance to the catacombs was close to the steps. On the top of the hill move about 200 metres forward of the wood for a view of the Messines sector. From here, Australian officers studied and sketched the front.

Dickebusch (Dikkebus)

West of Ypres, this village, or the remnants of it, was well known to every soldier who served in the Salient. It is by the side of a large artificial lake which is invisible from the road. Throughout the war, around the lake were huts, tents and trenches. Dickebusch was the site of main dressing stations, casualty clearing stations, advance dumps and various HQs.

Directions

From Ieper, cross the railway line near the station and keep going for 5 kilometres. The best landmark is the hotel on the left of the road as Dikkebus village is reached. Turn left into a short road and park in order to see the lake. You can be sure that Australian solders walked along the banks and bathed in the lake at every warm-weather opportunity.

Celtic Wood, Broodseinde

This is the site of an AIF mystery. At dawn on 9 October 1917, Lieutenant F. J. Scott led eighty-four officers and men of the 10th Battalion over Broodseinde Ridge and 400 metres down the gentle slope beyond to raid German positions in Celtic Wood. He was engaged on a diversionary raid to convince the Germans that an offensive planned for that day would develop on this part of the front. In fact, the major attack was to be against Passchendaele, a few kilometres to the north. If the Germans fell for the diversionary assault they would spread their counter-battery fire along the line and keep their infantry reserves away from the main front. Scott was instructed to destroy any enemy gunpits and dugouts, capture machine-guns and procure enemy identification and documents.

The 10th Battalion raiders suffered some casualties before the main party entered the wood — where they disappeared. Only fourteen wounded men returned to the Australian lines. The loss of so many men in an action was not unusual but certain circumstances made the Celtic Wood affair unique. The Germans never produced any list of survivors, dead or wounded, and gave no list of prisoners to the Red Cross, though they were generally meticulous in observing the practice. The defending battalion, 448th Infantry Regiment, did not mention the raid in its war diary, another unusual omission. When the fighting moved away from the Salient and the Graves Registration units entered the area they could find no graves, yet the Germans often marked enemy graves. Also, they found no human remains or pieces of equipment and uniforms which might have identified the 10th Battalion men. Obviously, the Australians were killed but we still do not know what happened at the eastern end of Celtic Wood. Tony Spagnoly, author of *Anatomy of a Raid*, exhaustively investigated the Celtic Wood affair. He traced certain names but reports that 37 Diggers are still totally unaccounted for.

It has to be said that the commander of the 3rd Brigade, Brigadier-General Gordon Bennett, complained strongly about lack of adequate artillery support for the 10th Battalion's raid, but this charge was refuted by Lieutenant-Colonel H. O. Caddy, commanding B Group, 5th Division RFA.

Directions

From Ieper, take the Zonnebeke road and continue to the Broodseinde crossroads. Turn right towards Beselare, signposted. After 1.3 kilometres, just after passing a garage on the right, turn left into Spilstraat. After 500 metres stop. The large area of fields to your left was once Celtic Wood but only a few scattered trees remain. In the field to the left, after a house with a large front vegetable garden, are the remnants of German bunkers. In 1951 the remains of two British or Dominion soldiers were found here. On another occasion, the bodies of three Germans were found in the opposite field. By turning from Spilstraat into Dragonerstraat you are travelling along the eastern edge of the old Celtic Wood. It was here that Lieutenant Scott's raiders of the 10th Battalion met their fate. On 2 May 1993 a memorial plaque to the raiders of 10th Battalion was dedicated in St George's Church, Ieper.

Hill 60

One of the most famous positions on the Western Front, the hill had been formed in the 19th century, from the spoil taken from a deep railway cutting. It made a mound of 230 metres by 190 metres, consisting of layers of clay, sand and quicksand. The hill's height of 60 metres gave it immense strategic importance in that flat country and both sides continually fought for it. The British tunnelled into the hill in 1915 and 1916 to plant mines which killed many Germans when they exploded. The 1st Australian Tunnelling Company, under Major J. Douglas Henry, took over the tunnels and mines on 9 November 1916.

The Company's primary job was to keep intact two great mines being prepared for a major assault to break the enemy front. The galleries' drainage and ventilation was poor and to improve them the Australians sank a metal-lined shaft 130 metres from

Above: A German pillbox on Hill 60, Ypres Salient. The devastated hill has never been reclaimed and is strewn with the wreckage of wartime emplacements.

Right: The 1st Australian Tunnelling Company memorial at Hill 60, Ypres. The hill remains scarred with mine craters and shell holes. The marks on the plaque are bullet holes from fighting here in World War II.

a main junction. Then they drove an additional gallery under the German line, about 400 metres distance. The shaft was coded Sydney, the drive leading from it Melbourne while defensive galleries were called Adelaide, Perth, Brisbane, Newcastle and Hobart.

Protecting the mines from the Germans involved the Diggers in ferocious underground fighting. The work was arduous and exhausting and six months' service in the tunnels of Hill 60 was regarded as the limit of strain any troops could stand. In one sector, the Australian listeners reported that enemy miners were so close that their tools were shaking the earth in the Australian tunnel. They packed a ton of ammonal into the end of their tunnel and on 16 December 1916 fired it. Recovering from this shock, the Germans continued their efforts to dig under the shallower Australian tunnels and blow them up. In March, April and May 1917 the Australians were tunnelling 5.5 metres a day in their efforts to prepare great mines for the impending attack on Messines Ridge.

Among the 1st Tunnelling Company were a father and son from the coal-mines of Wallsend, NSW, Sapper J. B. Snedden and Sapper W. F. Snedden. J. B. was killed in action on 7 April 1917 when German miners blew a camouflet and buried him.

Every moment underground was dangerous. Sapper J. T. Landrigan was entombed by a German explosion and survived only because of the frantic rescue digging by his comrades. On 25 May a German mine explosion separately entombed two Diggers, Sapper E. W. Earl and Sapper G. Simpson. Earl continued to listen to enemy noises and managed to write a report about them. He tapped out signals on the wall which twenty four hours later were heard. A close friend, Sergeant H. Fraser, led non-stop rescue digging and on 27 May Earl and then Simpson, were brought out. Earl handed over his valuable reports. Suffering from the effects of asphyxia, his breathing chronically hampered, he died three months later. Other Diggers died of asphyxiation while trying to rescue trapped mates.

Directions

From Ieper, take the Menin road. After 2 kilometres turn right into road signposted Zillebeke. Pass Perth (China Wall) Cemetery and at the T-junction, turn left and continue 1 kilometre to signpost Hill 60. The Hill 60 Museum has a large collection of wartime relics and is worth a visit. The 1st Australian Tunnelling Company monument is prominent by the side of the road. Be sure to read the description of the battles for Hill 60 on the bronze plaque near the gate. To see the big 1917 mine crater 'Caterpillar' walk across the bridge over the railway line and turn into a rough track along the lip of the cutting. After 150 metres turn right and push through the wood. You are soon at the crater, though it is much overgrown. There is another crater, though not so sharply defined, within the Hill 60 memorial park. Combat mining required a special kind of deliberate courage and Australians visiting Hill 60 should think about the cramped, filthy and ever-tense conditions underground, where lie the remains of Digger tunnellers.

Sapper J. B. Snedden is buried in Railway Dugouts Burial Ground (Transport Farm) Zillebeke (Grave 7.K.21). The gallant Sapper Earl, who died of paralysis on 28 July 1917, is buried in Wimereux Communal Cemetery, France (Grave 2.0.7).

Menin Gate (Menenpoort), Ypres

The Australian war artist Will Longstaff understood the sentimental and symbolic significance of this eastern entrance of Ypres and painted 'Menin Gate at Midnight', which hangs in the Australian War Memorial, Canberra. It shows the figures of soldiers on their way to the frontline and suggests, by their ghostly nature, that many did not return. Long before the outbreak of war the actual town gate had disappeared but its site was marked by two stone lions, one on either side of the road. They are now in Canberra. The gateway was exposed to enemy artillery and the ramparts here were much battered. After the war, a great marble archway, designed by Sir Reginald Blomfield, was erected over the roadway as a Memorial to the Missing of the Salient. It was inaugurated on 24 July 1927 by Field Marshal Plumer, who as commander of the British Second Army had much to do with the destiny of Australians serving in the Salient. They respected him more than most senior British commanders.

The 'Hall of Memory', the central passage of Menin gate, is 66 metres long by 36 metres wide. It is covered in by an arch in a single span. At either end of the hall is an archway 16 metres wide and 26 metres high. In the centre of both sides of the hall, broad staircases lead to the ramparts and to loggias running the length of the edifice. The names of 54 896 soldiers are engraved in Portland stone panels fixed to the inner walls of the hall, up the sides of the staircases and inside the loggias. There are 6176 Australian names. The greatest number of AIF

Menin gate, unveiled in 1927, is set into the ramparts of the ancient town of Ypres. As a memorial to the missing of the Ypres Salient, the walls behind the colonnades at right are covered with the names of 6176 Diggers. These men were killed in Belgium and have no known grave.

The great Cloth Hall of Ypres (Ieper). When the Diggers first saw it in 1916, German shelling had reduced it to rubble. Part of it now houses the Ypres Salient war museum.

missing belonged to the Machine-Gun Corps, 244 of them. Of the infantry battalions, the 45th (4th Division) lists 191 names and the 36th Battalion 148. The artillery, with 145 names, suffered a greater loss of men than any of the other battalions. Since gunners were not in the trenches this needs explanation. The German artillery observers constantly spotted for the flash and smoke from British guns and brought down counter-battery fire. The German shooting was accurate and shells bursting at a gun site blew many Digger gunners to pieces. Because of the attention given to the infantry, the sacrifices of the artillery have not been appreciated.

Within a recess of Menin Gate there is a visitors book. The playing of the 'Last Post' at Menin Gate is the most important experience of any visit to the Salient. It is sounded by buglers of the local fire brigade; there are usually two buglers although up to five take part on special anniversaries. The simple but moving ceremony takes place every evening of the year at 8 p.m., whatever the weather. Police hold up the traffic on the busy road. A special ceremony can be arranged for groups or individuals wishing to lay wreaths under one of the side arches. Contact the Last Post Committee through the Ypres Tourist Office in the Cloth Hall, which can also put visitors in touch with the Royal British Legion, Ypres branch. The idea for the 'Last Post' ceremony came from a one-time superintendent of police and the practice began in summer of 1928. It was discontinued in October of that year but restarted on 11 November 1929. With the exception of a break during the German occupation of Ypres (20 May 1940 to 6 September 1944) it has continued ever since. On the day the Germans left the town, the 'Last Post' was played at Menin Gate that evening.

Menin (Menen) Road

Menin road was one of the most famous names of the wartime Ypres Salient. Beginning at Menin Gate, Ypres, the road travelled due east towards the front line and was one of the main arteries of the entire battlefield. The wartime road was quite different from today's broad highway. When the Diggers saw it, it was little more than a single-track dirt (or mud) track, lined with the skeletal, shell-blasted trunks of trees. Along the road in both directions, throughout day and night, moved columns of men, wagons, ambulances and guns. The Germans used the road from the eastern end at Menin, a town which remained in their hands until the last few months of the war. During the early years of the war British control of Menin road extended only to Hooge Crater, on the first rise out of Ypres. Pioneers erected canvas or hessian screens along the road to conceal movement but they did not lessen enemy shelling. Infantry moving up to the attack reached their start lines along paths on either side of Menin Road.

Battle of Menin Road 20–21 September 1917

This was the first of four battles in September and October in which the AIF was engaged. The battles were a part of a general offensive to push the Germans off the Passchendaele-Messines Ridge and achieve a breakthrough. For the AIF it was a fight to control Menin Road ridge, the high ground which the road crossed on the way east. The 1st and 2nd Divisions, with a combined front of 1800 metres, were at the centre of a 13 kilometre British front. The Australians were positioned along Westhoek Ridge and faced enemy-held Glencorse Wood. When the battle began at dawn on 20 September, the Diggers closely followed their own barrage, overcame enemy infantry opposition and an unusually rapid advance took them to the north edge of Glencorse Wood, Hannebeek Swamp and the bogs of Nonne Boschen Wood.

In Glencorse Wood part of the 6th Battalion was held up by a machine-gun in a pillbox. Second Lieutenant Fred Birks, with Corporal W. Johnston, rushed the post. Johnston was wounded but Birks killed the enemy and captured the gun. At once he organised a small party and attacked another strongpoint occupied by about twenty-five Germans. Some of the enemy were killed and an officer and fifteen men were captured. Pressing on, Birks reorganised a large number of Australians who had strayed from their units during the attack and consolidated the sector he had captured. A shell burst in a post of his company, burying several men. Birks was desperately digging them out when another shellburst killed him. He was posthumously awarded the VC.

By noon that day (20 September) the 1st and 2nd Divisions had taken all their objectives and were at the western end of Polygon Wood. Despite orders not to go further than this, individual Diggers and small groups crept into the dangerous area ahead to search for souvenirs and take more prisoners.

Directions

From Ieper, take the Menen road, the N8. After 4 kilometres turn left at signpost Westhoek. After 100 metres ignore sign to Westhoek but go straight on to Nonne Boschen Wood. Turn left through this wood and within 200 metres reach what is left of Glencorse Wood. Lieutenant Birks' VC exploit took place at the point where Nonne Boschen and Glencorse Wood meet. His battalion, the 6th, was at the southern edge of the Australian line. This line extended 500 metres north. Return to the southern edge of Nonne Boschen Wood, turn left and cross over the motorway. The wood you then reach is Polygon Wood and the first corner is Black Watch Corner, the final objective for the Australians' Battle of Menin Road.

Battle of Messines (Mesen), 7–12 June 1917

The battle began with the blowing of nineteen great mines under the German positions along an 8 kilometre arc of Messines Ridge. The mines went up at 3.10 a.m. on 7 June 1917. The AIF 3rd Division (Major-General John Monash) and the New Zealand Division, with the AIF 4th Division in immediate support, were the spearhead formations. The 3rd Division, which knew the offensive by the code-name of 'Magnum Opus', had a front of 1.5 kilometres on the southern flank. The Australians' sector stretched from just south (right) of St Ives (St Yvon) north to Bethleem Farm.

The Germans were demoralised after the colossal explosions under their trenches, and the Diggers advanced rapidly. The main enemy opposition was on the right where the 33rd Battalion (Lieutenant-Colonel Leslie Morshead) came under machine-gun fire. After digging in, some Australians went prospecting into the Germans' Oosttaverne Line, named after a nearby village. The 4th Division made a follow-up attack in the afternoon. In this battle the Diggers of the 3rd and 4th Divisions encountered blockhouses for the first time in the war. The Germans used these miniforts to protect their machine-gun crews during enemy barrages. When the gunfire slackened, the crews speedily got their Maxims into position beside the blockhouse, on its roof or on the parapet of an adjoining trench. Lieutenant Rupert Grieve of the 37th Battalion won a VC capturing a key blockhouse position. The attack on the Oosttaverne Line succeeded largely because of Grieve's bravery.

In a single day's fighting the Australians and New Zealanders defeated the Germans on one of the strongest sectors of their entire front. The holding of the Messines gains led to another battle and on 8 June the 10th Brigade suffered one of the heaviest bombardments faced by the AIF during the war. The 45th Battalion was particularly hard hit. For four days the 33rd Battalion fought to hold the right flank and here the courage of Private John Carroll was especially notable and earned him the VC. His citation stated: 'During the 96 hours his battalion was in the line Private Carroll displayed the most wonderful courage and fearlessness. His magnificent example of gallantry and devotion to duty inspired all ranks in his battalion.' The AIF suffered 6800 casualties at Messines, which at the time was considered the greatest Allied victory of the war.

Directions
From Ieper, take the Armentières road through Mesen. On the southern edge of Mesen, watch for New Zealandstraat, to the right. It leads to the New Zealand memorial, which is signposted. The memorial roughly marks the left flank of the AIF's front. The German blockhouses in the New Zealand Memorial Park face the Douve River valley, (Douvebeek in Flemish) along which the 3rd and 4th Divisions made their advance on a broad front. Return to the main road and continue down the hill. Just before crossing the Douve notice the farm on the right. This was the scene of fierce fighting between Australians and Germans. Lieutenant Grieve's VC exploit took place at the hamlet of St Ives (St Yvon), about the centre of the modern village. Private Carroll's exploit occurred just behind, or west, of the modern village.

Neuve Eglise (Nieuwkerke)

While the AIF had units serving in Belgian Flanders, Neuve Eglise was one of the villages where the Diggers were in camps or billets. Their positions were heavily though sporadically shelled in March 1918 during the German offensive. This was the period when the Australians, heartily sick of the winter which was just ending, were having sporting competitions and the war was not going to put them off. On 21 March the 13th Battalion's tug-of-war team was having a final practice for the unit's sports on the athletics field when a shell crashed. Men ran to the site of the great explosion and found the entire team killed or wounded. Among the wounded was the trainer, Lieutenant N. J. Browne MC. A popular officer, Browne died next day. The shell was a British one which fell short. On 14 April the Germans captured Neuve Eglise but Australians were not at that time involved in its defence. Lieutenant Browne is buried in Westhof Farm Cemetery (Grave II.D.4).

Directions
From Ieper, take the N336 Armèntieres road, branch off right to Kemmel, across the railway line, and keep on through Kemmel to Nieuwkerke. For Westhof Farm Cemetery, continue through Nieuwkerke in the direction of Belle on the N331. Westhof Farm Cemetery is signposted to the right off this road.

Nieuport

The Belgian port and town of Nieuport lies at the mouth of the River Yser (Ijser) and south-west of Nieuport is Nieuport Bains. Here, in 1917 the French held a small piece of territory, mostly sand dunes, as an anchor to the entire Western Front. On either side of the Yser River, it was an exceptionally dangerous sector but the British felt that a breakthrough thrust could be made from there.

The British 1st Division took over and the 2nd Australian Tunnelling Company (Major E. N. Milligan) was asked to tunnel the dunes and plant mines under the German lines. It was an immensely difficult task requiring galleries of 400 metres and 270 metres, as well as communications trenches, through sand and soft ground. Milligan had 566 miners in No. 2 Company, plus 160 reinforcements and working parties of 500 British soldiers. The greater part of his force worked beyond the Yser and within eighteen days their tunnels were close to No Man's Land.

Above the miners, Australian gunners of the Australian Siege Artillery Brigade and the 3rd, 6th and 12th Australian Army Brigades supported them. The guns came under heavy fire from German artillery and by 10 July the entire British position was threatened by an enemy offensive. Two battalions of the British 1st Division were lost. Only eighty men escaped, most of them by swimming the Yser. Fifty AIF tunnellers in the dunes beyond the river were also trapped. Several tunnellers showed great courage in the fighting, notably Sapper C.G. McGlinchey and Sapper P. Minogue. Minogue was wounded through thigh, stomach and ankle in his game fight. Many of the sappers reached the river bank, where Sapper J. Coade took charge. He and Sapper Burke had a rope and Burke, a good swimmer, took one end across the river, Coade stayed on the enemy side to hold the rope taut while the non-swimmers, mostly British soldiers, struggled across. Then he followed.

The most astonishing performance was that of Sapper J. O'Connell, who had been wounded as well as burnt by a flamethrower. Bandaged, he lay on the river bank until he realised that capture was inevitable. He hauled himself on to a demolished bridge, hobbled as far as he could and swam the rest of the way. He had reached safety when he heard a British soldier in the water calling for help. O'Connell swam out, rescued the man and only then fainted.

Meanwhile, Sergeant F. Birrell and three other Australians as well as a British working party, had been trapped by a cave-in. They dug themselves out only to find that the Germans were at their rear. The Australians asked the British soldiers to give them 10 minutes' start before showing a white flag. The four tried manfully to escape under fire and Birrell was wounded. On the river bank, stranded and without weapons, they surrendered. Of the fifty tunnellers beyond the river only Lieutenant E. P. Hargraves, and Sappers Coade, Burke and O'Connell escaped. O'Connell won the DCM, the other two sappers the MM.

Directions

Like everywhere else in the Salient, Nieuport is easily reached from Ieper, through Dixmuide. The town has become a major tourist resort since the First World War and soldiers who were there would not recognise it. However, the course of the river remains the same and the sand dunes are still there. The tunnellers' exploits took place near the mouth of the river and on its right bank. The artillery men, who suffered many casualties, were a few kilometres to the rear. Nothing marks the AIF men's brief stay at Nieuport, a venture of great courage. While passing through Dixmuide en route to Nieuport visit the 'Trench of Death', a reconstruction of the trenches held by the Belgians along the River Yser.

Oosttaverne Wood, Wytschaete

This wood is notable for a small but gallant AIF action on 10 April 1918. The Germans had broken through in their 'George II' offensive. The sector was held by British troops already tired and strained from battle and the only AIF unit remaining there was the Australian Corps Heavy Trench Mortar Battery under Captain F. B. Darling. The battery was in action against the enemy when fired on from only 70 metres away to their right flank. Darling with three men, the crew of a medium trench mortar, conducted a fighting retreat from Polka Estaminet. Gunner Welsh was killed and Darling was wounded at Oosttaverne Wood. Corporal W. J. M. Hughes was killed while carrying Darling back. Lieutenants F. C. S. Bond and H. L. Newland took three machine-guns from retiring British infantry and got into position astride the Messines road to block the Germans. Bond rallied some stragglers and put them into trenches to cover the road. The general commanding the British division on the sector later sent a report complimenting the Australians on their 'admirable defences'. No more than a score of Diggers were involved.

Directions

Oosttaverne Wood was knocked flat by artillery fire but it recovered and grew again. From Ieper, take the N336 Mesen road and after 5 kilometres fork left at St Elooi, still on the N336, towards Waasten and Rijsel (Lille). Continue past Oosttaverne Wood Military Cemetery and two minor crossroads; 200 metres beyond the second crossroads, on the right, is an isolated house which was once Polka Estaminet. Captain Darling carried out his fighting retreat towards some woods south east of the estaminet. Built against the rear of the house is a German blockhouse, which is visible from the road. Two other blockhouses can be clearly seen in the fields in front of the new Oosttaverne Wood. Parking is dangerous on this part of the road; continue past the house 50 metres and park, right, in the farm road.

Battle of Passchendaele (Passendale), 9–12 October 1917.

Note: the entire Third Battle of Ypres is sometimes called the Battle of Passchendaele.

For the AIF the Battle of Passchendaele began on 9 October 1917 when the 2nd Division formed the flank for an attack by the British 66th Division. The 2nd Division's front was about 800 metres long with its left flank the Ypres-Roulers railway line. Its ultimate objective was higher ground known as The Keiburg, a spur on the Australian right flank from which the Germans controlled their battle operations. It was a desperate fight and the Australians suffered many casualties. German resistance was particularly fierce at two positions: at Assyria, a large barn turned into a fortress, and at the railway cutting. The 5th Brigade captured the cutting but at great cost. The RSM of the 17th Battalion, J. W. Raitt, was conspicuously courageous and effective here. The Australians were forced to withdraw that night.

The second phase of the battle began on 12 October with the 3rd Division and the New Zealand Division attacking side by side. The task of capturing Passchendaele was given to the 3rd's 38th Battalion. According to the plan the capture would be complete by 12.11 p.m. One unit carried an Australian flag to be planted in Passchendaele. After a night of rain and gas-shelling the attack went in after inadequate British shellfire. After much confusion, great loss — and great gallantry — the attack came to a halt. However, about twenty Australians, mostly of the 38th Battalion, actually reached Passchendaele Church. Completely isolated and unsupported, they were forced to withdraw to their own lines.

Meanwhile, the 4th Division which had been in support, was also under great pressure and suffered heavily before pulling back. The attack had failed. That night, dead and wounded of the 3rd Division lay in the filthy mud of Ravebeek valley. Others lay huddled in captured pillboxes. Stretcher bearers sent out to rescue these men found other Australians unwounded but stuck fast in the mud. The 34th Battalion's MO, Major G. R. C. Clarke, and members of his staff were killed while dressing the wounded. Corporal W. A. Murray gave up his place in a queue of wounded waiting for bearers and was never heard of again. The 3rd Division suffered 3199 casualties in the twenty-four hours of battle.

Directions

From Passendale, go to Tyne Cot Cemetery via the Broodseinde road. Drive north past the cemetery and, after 1 kilometre, through the crossroad. Within 400 metres you reach the Ravebeek, the shallow ditch which formed part of the 3rd Division's approach line. To your right it points towards the direction of Passendale. Within 20 metres the road crosses a branch of the Ravebeek. Stop and look along the beek. On the night of 12 October 1917 hundreds of dead and wounded Diggers lay here, hoping for rescue. The entire area, for more than a square kilometre, is one of Australian endurance and sacrifice. In Passendale, the church reached by the Australians lies at the six-ways in the middle of the village.

Battle of Pilckem Ridge, 31 July — 2 August 1917

Geographically misnamed, this battle was the opening of the Third Battle of Ypres. The brigades of the AIF 1st and 2nd Divisions were engaged as supports for British divisions. The jumping-off line for the Australians was from just right of Hooge Crater on the left flank to just right and forward of Hill 60 on the right. Among their objectives were Shrewsbury Forest and Inverness Copse. The AIF infantry was not heavily engaged but the Australian artillery lost many men that day — sixteen officers and 137 men hit. Despite their losses, the two brigades carried out their long fire programme to the last shell.

Directions

From Ieper, take Menen road to the Potize-Zillebeke crossroads (Hellfire Corner). Turn right and continue until Hooge Crater Cemetery is on your left. In the depression below the cemetery was the AIF artillery forward position. Early on the morning of 31 July 1917 seven batteries assembled here before diverging to take up their stations. Lieutenant A. Walker of 1st Division Signals was killed while connecting telephone lines to the forward exchange at Stirling Castle, east of Hooge. He has no known grave and his name is commemorated on Menin Gate Memorial, panel 7.

Plugstreet (Ploegsteert) Wood

Inevitably known to all British and Dominion soldiers as Plugstreet throughout the war, this large wood was 2 kilometres by nearly 1 kilometre. It was really more of a forest and over a period of four years probably one million soldiers found a form of shelter among its trees. The Germans often fired high explosive, shrapnel and gas shells into it. It covered much of Hill 63 as well as the lowland east of Hill 63, and the front line ran along its northern edge.

The AIF's first experience of Plugstreet Wood came on the night of 6 June 1917 when units of the 3rd Division came under phosgene gas-shell attack as they headed to the start lines for the Battle of Messines.

The Germans broke through the British defences of the Ypres Salient on the night of 9-10 April 1918 and reached Ploegsteert village. On the soggy ground the 2nd Battery Australian Siege Artillery had great difficulty in withdrawing its guns that night. By hitching three tractors together the gunners got one gun carriage out. The other guns were overrun but were later recovered.

Directions

From Ieper, take the Mesen-Armentières road which passes through the wood south of Mesen. Turn left at the crossroads in Ploegsteert and left again at Le Gheer to circumnavigate the wood. Several military cemeteries are in the area. *See* **Catacombs**.

The plaque on the 5th Division's memorial in Polygon Wood, Ypres Salient. The 5th is the only AIF division with Fromelles among its battle honours.

Battle of Polygon Wood, 26–28 September 1917

The battle began at 5.30 a.m. on 26 September 1917, when the British and Dominion guns opened on a 10 kilometre front. The intention was to build on the gains made during the Battle of Menin Road. The AIF 4th and 5th Divisions were responsible for a 2500-metre sector and one of their main objectives was Polygon Wood Butts, in peacetime the target on the Ypres district rifle range. It was now a small plateau from which the Germans dominated the nearby ground with machine-guns. The 14th Brigade captured the position and then a second objective of several strongpoints. Dash, gallantry and good leadership held the advance together at critical moments. At one time, men of the 14th Battalion ran into their own bursting shells and were badly shaken until steadied by Captain Albert Jacka, of Gallipoli, Pozières and Bullecourt fame. Private Patrick Bugden, 31st Battalion, led a small party to attack German machine-gun posts. He captured the posts with bombs and bayonet and then, single-handedly, charged some Germans who had captured a corporal. On five occasions during the next few days he risked his life to rescue wounded men but his luck ran out and he was killed.

The 4th Division's battalions captured all their objectives — woods, blockhouses, trenches — and suffered 1717 casualties. The even more heavily engaged 5th Division suffered 5471 dead and wounded in the period 26–28 September.

A much eroded trench in Polygon Wood. It was probably dug by Australians during their advance through the wood in September 1917.

Directions

From Ieper, take the Zonnebeke road to reach the north-eastern entrance to Polygon Wood. In the

A wartime postcard shows the AIF's heroic capture of Polygon Wood.

The entrance to a deep dugout discovered in the claypits of a brickyard at Zonnebeke, Ypres. The place may have been an HQ or a signals exchange. The brick company has preserved this site.

middle of Zonnebeke on the right, the AIF 5th Division memorial and Buttes New British Cemetery are signposted. Stop next to a small cemetery, Polygon Wood Cemetery, which is just opposite a lawn path leading to the 5th Division memorial and the wood.

Polygon Wood today, though smaller than in 1917, is still large. The remains of three German pillboxes captured by the Australians lie deep among the trees but few trench lines remain. The Butte is still prominent and mounted on top of it is the AIF 5th Division memorial, the usual obelisk. It faces the Butte's Military Cemetery at the other end of which is a New Zealand memorial to the missing of the sector. It is well worth walking through the woods from the east or Ypres end towards the 5th Division's memorial to gain some idea of the dangers of approaching the commanding German machine-gun positions.

Within prewar Polygon Wood, Ypres district trotting course was located but it had been pounded out of all recognition when the Diggers reached it and it was never afterwards restored. In the 1960s older people living near Polygon Wood told me that they remembered how the Butte, which had been much reduced by shellfire, was rebuilt. After September 1918 lines of slouch-hatted Australians, each with a sandbag of soil, climbed the Butte to deposit his load on the top. They dug the soil from the ground behind the Butte where there is now a large depression.

Poperinge

All soldiers knew this large Flemish town, 11 kilometres west of Ypres, as 'Pop'. It had great importance as the railhead of the main line serving Ypres and as the largest Flemish town in British hands, other than battered Ypres itself. Over a large area throughout the hopfields were training camps, transit depots, hospitals, depots and dumps. The railway station, despite often being the target for German guns, was always busy. Many civilians remained in Poperinge, so that estaminets and restaurants stayed in operation.

The main attraction for many soldiers was Talbot House, better known in army signalese as 'Toc H'. An old three-storey home, Talbot House became a club or recreation centre. It was run by one of the Western Front's most engaging and vigorous characters, Chaplain Philip Byard Clayton of the British 6th Division. An Australian by birth and known affectionately as 'Tubby' (for obvious reasons), Clayton made Talbot house the talk of the Salient. Rank was irrelevant to Clayton and Talbot House was open to everybody. For a few hours, perhaps even overnight, men could get away from the war. The most important place was the chapel which Clayton had set up in the former hop store at the top of the house. It became known as the Upper Room and here Tubby held services, arranged baptisms and confirmations and gave advice.

He kept Talbot House open until May 1918 when enemy bombardment forced its closure, but it was open again in September. The Toc H movement grew out of Talbot House and the Christian spirit it had awakened. In 1929 the 'Old House' of Poperinge was bought for Toc H by Lord Wakefield, who was later Governor of New South Wales.

'Skindles' is another interesting building in Poperinge. During the war it was a popular restaurant and estaminet much patronised by officers, perhaps partly because the proprietress had two attractive daughters. For a time General Haig used it as a HQ. Now a private home, it is close to Talbot House.

Directions

From Ieper, take the N9 or N308 for 11 kilometres into Poperinge Great Square and stop there or close by. Talbot House is a short distance along Gasthuisstraat, No. 43, and easily identifiable from its sign and the Union Jack flag. The warden welcomes visitors. Talbot House has accommodation for guests, who need not be members of Toc H. They sleep in the very rooms used by soldiers in the war. The kitchen is a communal one where many visitors prefer to get their own meals rather than buy them in the town. During the summer and at special times, such as Armistice Day, it is advisable to book accommodation. It is always advisable to arrive before 4 p.m.

Spanbroekmolen, 'Pool of Peace', Wytschaete

This was not an AIF place of battle, but as the largest of the 1917 mine craters it is worth a visit. It is one of the nineteen mines blown to precede the Battle of Messines on 7 June, in which many Diggers were involved. The charge was 41 278 kilograms of ammonal, which blew a hole now 129 metres in

The author at the site of Lone Tree Crater on Messines Ridges, Ypres. The dimensions of the vast hole give some idea of the extent and enormity of the explosion on 7 June 1917. The crater is now known as the Pool of Peace.

diameter and 27 metres deep. The crater filled with water and became a tranquil pool, known for some years as Lone Tree Crater. In 1930 Padre Tubby Clayton (see *Poperinge*) thought that at least one crater should be preserved and he induced Lord Wakefield to buy Lone Tree Crater for Toc H. It was dedicated the 'Pool of Peace'. As you stand near it remember that many German soldiers died when the mine exploded.

Directions

From Ieper, take the Mesen road and in the large village of Wytschaete turn right towards Kemmel. After 2 kilometres turn left into a narrow road signposted Lone Tree Cemetery. Park next to the rim of the 'Pool of Peace' and walk 100 metres to the gate.

Warneton (Waasten)

On the Belgian bank of the River Lys, which marks the France-Belgium border, the town of Warneton was fortified by the Germans and held by a strong garrison. No Man's Land here was 600 metres wide, largely because of flooding and the consequent impossibility of holding a continuous trench. From November 1917 the AIF 5th Division, with the help of the 3rd Division, covered this part of the Flanders front. Australians and Germans made nightly patrols to kill or capture the garrisons of small posts. The Germans had the better of it until Major-General J. J. T. Hobbs, GOC 5th Division, repositioned and strengthened his own posts. From this strong base line, AIF patrols swarmed over No Man's Land.

Warneton town and district quickly became familiar to the Australians as they patrolled the outposts at Pond House, Estaminet House, Crown Prince Farm and White Farm. In the heavy mists, the Belgian (or right bank) of the Lys often gave them their direction. They were always on the alert for enemy machine-guns firing from the Soaphouse and Dyeworks. The most important operations were by the 3rd Division, which made a specialty of large-scale raiding. Some raids, which began from the Australian lines in Plugstreet Wood, were made towards Pont Rouge (Red Bridge) in the hope of catching Germans crossing the bridge over the Lys. Much AIF activity took place around the northern end of the bridge. Some patrols, sent out to capture Germans, crossed the Lys into enemy territory. So spirited were Australian attacks that the Germans were convinced that they were not raids at all but serious attempts to capture their Warneton defences. On the night of 30 November 1917 the 40th Battalion killed eighteen men and wounded thirty-six others of the German 103rd Regiment.

On the evening of 30 November the 39th Battalion of the 10th Brigade raided enemy posts near the railway, killed about thirty Germans and took two prisoners. Brigade HQ waited until the Germans were likely to be repairing their defences and then sent out a strong raiding party of the 40th Battalion. The Germans were trapped in the open and about seventy of them were shot. On 10 February 1918 the two other battalions of the 10th Brigade, the 37th and 38th, sent out a joint patrol to raid south-west of Warneton. The Australians claimed to have killed 102 enemy and to have captured thirty-three prisoners, though they themselves had thirty-nine men hit.

Directions
From Ieper, take the N369 to Mesen, where Warneton (Waasten) is signposted. Other than Pont Rouge, which is 2 kilometres from Warneton, no particular wartime site of action is now identifiable. However, the railway embankment just west of the town was a satisfactory area of operations for the Diggers. Some of the most outstanding raids of the war were made in the fields on either side of the railway. Australian scouts actually penetrated into Warneton, near where the small bridge crosses the Lys into France.

Ypres (Ieper)

Most AIF men who reached the Western Front in 1916, 1917 and the early months of 1918 saw this walled and moated town of Belgian Flanders. In peacetime it was an attractive, picturesque place, noted for its great medieval Cloth Hall, centre of Ypres' weaving trade. It stood in the Grote Markt (Great Market Square), a place of bars, hotels and cafes. By the time the Diggers reached Ypres and the surrounding villages it had been the scene of two great battles, so that all the Diggers saw was ruin and rubble. The Germans bombarded the place continuously early in 1915 and fire reduced it still further. The massive and sturdy ramparts, designed by the French military architect Vauban, withstood the bombardment. The troops built pathways, tunnels and dugouts into the ramparts and many Australians, mostly gunners, pioneers, engineers and headquarters' staffs, worked and slept there in 1917. Field dressing stations and casualty clearing stations also operated within the ramparts. AIF men entered the town from the direction of Poperinge or Kemmel and often formed up in the spaces of the battered town before leaving for the front through Lille or Menin gates. Descriptions follow of the most interesting sites for Australian visitors. *See also* **Menin Gate**.

Commonwealth War Graves Commission, North-West Area

The CWGC office (82 Elverdingestraat, Ieper) can provide information about the whereabouts of any soldier with a known grave. If a soldier is commemorated only by a name engraved on a wall of remembrance, the staff can give this information too. Michelin maps showing the position of all CWGC cemeteries on the Western Front may be bought at this office.

Lille Gate (Rijselpoort)

While Menin Gate is the primary focus of visitors' interest, Lille Gate is also important in AIF history. Menin Gate was open to enemy artillery fire and was too dangerous for use as a routine exit to the front line. Lille Gate, on the town's southern side, was much more frequently used. Troops left for the trenches by this gate and made a looping movement around the town when heading for the north-eastern part of the front line. The stretch of town wall adjoining Lille Gate is very much as it was in 1918. Clearly visible to the left of the gate is Ramparts Cemetery, which should be visited.

Hell Fire Corner

Probably the most famous — and certainly the most notorious — spot in the Ypres Salient. The Corner was actually the crossroads of the Ypres-Menin road and the Zillebeke-Potize road. It was referred to as 'the hottest spot on earth'. As a route junction and an easily identifiable place, it was under constant observation by the Germans on the higher ground beyond. They ranged their artillery on to the corner in the expectation of catching transport and infantry moving up Menin Road. Drivers of the Australian Army Service Corps whipped up their horses as they approached Hellfire Corner. Pioneers erected great canvas and hessian screens along the road to conceal movement but they did not dissuade the Germans from firing their guns.

Directions
Hell Fire Corner is only 1 kilometre from Ypres along Menin Road and identifiable by the demarcation stone set prominently at the crossroads. The stone marks the limit, at this part of the front, of the German breakthrough towards the Channel ports in their 1918 offensive.

Ramparts British Cemetery (Ieper)

This tranquil cemetery is visible across the moat at Lille Gate. Six of the eleven Australians here are buried in a row, which is not surprising as they were killed on the one day, 29 October 1917. Two were members of 2nd Division HQ, one belonged to 1st Division HQ, two to Australian Army Medical Corps, one was a gunner and one a pioneer. They were killed by a single shellburst.

Shrapnel Corner

From the Grote Markt in Ieper, take Rijselstraat to Rijselpoort (Lille Gate) in the direction of Armentières. Shrapnel Corner, though it does not carry this label now, is only 0.5 kilometre along this road, immediately before it crosses the railway. The junction was frequently shelled by German artillery and it was as dangerous as Hell Fire Corner. No infantry fighting took place here but Australians were killed or wounded at this spot while making their way forward to the battle lines or to the rear.

St George's Memorial Church

The church, in Elverdingestraat, was built in 1928–9 as a place of worship for the large British postwar colony in Ypres. It is now a memorial to all who died in the Salient, and everything in it, from windows to furnishings, is a memorial to units or individuals. The RSL placed a general memorial plaque in the church in 1953 to commemorate all Australian servicemen and women who lost their lives during the two great wars, but it has no specific reference to the Ypres Salient or Flanders. This is left to a private plaque, which reads: 'To the glory of God and in grateful remembrance of Driver Joseph Green, 25th Machine-Gun Company and his comrades of the Australian Commonwealth Forces who fell in Flanders'. Note also the plaques for Private G. Downton, whose grave is in Strand Cemetery, and for Lieutenant H. J. F. Watson of the 13th Battalion, who has no known grave. His name is inscribed on panel 29 of Menin Gate. Services are held in St George's each Sunday evening.

Ypres Salient War Museum, Great Square (Grote Markt)

The museum takes up a large part of the first floor of the rebuilt Cloth Hall and is the best starting point for a tour of the Belgian battle fields. Many relics of the fighting are on display, together with some good quality though small scale dioramas. A study of the illuminated wall map showing the front line at various stages during the war is useful preparation for a tour. A life-size model of a uniformed Digger, a gift from the Australian War Memorial, graces the far end of the hall. At least an hour is necessary in this professionally laid out museum.

Zonnebeke Redoubt

One of the strongest German positions in the Ypres Salient was Zonnebeke Redoubt. Its shafts, dugouts and underground shelters were deep in heavy clay and impervious to shellfire. Built into the rubble of Zonnebeke, the redoubt was a formidable obstacle. It was on the left edge of the 18th Battalion's front during the attack of 20 September 1917. Close by was a German two-storey observation blockhouse which interested the Diggers and after its capture Lieutenant A. V. L. Hull of the 18th Battalion claimed it with a miniature Australian flag. When the war ended the blockhouse was removed to make way for brick kilns.

In 1985 a wartime underground position was found during clay-digging for making bricks. The beams used, together with the construction of the supports and of the two-tier wooden frames to form soldiers' beds, have led engineers to believe that the work is Australian. A spade which I found during the excavation is British or Australian and a length of rubber concertina-type hosepipe for ventilation seems to be of British manufacture. The dugouts also had fittings and wires for electricity supply and they too seem to be British rather than German. The dugout's position, giving protection against gunfire from the east rather than the west, suggests that it is a British or Australian post rather than a German one.

In 1989 wartime dugouts or chambers were found under Zonnebeke church during repairs. Again, from the timbering they seem to be Australian-built. They might well have been extensions of the cellars and crypts of the demolished church. Australians were in Zonnebeke for six weeks, September-

November 1917, plenty of time for AIF Engineer units to build HQ dugouts or ammunition depots under the church.

Directions:
From Ieper, take the Zonnebeke road to the giant brickyards on the western edge of Zonnebeke. Apply at the brickworks' office for the key to the dugout. In case of difficulty (which is unlikely) explain that you are Australian. The church dugouts cannot be visited but the rebuilt church itself is in the centre of the village.

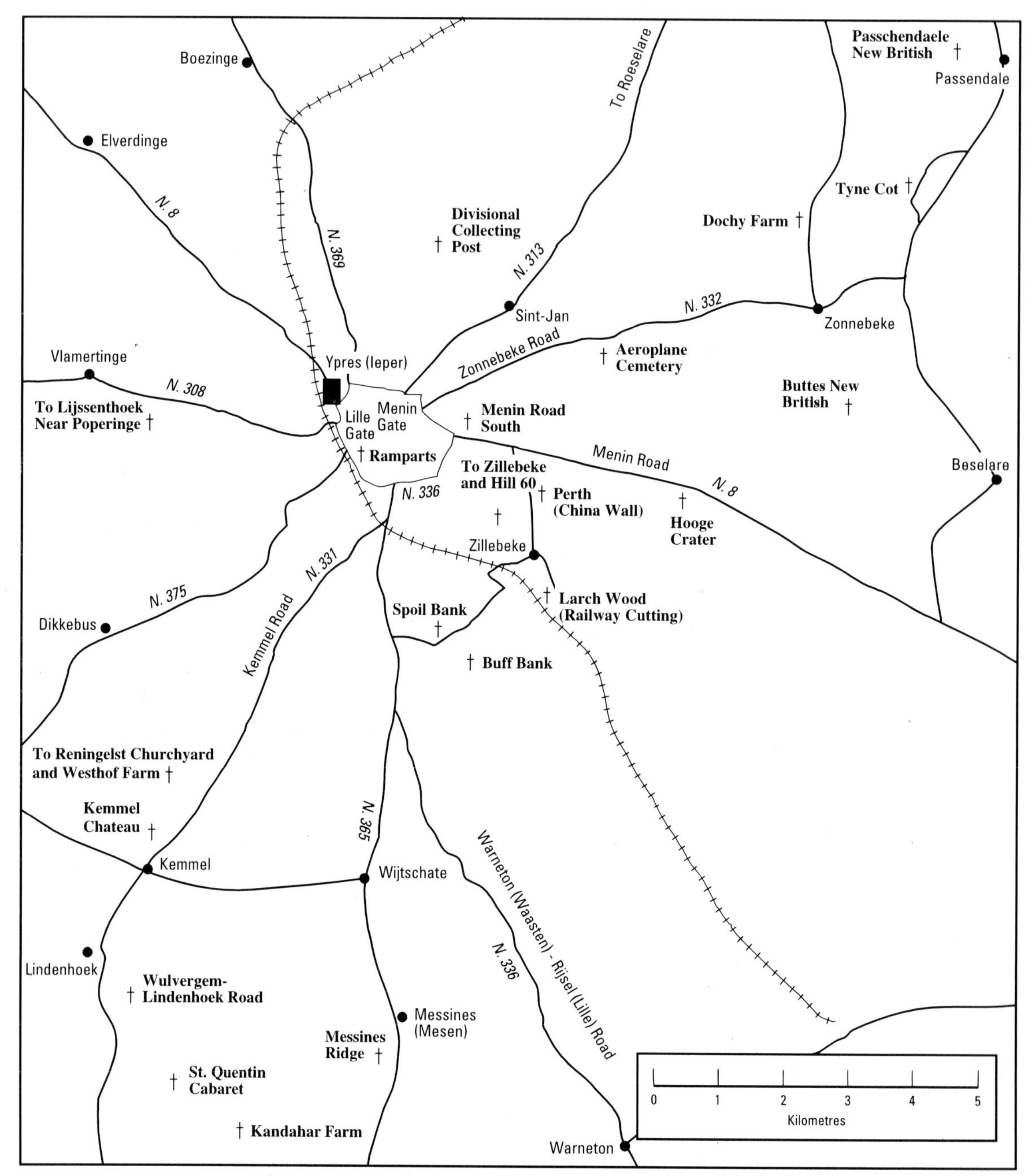

Map 3. Ypres Salient: Cemeteries

Chapter 2

Cemeteries in Belgium of Australian Interest

Australian servicemen are buried in 163 cemeteries in Belgium, in numbers ranging from 1368 to just one soldier. In a book of this size it is impossible to cover all cemeteries, so I have dealt with those of the greatest AIF interest.

Buttes New British Cemetery, Polygon Wood, Zonnebeke

This large and beautiful cemetery, entirely within Polygon Wood, has 564 Australian burials out of 2066. However, more than four-fifths of the total number of graves and 407 of the Australians are unnamed. The fighting here was so savage and the shelling so intense that many bodies could not be identified. The burial ground was made after the Armistice and soldiers who had been buried singly or in groups for several kilometres around were brought here. The AIF 5th Division's memorial is atop the mound and faces the gravestones. All five AIF divisions, all brigades and most battalions are represented in the cemetery. There are many casualties from the Battle of the Menin Road (20–21 September 1917), Battle of Polygon Wood (26–28 September), Battle of Broodseinde Ridge (4 October), Passchendaele (9–12 October). The battles in which men were killed can be read from the dates; that of 4 October is the most frequently found.

Other units, such as Field Ambulance units of the Australian Army Medical Corps, had their casualties. Note the grave of Private Arthur Joyce, 15th Field Ambulance, killed 2 October; he was aged 19 (Grave X.B.8). A late Australian casualty for this cemetery is Private Joseph Raine MM of the 9th Battalion, killed on 4 November 1917. (Grave V.B.1). The most distinguished of a gallant company is Lieutenant-Colonel Alan Humphrey Scott, commanding officer of the 56th Battalion. Scott had first shown himself to be an outstanding leader at Lone Pine, Gallipoli, in August 1915 and was only 24 when given command of the 56th Battalion. The battalion was relieved on 1 October but Scott stayed behind to show his British successor the Polygon Wood front. While standing with this officer at the Butte, Scott was killed by a sniper. He was 27 (Grave II.A.12).

Directions

From Ieper, take the Zonnebeke road. Almost in the centre of Zonnebeke, to the right, the AIF 5th Division Memorial is signposted. The cemetery lies in front of the memorial, which is visible from the road.

Divisional Collecting Post Cemetery Extension, Boezinge

The original Collecting Post Cemetery was a small Field Ambulance cemetery but during the 1920s it was enlarged by the concentration of 676 graves from smaller burial grounds and from battlefields north and east of Ypres. The Extension contains the graves of 102 Australian soldiers, seventy-one of whom are unidentified. The majority of the identified Australians were killed on 20 September 1917 during the Battle of the Menin Road, though the fighting took place several kilometres from this cemetery. Lieutenant Frederick Cochran of the 24th Company Australian Machine-Gun Corps was killed on 17 October, during the later fighting for Passchendaele. Formerly a sergeant-major of the 35th Squadron Australian Light Horse, Cochran, a Victorian, had transferred to the infantry in order to see action on the Western Front (Grave II.H.19).

Directions
From Ieper, take the St Jan Road. At the church in St Jan turn left. After 0.5 kilometre, at a T-junction, turn right. In another 0.5 kilometre, at a crossroads with a cemetery (New Irish Farm), turn left. Divisional Collecting Post Cemetery Extension is a short distance along this road.

Dochy Farm New British Cemetery, Langemarck

The Germans had turned Dochy Farm into a major strongpoint which was captured by the New Zealanders on 4 October 1917, during the Battle of Broodseinde. The cemetery was made after the Armistice by the concentration of graves from Boezinge, St Julien, Frezenberg and Passchendaele. AIF burials number 305 out of 1437 graves. Inevitably, considering the conditions, a large number of men (958) are unidentified.

Directions
From Ieper, take the Zonnebeke road. Turn left in the centre of town towards Langemarck. After 2 kilometres, Dochy Farm Cemetery is on the left. On higher ground and almost in the centre of the Passchendaele-Broodseinde battlefield, it is an excellent position for the visitor to study the battlefield. Stand at the entrance with your back to Ieper and look east towards Tyne Cot Cemetery, which is clearly visible. The entire area before you was mud which had to be crossed under fire by infantry. Probably nowhere within the Salient is there a better place from which to understand the importance of the higher ground along the Passchendaele-Broodseinde line.

Aeroplane Cemetery, Ypres

Before 31 July 1917, the site of the cemetery was in No Man's Land but on that day British troops captured it while the Australians were active on the British right. The cemetery was begun in August and by October it had acquired its present name because of a wrecked British plane near where the Great Cross now stands. After the Armistice, 966 graves from the battlefields and smaller burial grounds were concentrated in Aeroplane Cemetery. Now there are 1097 graves, of which 636 carry no name. Australian graves total 204, including eighty-nine unnamed, and there is a special memorial to four Diggers known or believed to be buried here. Many of the Diggers were killed either on 26 September 1917 during the Battle of Polygon Wood or during the fighting at Passchendaele.

Directions
From Ieper, take the Zonnebeke road. After 2 kilometres, just past a large French military cemetery, Aeroplane Cemetery is on the right.

Kandahar Farm Cemetery, Neuve-Eglise (Nieuwkerke)

The cemetery lies in the valley of the Douve River, between Kemmel Hill and the Ploegsteert Ridge. The British front ran a little east of this cemetery from the autumn of 1914 until the summer of 1917, when Messines was captured. Kandahar Farm Cemetery was used by the divisions holding that sector from November 1914 until April 1918. The cemetery fell into German hands in that month and was held by them until September 1918. Of the 433 British and Dominion burials 186 are Australian. The greatest number are 3rd Division men killed during the Messines fighting of June–July 1917. One of the Australians is Captain William Connell of the 12th Battalion, who died of wounds on 28 December 1917. He had won the DCM as a sergeant at Gallipoli, rose through the ranks and was one of the most popular officers of his battalion (Grave II.H.6). There are also 1st and 4th Division men killed at the same time. Other Diggers died during the intense raiding activity of winter 1917–18.

Directions
From Ieper, take the Kemmel-Armentières road. Soon after leaving Kemmel there is the hamlet of Lindenhoek. About 1 kilometre down the hill take a right turn signposted Wulvergem. Kandahar Farm Cemetery is on the south side of the road Nieuwkerke-Wulvergem but nearer to the village of Wulvergem.

Lijssenthoek Military Cemetery

Lijssenthoek is a hamlet between Abeele and Poperinge, close to the French frontier. Just behind the extreme range of enemy shellfire and on a railway line, it was a natural place for hospitals to establish themselves. The hospital staff began to bury their dead in a hopfield, which became the second greatest British war cemetery after Tyne Cot. More Australians (1131) are buried here than anywhere except Tyne Cot. All are known by name because they died of wounds or, in a few cases, from accidental injuries. Thus, they left the battlefield still wearing identity discs. They were not killed on the battlefield but survived long enough to be treated in a field ambulance, casualty clearing station, advanced dressing station, main dressing station or one of a variety of hospitals. Many of the AIF men in Lijssenthoek died in field hospitals around the region, some in general hospitals. Lijssenthoek is, in effect, the quintessence of collective suffering. As the cemetery visitors' book shows, relatively few foreign visitors reach it. Most are drawn to the much better known Tyne Cot. I have yet to see a touring party in a coach at Lijssenthoek but, in summer, many coaches visit Tyne Cot each day.

Among the Australians buried at Lijssenthoek is Major Frederick Tubb VC, of the 7th Battalion. Tubb won his VC at Lone Pine, Gallipoli, on 9 August 1915. During the Battle of Menin Road on 20 September 1917 he led his company in the capture of nine enemy pillboxes south of the wood and was wounded by shells of the British barrage. He died that evening in an advanced dressing station (Grave XIX.C.5). His inscription reads: 'Our dearly beloved son and brother. Called to higher service'. One of the soldiers who died of accidental injuries was Lieutenant David Hardy MM of the 11th Battalion (Grave XX1.AA.19).

Directions

From Poperinge, take the A33, signposted to France. After 0.5 kilometre the cemetery is signposted on the left.

The grave of Major F. H. Tubb VC, in Lijssenthoek Military Cemetery, Ypres Salient. Tubb died of wounds sustained during the Passchendaele fighting of 1917.

Private Patrick Bugden, awarded the VC for gallantry during the Battle of Polygon Wood, is buried in Hooge Crater Cemetery, Ypres Salient.

Hooge Crater Cemetery, Zillebeke

This cemetery is opposite the site of the château where fierce fighting occurred in 1914–15. Many soldiers were killed during struggles for possession of the crater but Australians did not enter the area until late 1916. It was not possible to begin the cemetery until October 1917 and after the Armistice it was greatly increased in size by the concentration of graves from various battlefields. It now contains

A total of 1131 Diggers are buried in Lijssenthoek Military Cemetery. The Australian graves lie behind the German graves in the foreground. All but a few of the Australians died of wounds.

the graves of 5878 men of whom 2343 are identified by name. Australians number 513, including 178 unidentified. The design of the long, sloping cemetery is notable for the symbolism of the landscaped crater at the entrance. Of particular Australian interest is the grave of Private Patrick Bugden VC of the 31st Battalion, who was killed during the Battle of Polygon Wood (Grave VIII.C.5). Most of the Diggers buried in Hooge Crater Cemetery are Polygon Wood casualties.

Directions
From Ieper, take the Menin road for 4 kilometres. The cemetery is by the roadside on the right.

Kemmel Château Military Cemetery

Various British units had HQs in the old château in the earlier years of the war. The pretty village of Kemmel was only 10 kilometres south-west of Ypres and at the foot of Mont Kemmel, which was an excellent position for observation and for direction of gunfire. The cemetery was begun in the château grounds in December 1914 and was used until March 1918. It fell into German hands in April and was recaptured in September. The cemetery contains 1135 graves, of which twenty-four are Australians. Most of them are artillerymen who were killed during the massive German bombardments which accompanied the enemy breakthrough in March 1918.

A casualty of 18 August 1917 is Captain Bruce Arnott of the 52nd Battalion. Only 20 years of age, Arnott was highly regarded in the 4th Division and had been awarded the French Croix de Guerre. On the day of his death he and his close friend, Captain Arthur Maxwell, had set off on different tracks for the Messines front, where they were to rendezvous in thirty minutes. Arnott was killed on the way and when Maxwell heard of this he collapsed. An Anzac veteran, Maxwell had fought with distinction in many battles but the death of his friend was just too much. He finished the war as aide-de-camp to Major-General Glasgow, GOC 1st Division. Maxwell paid several visits to Bruce Arnott's grave before returning to Australia. (Arnott's grave B.5)

Directions
From Ieper, take the Kemmel road through the Lille gate. At Kemmel, turn right into the village, continue 200 metres and turn right opposite the church. The beautiful cemetery is 300 metres along this street.

Larch Wood (Railway Cutting) Cemetery

Between the hamlets of Verbrandenmolen and Zwarteleen, Ypres, was a small plantation of larches and a cemetery was made at the north end of this wood. After the Armistice many more graves were brought in. It now contains 768 burials, including thirty-five Australians. Note the grave of Gunner Ernest Grenfell Greer of 5th Bde Australian Field Artillery, killed on 6 August 1917. The cemetery register records that Greer is 'buried near this spot'. (Grave I.H.9) He is an example of the meticulous care taken by the Commonwealth War Graves Commission to be precise in its burials. Greer is one of many AIF gunners buried in Larch Wood. Sergeant Dallas Love, 3rd Battalion, is one of the earliest AIF casualties in this sector. He was killed on 4 September 1916 (Grave I.L.16).

Directions
From Ieper, take the Hollebeke road, which passes Shrapnel Corner. About 1 kilometre after crossing the railway line for the second time, Larch Wood is signposted on the left. It is not visible from the road and is reached by an access path. Ieper, Hill 60 and Zillebeke can be seen from the cemetery.

Lindenhoek Chalet Military Cemetery, Kemmel

Lindenhoek contains the graves of 248 British and Dominion burials of which ten are Australian. All are identified but four, while believed to be in the cemetery, have no known grave. Most were killed in the fighting of mid-1917 and one, a machine-gunner, in December 1917. The 'buried but without grave' men were killed in March 1918 during the German breakthrough.

Directions
From Kemmel, take the road towards Armentières. Lindenhoek hamlet is 1 kilometre from Kemmel and the cemetery is signposted there. Kemmel Hill and Messines Ridge can be seen from the cemetery, also several villages east and south. All this was AIF territory in the period June 1917–April 1918.

Messines Ridge British Cemetery

This large cemetery occupies ground where a convent stood before being destroyed by shellfire in 1916. The Germans built an elaborate system of cellars and tunnels under the convent and turned it into a powerful bastion. Included in the 1490 burials are 332 AIF men, nearly all killed in the great attack on Messines Ridge on 6 July 1917. A special memorial commemorates ten Australians believed to be buried here. After the war, bodies were brought in from nearby smaller burial places, such as Queensland Cemetery. Thirty Australians came from there, including twenty-three from the 41st Battalion, a largely Queensland unit. The cemetery incorporates yet another New Zealand memorial, this time to the 840 New Zealand troops who fell in the neighbourhood and have no known grave.

Directions
From Ieper, drive to Mesen. At the entrance to the town, on the right, the cemetery is signposted.

Menin Road South Military Cemetery

This cemetery, beside the main route to the Ypres Salient front line, was always within the British lines. It was first used in January 1916 by British regiments and in 1917 Australians were buried there by their units or Field Ambulancemen. After the Armistice 203 graves from Menin Road North Military Cemetery (no longer in existence), and from isolated positions on the battlefields, were brought in. Out of 1755 graves 263 are Australians, eight of whom are unknown.

Since this cemetery was by the side of a route much used by wagons, it received many bodies deposited by passing drivers. Consequently, many infantry battalions are represented, as are the pioneer battalions, machine-gun companies, artillery batteries, engineering companies and the Army Service Corps. Several members of the 3rd

Australian Light Railway Operating Company are also buried here. The Company strove throughout the period July to November 1917 to build and maintain a narrow-gauge railway from Ypres to the front.

With only two exceptions, the Diggers in this cemetery are 1917 casualties, killed between September and November 1917 in the battles of Menin Road, Polygon Wood, Broodseinde or Passchendaele. Some got back this far from the front because they were still alive, though dying of their wounds.

The grave of Captain Fred Moore of the 5th (Victorian) Battalion (Grave I.T.4) evokes memories of a notorious incident which occurred on 20 September 1917 at a blockhouse at Black Watch corner, Polygon Wood. Captain Moore led his company in an attack on the formidable place, which was not only dangerous to his own men but to the battalion which would follow in the next advance. Moore ran towards the blockhouse, apparently to receive its surrender. When the German who had surrendered saw that his approaching enemy was an officer he is believed to have picked up his weapon, killed Moore with it and then surrendered again. Moore, who was only 22, was a much admired officer and the Victorians at once killed the German. Angry and bitter, they would have wiped out the garrison had not some other Australian officers stopped them. In a few similar incidents where the Diggers believed, sometimes wrongly, that treachery had occurred, entire garrisons were killed in retribution.

Mud Corner British Cemetery

While this cemetery is nominally within the commune of Warneton (Waasten), it is 2 kilometres from the village. It lies just outside the extreme northern edge of Plugstreet (Ploegsteert) Wood and is really an Anzac burial ground, with 53 New Zealanders and 31 Australians, together with one British soldier. Most of the Diggers are 9th Brigade men killed during the Battle of Messines in June 1917 but the burial period continued until December of that year. A soldier of the 3rd Australian Pioneers, Private Albert Victor, was killed on 1 December. A brave young second-lieutenant, Thomas Denton-Clarke, 35th Battalion, is among the Diggers of Mud Corner. Aged 24, he was the son of parents at the Institution of the Deaf, Dumb and Blind at Darlington, Sydney. Mud Corner was very much a battlefield cemetery, as one of the epitaphs implies. It is for Private C. G. Keogh, 43rd Battalion, killed on 9 June 1917. 'They laid him by with prayer and sigh, the spot where he was killed'.

Directions

From Ieper, take the N336, signposted Armentières. Pass through Mesen and after 2 kilometres note a cluster of five military cemetery signs, including Mud Corner. Turn left here on to a narrow road for 0.5 kilometre and then right on to a dirt farm road, which is passable for vehicles. It leads to Mud Corner within 100 metres. *See* **Toronto Avenue Cemetery**.

Passchendaele New British Cemetery

Made after the Armistice by the concentration of graves from the battlefields of Passchendaele and Langemarck, this cemetery contains 2091 graves. They include 292 Australians but 170 of them are unidentified by name. Most were killed during the Battle of Broodseinde Ridge on 4–5 October 1917 or during the Battle of Passchendaele a week later. However, seven were killed in November, which was late for AIF participation in the battle. Five are from the 1st Division which was ordered to leave some battalions to support the Canadians when the bulk of the AIF had been withdrawn. Visitors might care to linger at the grave of Lieutenant Talbert Pitman of the 44th Battalion and reflect on the manner of his death on 5 October 1917. Signals officer of the battalion, Pitman gave up his place in an advanced blockhouse to allow some of his tired men to sleep inside. He lay down outside beside the wall, where a shell killed him (Grave XIII.G.11).

Directions

From Passendale centre crossroads take the Westrozebeek road. Within 1.5 kilometres of Passendale centre the cemetery is signposted on the left.

Perth Cemetery (China Wall), Zillebeke

It is not known why this cemetery was called Perth but its China Wall label comes from a nearby communications breastwork (an above-ground 'trench') known as the Great Wall of China. It was used as a frontline cemetery until October 1917, when it contained 130 graves, and then not used again until after the Armistice. It now has 2763 graves including 134 Australians, nineteen of them unidentified. Special memorials bear the names of another thirteen Diggers buried in the cemeteries concentrated here but whose graves could not be found. Remains were brought from nearly thirty small cemeteries in the years after the Armistice.

Second Lieutenant Frederick Birks VC, MM, of the 6th Battalion, killed during the Battle of Polygon Wood, is buried here (Grave I.G.45). The cemetery is notable for the large proportion of gunners from the Australian Field Artillery, about half the AIF burials. One of these casualties is Bombardier Ambrose Crawford MM, killed on 26 October 1917. The other VC winner in the cemetery is an Englishman, Major W. H. Johnston of the Royal Engineers, a 1915 casualty (Grave III.C.12).

Directions
From Ieper, take the Menin road and after 1.5 kilometres at a crossroads, turn right to Zillebeke, which is signposted. Perth Cemetery is on the left within 1 kilometre.

Reningelst Churchyard and Extension

One Australian lies amid fifty-five British soldiers. He is Australian Army Chaplain M. Bergin MC, who was killed during the Battle of Passchendaele on 12 October 1917. Father Bergin, a missionary, had joined the AIF in Egypt. He served in the front trenches at Pozières and a soldier said of him, 'If ever an angel walked among men, it was he'.

Directions:
From Ieper, take the Dikkebus road and continue to the village of Le Clytte. At the crossroads here, turn right to Reningelst, which is signposted.

Segard, Château, Voormezeele, Ypres

Château Segard and its grounds were much used by the AIF late in 1916 and for much of 1917. Battalions finally formed up there before moving towards the front. Support battalions, waiting for their turn to go forward, rested there. When operating in the Ypres Salient most AIF divisions kept a small staff at the chateau for administration. The Diggers called the place 'Château Cigar'.

Directions
From Ieper, pass through the Rijselpoort and take the Kemmel road. 1 kilometre after crossing the railway note two broken pillars at a farm road on the right. This was the entrance to the château's grounds. The present farm stands on the site of the demolished château.

St Quentin Cabaret Military Cemetery, Ploegsteert

St Quentin Cabaret was an inn about 650 metres east of Kandahar Farm, on the south side of the road from Neuve-Eglise to Messines. At times it was used as a battalion HQ. British units began the cemetery in February 1915. Of 460 British and Dominion burials only seven are Australian. Five of them are 3rd Division men killed in the early fighting at Messines in June 1917, together with one 4th Division soldier. Driver Arthur O'Connor, a gunner, was only 18 (Grave II.B.21). An eighth Australian is buried in St Quentin Cabaret Cemetery, though he served in the 1st Canadian Infantry (Western Ontario Regiment). He was Private John Harold Davis of Millthorpe, near Orange, NSW. He was killed on 24 December 1915, long before any of his AIF countrymen reached the Western Front (Grave I.B.17).

Directions
At the larger cemetery of Kandahar Farm, 650 metres from St Quentin Cabaret, check the local map in the cemetery register.

Sanctuary Wood Cemetery, Zillebeke

Sanctuary Wood was so named because it was used to screen troops behind the front line. There was also a story that a certain senior officer, in charge of a troops collecting depot here, refused to allow soldiers to go forward until they were rested and thus provided temporary sanctuary. One of the largest and most beautiful of cemeteries in the Ypres Salient, Sanctuary Wood Cemetery is fan-shaped and contains the graves of 1989 soldiers, of whom 1353 are unidentified. This large proportion of unknowns is because of the heavy fighting and shellfire which obliterated earlier burials. Australian burials total eighty-eight of whom fifty-three are unidentified. Most were killed in the summer of 1917 in the Polygon Wood sector and brought in to Sanctuary Wood Cemetery from isolated graves. Lieutenant G. W. L. Talbot, in whose memory Talbot House at Poperinge was established, is buried here (Grave I.G.1).

Directions
From Ieper, take the Menen road 2 kilometres to Café Canada and turn right into Maple Avenue where the Canadian Memorial is signposted. Just beyond Sanctuary Wood Cemetery is Hill 62, and a trenches museum, which should be visited.

Spoil Bank Cemetery, Zillebeke

The cemetery is by the side of the now disused Ypres-Comines canal, which runs south-east from Ypres between Zillebeke and Ypres. The canal bed lies between banks of spoil thrown up when it was dug. The cemetery was begun in February 1915 and the first AIF casualties were interred there in the autumn of 1917. Total graves number 509, of which sixty-seven are Australian, including six unknown. AIF dead include Major Horace Henwood of the 10th Battalion. While the 1st Division was relieving the 4th on 1 March 1918, a strong patrol of Germans raided several posts. Major Henwood had just taken over a captured pillbox as his company HQ, when the Germans struck. Taken by surprise he was captured, but while the German patrol was retiring it was spotted by other Australians, who opened fire. Men were seen to fall and the dead included Henwood, whose body was found by a patrol from his own company (Grave II.D.9). Most Diggers buried here fell during the winter of 1917–18 and many of them were machine-gunners. *See* **Buff Bank**.

Directions
Precisely as for Buff Bank.

Toronto Avenue Cemetery

Officially, this cemetery is in the commune of Warneton (Waasten) but it is 2 kilometres from the village. It lies within the northern part of the famous Plug Street (Ploegsteert) Wood. The cemetery was named from one of the paths in the wood but if ever a war burial ground warranted the name Australia, this is it. Every one of the 78 soldiers buried here is Australian, 44 of them being from the 33rd Battalion. The 36th Battalion erected a wooden memorial to its dead in 1917 but it rotted away decades ago. All the Diggers of Toronto Avenue were members of the 9th Brigade, 3rd Division, and they were killed close by in the period 7–10 June, during the Battle of Messines. Three were only 18 years of age. The most senior soldier was Captain F. J. Piggott of the 36th Battalion, whose family left this epitaph: 'A career so brilliant laid aside for the call to arms'. Sadly, the cemetery has no provision for a register of graves or a visitors' book, but as it is completely hidden in the wood and away from a road, it has few visitors. The Commonwealth War Graves Commission has gone to great lengths to keep forest animals out of the cemetery. Steel mesh has been sunk several feet into the surrounding earth. Under the overhanging trees, the white stones became badly stained with green mold but coated with a special substance, they now remain white.

Directions
From Ieper, take the N336, signposted Armentières. Pass through Mesen and after 2 kilometres note a cluster of five military cemetery signs, including Toronto Avenue. Here turn left on to a narrow road for 0.5 kilometre and then right, immediately after passing Prowse Point Cemetery, on to a farm dirt road. Passable for vehicles, this road leads within 100 metres to Mud Corner Cemetery. After visiting Mud Corner, continue 50 metres to a gate. It is never locked and you may safely ignore the 'no entry' sign. Drive or walk along this road for 0.5 kilometre and watch for Toronto Avenue Cemetery at the end of a short branch to the left. During the hunting season, November to February, it is unwise to go further into the wood. *See* **Mud Corner Cemetery**.

Tyne Cot Cemetery, Passchendaele

Tyne Cot or Tyne Cottage was the name given by the army to a barn which stood west of the Passchendaele-Broodseinde road. The barn became the centre of five German blockhouses and was captured by the AIF 2nd Division on 4 October 1917. One

An English schoolgirl on a study tour takes notes from the grave of Captain Clarence Smith Jeffries VC, in Tyne Cot Cemetery.

of the blockhouses was then used as an Advanced Dressing Station. From 6 October 1917 until the end of the war 343 graves were made on either side of the ADS. After the Armistice the cemetery was enlarged until it held 11 956 graves, the largest British cemetery, and covered 35 103 square metres. The unnamed graves number 8366.

There are 1368 Australian graves, the majority being unidentified. A special memorial records the names of fifteen other Australians known or believed to be buried within the cemetery. Of particular interest to Australians is the Cross of Sacrifice which, at the suggestion of King George V, was built over one of the blockhouses. It is one of several captured by the AIF and a plaque commemorates the heroic deed. A small part of the original blockhouse concrete is visible through a 'window' in the gleaming white cement which forms the base for the cross. Two Australian VC winners are buried in Tyne Cot

Sergeant Lewis McGee showed great courage and exemplary leadership in the Passchendaele fighting of October 1917. Killed in action at Broodseinde, he is buried in Tyne Cot Cemetery not far from Captain Jeffries VC.

Cemetery, Captain Clarence Smith Jeffries of the 34th Battalion (Grave XL.E.1) and Sergeant Lewis McGee of the 40th Battalion (Grave XX.D.1).

Tyne Cot is a magnificent garden cemetery and a blaze of colour during the growing seasons. The view up the slope from the lich-gate, through the headstones, garden and lawns to the Great Cross and the Memorial to the Missing, is profoundly moving. All major memorial ceremonies are held in Tyne Cot Cemetery. Note the two large blockhouses towards the front of the cemetery. Both were captured by the AIF, but by the 3rd Division, not the 2nd, as implied on the memorial.

Directions
From Ieper, take the Zonnebeke road until you reach the major crossroads of the Passendale-Broodseinde road. Turn left and in 1 kilometre Tyne Cot is signposted left.

Wulvergem-Lindenhoek Road Military Cemetery

The cemetery contains 658 soldiers, including thirty-nine from Australia. Five of the Diggers are unidentified. Roughly half of these men were killed during the Third Battle of Ypres, July-November 1917, the others during the AIF raids in the Lys River sector of winter 1917–18. The great majority are infantry, together with five pioneers, two artillery men and a machine-gunner. One of the pioneers is Lieutenant John Drury Reid MC, of the 4th Pioneers, who died of wounds on 10 June 1917 (Grave II.A.29). Some of the Australians had first been buried alone or in small cemeteries and were brought together at Wulvergem-Lindenhoek Road after the war.

Directions
From Ieper, take the Kemmel-Armentières road. About 2 kilometres from Kemmel, the cemetery is signposted on the left.

Other Belgian Cemeteries with Australian Graves

Adinkerke Military Cemetery, Furnes; Arvaing Churchyard, Province of Hainault; Artillery Wood Cemetery, Boezinge; Audenard de Communal

Cross of Sacrifice in Tyne Cot Cemetery, Broodseinde Ridge, Passendale, Ypres. The cross is built over a blockhouse captured by the AIF.

Cemetery, Province of East Flanders; Bedford House Cemetery, Zillebeke; Belgian Battery Corner Cemetery, Ypres; Belgrade House Cemetery, Namur; Bethleem Farm East Cemetery; Bethleem Farm West Cemetery; Birr Cross Roads Cemetery, Zillebeke; Brandhoek Military, Vlamertinge; Brandhoek New Military Cemetery; Buffs Road Cemetery, St Jean-Les-Ypres; Bus House Cemetery, Voormezeele; Cabin Hill Cemetery, Wytschaete; Chester Farm Cemetery, Zillebeke; Courtrai (St Jean) Communal Cemetery; Coxyde Military Cemetery; Derry House Cemetery, Wytschaete; Dickebusch New Military Cemetery; Dickebusch New Military Cemetery Extension; Dinant Communal Cemetery; Dozinghem Military Cemetery, Westvleteren; Dranoutre Military Cemetery; Duhallow ADS Cemetery, Ypres; Escanaffles Communal Cemetery, Province of Hainault; Godezonne Farm Cemetery, Kemmel; Gunners Farm Cemetery; Gwalia Cemetery, Poperinge; Hagle Dump Cemetery, Hal Communal Cemetery; Haies Communal Cemetery, Nalines;

Hantes-Wiheries Communal Cemetery; Haringhe (Bandaghem) Military Cemetery; Harlebeke New British Cemetery; Houyet Churchyard; Hyde Park Corner (Royal Berks Cemetery); Irish House Cemetery, Kemmel; Kemmel No. 1 French Cemetery; Klein-Vierstraat British Cemetery, Kemmel; La Brique Military Cemetery, St Jean-Les-Ypres; La Clytte Military Cemetery; La Laiterie Military Cemetery, Kemmel; La Louvaine Communal Cemetery; Lancashire Cottage Cemetery, Ploegsteert; La Plus Douve Farm Cemetery; Liege (Robermont) Cemetery; London Rifle Brigade Cemetery; Maple Leaf Cemetery, Neuve-Eglise; Marcinelle New Communal Cemetery; Mendinghem British Cemetery, Proven; Menin Road South Military Cemetery; Mons Communal Cemetery; Morville Communal Cemetery; Motor Car Corner Cemetery; Mud Corner British Cemetery, Warneton; Neuve-Eglise Churchyard; New Irish Farm Cemetery, St Jean-Les-Ypres; Nine Elms British Cemetery, Poperinge; Nivelles Communal Cemetery; Oak Dump Cemetery, Voormezeele; Oosttaverne Wood Cemetery, Wytschaete; Oxford Road Cemetery, Ypres; Potijze Burial Ground, Potijze Château Grounds Cemetery; Potijze Château Lawn Cemetery; Ploegsteert Wood Military Cemetery; Poperinge New Military Cemetery; Prowse Point Military Cemetery, Warneton; Ramscappelle Road Military Cemetery; Ration Farm (La Plus Douve) Annexe; Reningelst New Military Cemetery; Ridge Wood Military Cemetery, Voormezeele; Russeignies Churchyard; Somer Farm Cemetery, Wytschaete; St Julien Dressing Station Cemetery; St Maur Churchyard, Province of Haincourt; Strand Military Cemetery, Ploegsteert; Tancrez Farm Cemetery; The Huts Cemetery, Dickebusch; Toronto Avenue Cemetery, Warneton; Torreken Farm Cemetery, Wytschaete; Tournai Communal Cemetery Allied Extension; Underhill Farm Cemetery, Ploegsteert; Vlamertinge Military Cemetery; Vlamertinge New Military Cemetery; Voormezeele Enclosures; Westhof Farm Cemetery, Neuve-Eglise; Westouter Churchyard Extension; White House Cemetery, St Jean-Les-Ypres Woods Cemetery, Zillebeke; Wytschaete Military Cemetery; Ypres Town Cemetery Extension, Menin Gate; Ypres Reservoir Cemetery; Zandvoorde British Cemetery.

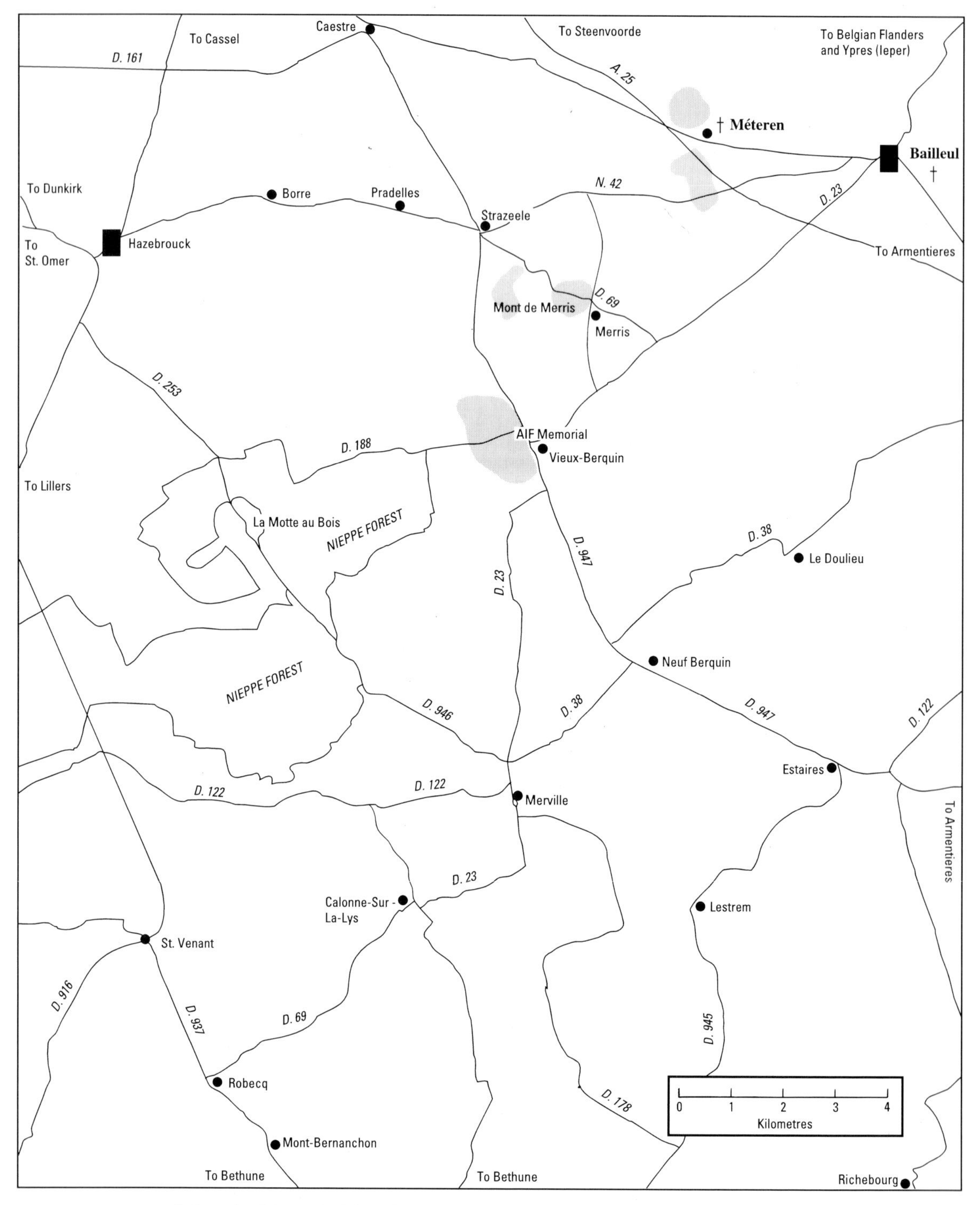

Map 4. French Flanders: Towns, Battle Areas, Cemeteries

Chapter 3

French Flanders and Northern France

This lowland region was the sector in which the AIF first began its active service operations on the Western Front. The Diggers fought their first big battle here, at Fromelles in 1916, and during the German breakthrough of spring 1918 they achieved some of their most spectacular successes.

The 2nd Division began to take over a 14.5 kilometre sector of the line south-east of Armentières on 8 April 1916. This was the 'Nursery', a region of ditches, boggy ground and hedges which made active operations difficult, especially in winter. British and Dominion troops were given experience in the Nursery before being sent to more active parts of the front. The Australians discovered that the trenches were not trenches at all but breastworks, made of earth and rubble piled above the level of the land. In effect, the breastworks were above-ground trenches. Even the communication trenches were carried on footbridges whenever they crossed a ditch. The accuracy of German snipers made it dangerous to look over the parapet. Behind the breastworks were rectangular shelters for officers and men, for company bomb stores and headquarters.

The Diggers had many complaints about the inadequacy of the defences. The parapet was not bullet proof, no dugout could withstand the impact of a heavy shell and the soggy ground and sheets of water made life unpleasant.

Before the AIF took over the line the British sentries did not fire on the enemy lines on the supposition, correct as it turned out, that if the Germans were not stirred up they would not retaliate. The Diggers changed all that. From the moment they went into the line many of them were looking for good targets and sniping became a keen pastime. Within a few weeks of the AIF taking over the line, numerous patrols were at work after dark, going right up to the enemy's wire and sometimes through it. Patrols often tossed bombs into the German trenches.

Behind the lines, the towns of Merville, Strazeele, Merris, Meteren and Hazebrouck, among others, loomed large in the lives of the Australians because of their billets and estaminets. Here they discovered the 'real' France and met French people. They flirted with the girls, played with the children and bought what they could from every farm Madame. There can be few farms in the region where Diggers did not once sit in family intimacy with Madame and her children and the few men not away at the war.

Armentières

Being just behind the lines, Armentières was a great forward base and a popular recreation centre. One of its main industries was brewing and in the Diggers' judgment Armentières beer was good. Despite intermittent shelling, the town was not greatly damaged before 1918. The Germans captured it on 10 April 1918 during the Battle of the Lys. When they seemed about to lose it during a British counter-offensive in September, the Germans destroyed all the main buildings and factories. The town was well known to the Australians, who patronised the many estaminets around the main square.

Bois Grenier

A commune and small village on the D222 road 3 kilometres south of Armentières, Bois Grenier had been the scene of much fighting long before the Australians reached France. In the summer of 1916 Australian battalions were involved in frequent large-scale raiding in the fields of Bois Grenier, as diversions before the imminent great British Somme offensive of 1 July. On the night of 25 June the AIF won its first VC in the European war at Bois Grenier. Captain K. Heritage led eight officers and seventy-three other ranks, all volunteers of the 5th Brigade, to harass German positions. After a successful raid, the Australians were returning when they came under shellfire in No Man's Land. Private William Jackson of the 17th Battalion brought a prisoner into the Australian lines and then ran out into a storm of exploding shells to rescue a wounded mate. Having done this, he went out again and was bringing in another wounded man when a shell practically blew off his own arm. Despite this terrible wound, Jackson persisted in his rescue attempt before allowing his arm to be amputated in the trench.

Directions
Jackson actually won his VC 2 kilometres west of Bois Grenier village. From Fleurbaix, take the D176 towards Bois Grenier. After 1 kilometre there is a sharp left elbow where the road becomes the D222. Jackson's exploit took place in the field to the left of this turn in the road.

Calonne-sur-la-Lys

This village, 3 kilometres south-west of Merville, was the scene of great Australian initiative on 12–14 April 1918 during the German Lys offensive. Some AIF Field artillery units — the 12th, 45th, 47th, 46th and 112th Brigades — had been firing from just behind the Clarence rivulet which flows through the village, and the rapidity of the German infantry advance surprised them. When the Germans were no more than 200 metres away, Sergeant P. H. George, 45th Brigade, brought up the horse teams to get his guns away before the road to Robecq was cut. As the teams galloped down the road other AIF gunners steadied the retiring British infantry. Gunner A. Medcalf, 47th Brigade, rallied some dispirited British to help soldiers of the Warwickshire Regiment who were making a stand, and stayed with them until night. Gunners W. G. Parkinson and T. W. Kelly 45th Brigade, and G. T. White, 112th Brigade, also fought with the infantry. Gunner O. E. Cohen, medical orderly of the 47th, formed an aid post on the Calonne road. Here he tended the wounded and retired with his last patient. When the batteries withdrew across the La Bassee Canal the canal drawbridges were guarded by scratch units formed by Lieutenant R. T. Watt, 112th Battery, and other AIF officers. The canal became the British front line. Calonne has changed little since 1918. Gunner Cohen's makeshift aid post was at the junction in Calonne of the Robecq and St Venant roads.

Directions
From Merville, take the D23 south to Calonne for 3 kilometres. In Calonne, near the junction of the road to St Venant, the D23 becomes the D69. The AIF batteries were positioned on the west side of the river, which runs parallel to the D69.

Battle of Fromelles, 19–20 July 1916

The farm fields of Fromelles were the scene of the AIF's first great battle on the Western Front. The battle, the brainchild of the British General Sir Richard Haking, was a terrible blunder and the AIF 5th Division (Major-General J. W. McKay) suffered 5533 casualties in twenty-seven hours of incessant fighting, 19–20 July 1916. Haking used the 5th Division, together with the British 61st Division, in a virtually impossible attempt to capture enemy positions protecting Fromelles, which lies on Aubers Ridge. The British High Command also hoped that the attack would hold to that part of the front German divisions which might otherwise be sent to the Somme, where a great battle had been raging since 1 July.

During 1915 the British had twice lost heavily in abortive attacks on Aubers Ridge and Haking himself had already suffered losses in a similar operation in June 1916. The Germans on the higher ground dominated the plain west of the ridge and little British activity there escaped their observation. Their trench lines in front of Fromelles were strong and well defended by many machine-guns. No Man's Land was from 100 metres to 450 metres wide and without cover for attackers. For the Allies much depended on their artillery barrage being effective and on close co-ordination between the 5th and 61st Divisions. The key German trenches were those of the Sugar Loaf, a salient where the German lines jutted forward of their otherwise straight line.

Responsibility for capturing the Sugar Loaf fell on the 61st Division. On the 61st's left, the 5th Division had a front of about 2400 metres, with the 15th Brigade on the right, the 14th in the centre and the 8th on the left. Despite an inadequate supporting artillery bombardment, the 8th and 14th Brigades made a good start. They crossed No Man's Land, stormed the enemy front trenches and broke through.

On the right, however, the British did not capture the Sugar Loaf, enabling the German machine-gunners to enfilade the 15th Brigade's battalions — 57th, 58th, 59th and 60th Battalions — as they strove bravely to cross the widest part of No Man's Land. A few Diggers almost reached the enemy wire, the rest were killed or wounded within a few minutes of the battle's commencement. The survivors dug in and fought on.

The 8th and 14th Brigades captured the German second line, hundreds of metres beyond the first line, and worked long into the night to organise a defensive line. As the hours passed they steadily lost officers and men to every type of German fire. That night a supporting attack by the 61st Division was cancelled, leaving the Australians surrounded in the trenches they had captured. Meanwhile, Australian engineers worked frantically to drive communications trenches across No Man's Land and to their infantry in the enemy trenches. Hand-to-hand fighting and bombing lasted all night and into the next day. Several officers distinguished themselves; they included Captain Norman Gibbins of the 55th Battalion, Captain C. Arblaster, 53rd, Lieutenant C. T. Agassiz, 55th, and Captain F. L. Krinks, 30th. Chaplain S. E. Maxted, 54th Battalion, ignored an order to stay in the rear and became a stretcher bearer. He was killed in No Man's Land while attempting to rescue wounded men.

As early as dawn on the 20th it was clear that the position was hopeless. None of the positions held by the Australian brigades had any natural advantages and the High Command had not contemplated any reinforcement with fresh troops. As an organised force, the 15th Brigade had ceased to exist. Fighting to the last, the exhausted men of the 8th Brigade and then the 14th were slowly forced back by relentless German pressure.

The appalling losses shocked the senior Australian officers. The 60th Battalion (Victoria) went into the fight with 887 men and came out with one officer and 106 men. The 32nd Battalion (Western Australia, South Australia) had seventeen officers and 701 men hit. Brigadier-General H. E. Elliott, commander of the 15th Brigade, wrote a scathing indictment of the British decision to attack Fromelles and of the battle plan:

Australians taken prisoner at Fromelles are marched through the streets of La Bassée by their German captors. Steel helmets were not then universal in the AIF and some Diggers are wearing their slouch hats.

The whole operation was so incredibly blundered from beginning to end that it is almost incomprehensible how the British staff, who were responsible for it, could have consisted of trained professional soldiers . . . and why, in view of the outcome of this extraordinary adventure, any of them were retained in active command.

Lieutenant-Colonel J. W. Clark, CO of the 30th Battalion, wrote: 'We are supposed to have accomplished what the British command was strategically working for, the pinning of German troops to the front, and preventing them from being sent to the Somme. But this could have been achieved by massing troops and making a demonstration.'

Fromelles was the only battle which the AIF fought on the Western Front which failed to produce any positive result, but flesh and blood could have done no more. Nobody has ever suggested that the slaughter was in any way the fault of the 5th Division's commanders.

Directions

Fromelles is most easily approached from Armentières. From the centre of Armentières take the D933 to La Chapelle d'Armentières and cross the A25 motorway. Follow signposts to Bois Grenier and at the crossroads in the centre of the village turn left on the D62, signposted Radinghem-en-Weppes. After 5 kilometres immediately after passing through this village, and through another crossroads, turn right on the D141b to Le Maisnil and Fromelles. From here, the plain on which the battle was fought is clearly visible. Turn right through Fromelles village. After 1.5 kilometres there is a T-junction at the hamlet of les Rouges Bancs. From here, VC Corner Australian Cemetery is signposted. The cemetery is in the middle of the battlefield. Stand on the cemetery steps and turn half left to place yourself in the direction in which the Australians were advancing. The River Laies (actually little more than a ditch) is only thirty paces to your right and crosses the battlefield diagonally. In the field across the road from the cemetery was the German frontline position which the British called the Sugar Loaf.

Note the line of church spires to your front. In the centre is that of Fromelles, right of it is Aubers and left is Le Maisnil. They mark the line of Aubers

VC Corner Australian Cemetery, Fromelles, is the only cemetery without headstones. Under two crosses, right and left of the central path, lie the remains of 410 unidentified Australians killed during the Battle of Fromelles. Names of the missing are listed on the rear wall.

Ridge. Parking at VC Corner Australian Cemetery is difficult. Approach the family in the farm next to the cemetery, explain that you are Australian and they will gladly permit you to park. The Australians' forming up area for the Battle of Fromelles was Rue Tilleloy, near Picantin. Brigadier-General Elliott had his HQ in an estaminet called Rouge Debout at Trou Post.

The entrance to VC Corner Australian Cemetery on the battlefield of Fromelles.

La Croix Blanche, Fleurbaix

This hamlet lies at the crossroads of the D171 (Fleurbaix to Neuve-Chapelle) and the D175, 2 kilometres south of Fleurbaix. It is an interesting spot because at the crossroads on 20 July 1916 the 30th Battalion held its roll call after the Battle of Fromelles. Major M. Purser was in charge of the parade, as the men stood in the road and answered their names. The CO, Lieutenant-Colonel J. W. Clark, wrote, 'The greatest shock of my life was the heartbreaking feeling that I had lost so many fine men from a battalion I had watched grow from a motley mob into an efficient unit.' In fact, Clark's casualties were nine officers and 343 men, a terrible loss, but a low total compared with other battalions. The 30th Battalion was held for three days in reserve at La Croix Blanche while parties ventured out from time to time at night to bring in wounded men from No Man's Land. It is not often possible so closely to pinpoint the place at which an after-battle roll call took place.

Hazebrouck

This large town with its railway junction was a major base throughout the war. Within an 8-kilometre radius of the town were camped or billeted tens of thousands of soldiers and scores of units and many depots. Close behind the town to the west were transit and reinforcement camps and to the south-west were casualty clearing stations and hospitals. During the German spring offensive of 1918 Hazebrouck was in danger of capture but the AIF 1st Division held firm and, with support from some British troops, blocked the German advance and saved the town. It remains much as the Diggers knew it in 1918, especially around the town hall and great square. AIF bands played in the square on several occasions.

Hill 70, Lens

While nothing of the war remains to be seen at this site, it is important in Australian military history on the Western Front for the work, fortitude and courage of the 3rd Australian Tunnelling Company, a West Australian unit with a large proportion of Tasmanians. In November 1916, the unit was ordered into the mines of Hill 70, 2 kilometres north-west of the mining centre of Lens. The Germans were aggressively mining in the white chalk, but the Australians did not then have an accurate idea of the enemy's whereabouts underground. On 27 November the Diggers were almost ready to fire a mine when the Germans beat them to it with a *camouflet*. Twenty miners were killed and others were gassed. Two more Australians were killed next day. Their mates hit back at the Germans as they learned more about the enemy tunnels and blew their own *camouflets*. Underground fighting continued and on 26 March 1917 the Australians finally closed the gap in the underground defensive system with a charge of 4990 kilograms of ammonal.

On 26 June 1917 three parties of tunnellers were to raid overland to destroy three enemy shafts within enemy lines. Major L. J. Coulter DSO, the CO of the Company, returned from leave an hour before the patrol was due to start and accompanied the infantry patrol. He was killed during a fight with German infantry.

On 24 July the tunnellers followed up their destruction of enemy shafts by breaking into the German underground system and capturing it. Their struggle for Hill 70 ended in August but 3rd Tunnelling Company was busy well into 1918.

Directions
Hill 70 was not a single hill but an area of high ground, largely created from the spoil brought from the mines. Much of the area has been levelled since the war but the old battle arena can be seen from the Bethune-Lens road, the N43. It is on the north side of the road about 6 kilometres from Lens. (*See* **Hersin Communal Cemetery Extension**.)

Le Waton

This hamlet, between Meteren and Merris, was the scene of a fine action by platoons of the 9th Battalion on 19 July 1918. After capturing Le Waton in April the Germans had prepared strong positions, in Le Waton itself and between the hamlet and Meteren Becque (stream). Australian platoons advanced along the hedges and through wheatfields until stopped by a well-handled machine-gun. Lance-Corporal J. E. Young (serving under the name of Bartle) worked his way from shellhole to shellhole and, when 40 metres away, charged the position while firing his Lewis gun from the hip. He killed the crew and captured the gun and repeated the feat with two other guns and crews. He was awarded the DCM for this feat but many VC winners did less for their more exalted award. Young's exploit took place at what is now Joye Ferme (farm) on the northern edge of the hamlet.

Lys River

AIF activities along the Lys River in Belgian Flanders are described in Chapter 1 of this book. Australians were also busy in the Lys River sector of French Flanders. The Battle of the Lys began on 9 April 1918 when the German Sixth Army, with Armentières as its base, struck the British lines in a great effort to break through to the Channel ports. When the Germans overwhelmed a Portuguese division in the centre of the British First Army, the entire Allied line was pushed back by 7 kilometres. Next day the German Fourth Army pushed back the British Second Army and Messines Ridge, won at great cost in 1917, was lost. On 12 April Haig issued an order forbidding any further retirement. The AIF 1st Division, which had been sent from Flanders to the Somme, had no sooner arrived there than they returned to the Lys sector to plug the breakthrough. What the Australians achieved here is described under the headings of various places, Vieux-Berquin, Hazebrouck, Merris, Strazeele, Meteren and others. Small AIF units, sometimes mere detachments under a junior officer or NCO, held the front together at many points. As a river, the Lys was not important in AIF or even larger Allied operations. It was merely the stream in the broad, shallow valley along which the Germans made their massive advance.

Merris Patrols – North-West

On the night of 10 June 1918 Lieutenant R. E. Taylor, the Intelligence Office of the 4th Battalion, made a reconnaissance patrol of the area north-west of Merris and came across an enemy trench containing about twenty enemy. Following his report his CO, Lieutenant-Colonel C. D. Sasse, asked him if he wanted to raid the trench. Taylor, well known for his audacity, took six men with him on the morning of 12 June and crept through standing wheat to the German wire. Here he left one man as rearguard while he and others cut the wire and jumped into the trench. By now there were thirty enemy, and a fierce fight took place. The Australians killed about ten Germans and grabbed two as prisoners but the Germans, having recovered from their surprise, regrouped and counter-attacked. German bombs killed the Australians' prisoners and slightly wounded Taylor and some of his party but they returned safely. Taylor handed over a Bavarian cap and shoulder strap marked '5'. This was valuable intelligence. Taylor won the MC for his daring raid.

Nothing remains of the wartime positions but the site of Taylor's raid can be visited. From Merris, head north on the Flêtre road for 0.3 kilometre and turn left to the local cemetery. The trench which Taylor attacked was in the field immediately beyond the cemetery towards Strazeele.

Merris Patrols – South-West

On 11 July 1918 a patrol of the 1st Battalion, commanded by Lieutenant G. E. Gaskell and Sergeant D. H. Scott, carried out a patrol along the railway between Merris and Strazeele. It was later considered to be such a perfect patrol action that for thirty years it was used as a model in British Army training.

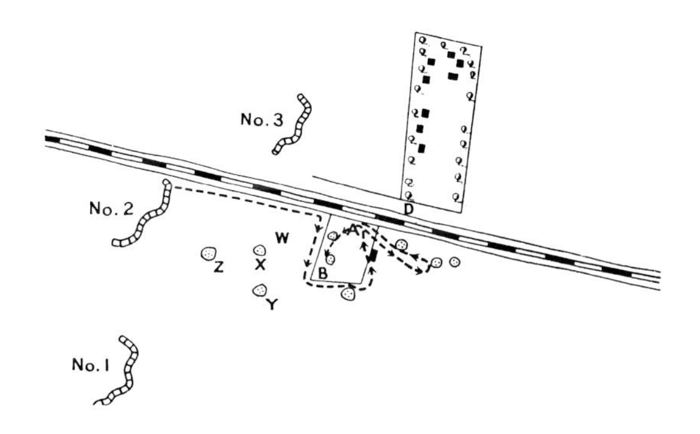

In the summer of 1918 the AIF was engaging in what the Diggers called 'peaceful penetration', a form of aggressive patrolling which had a demoralising effect on the Germans facing them.

It is possible to see where Gaskell's 'Merris patrol' took place. His platoon, in three posts, straddled the railway about 600 metres west of where the Merris-Vieux-Berquin road crosses the line. Gaskell, Scott, Corporal A. London and one man first made a reconnaissance, using as cover an embankment about 3 metres high. They searched a house and noted three suspicious looking shellholes, marked X, Y, Z on the sketch. Crawling through crops, Gaskell and Scott worked their way to the back of X and saw a machine-gun facing towards the Australian posts. Two German soldiers were sitting in the craters and talking. Taken by surprise at revolver point they cried for mercy but were ordered to keep quiet and to point out the other German posts. They indicated Y and Z. Gaskell and Scott took the prisoners back to Corporal London and his mate at W, with the Germans carrying their captured machine-gun.

Gaskell decided to rush post Y while Scott did the same at Z, the attacks to be simultaneous. Each stalked to within ten paces of the shellholes, then Gaskell waved his helmet and the two men charged. Gaskell jumped eight Germans at Y and Scott four at Z. In each post was a machine-gun aimed at the Australian lines but the raiders, attacking from the rear, were safe from machine-gun fire. The Germans fired a single rifle or pistol shot at each of the two Diggers but missed. Gaskell shot the NCO in charge of post Y and the crew surrendered. Scott achieved the same result at his objective, Z.

The whole party of prisoners was quickly disarmed, taken back to No. 2 post and then marched away through the crops towards the rear. Gaskell's CO ordered him to undertake further immediate 'clearance'. With the same patrol plus two other men, he worked through the crops towards other shellholes near the posts already captured. The Diggers captured another eighteen Germans in these posts, all observers or members of the gun crews. Their living position was in the form of an undercut driven into the side of the shellhole facing the Australian posts and then sunk some feet down. The opening was covered by a sheet and so well concealed that it was not easy to spot even when looking straight down.

During this operation, German snipers became active and one Australian was wounded. Corporal London, with two men, was placed in the house, shown at S, to prevent the Germans from reoccupying it. Later, three machine-guns and their crews were sent up to strengthen the post in the house.

Gaskell's patrol had been out over 3 hours and had taken thirty-two prisoners and three machine-guns. Meanwhile Lieutenant C. R. Morley, also of the 1st Battalion, had been on patrol on the other side of the railway and in the lightly timbered wood shown on the sketch he and his small party captured thirty-six prisoners and four machine-guns. Spurred by these successes several other young officers and sergeants carried out daring and successful patrols, north and south of Merris.

As a result of the patrols, the battalion line was advanced to the wood shown on the sketch. Gaskell was awarded the MC, Scott the DCM and London the DCM. Both these NCOs were later decorated a second time.

Directions

From Merris, take the road through the town toward Strazeele. After 1 kilometre, at a bend in the road, turn left on to a farm road, Lynde Streete. After 1 kilometre this road reaches the railway. Gaskell's patrol took place just across the railway line and the embankment which he used in his approach. Morley's patrol took place to the right of the farm road but the wood in which he operated has disappeared.

Merris – VC action

Merris was the scene of an AIF VC action on 28 June 1918. The 10th Battalion (Lieutenant-Colonel Wilder-Neligan) was in position about 500 metres south-west of Merris and preparing to make an attack on the place, now held by the Germans. During the attack a platoon was digging in when it came under machine-gun fire which killed its commander. Some survivors sheltered in a ditch, others made a rush for the Australian lines. In this desperate situation, Corporal Philip Davey, though under point-blank fire, attacked the gun with hand grenades, putting half the crew out of action. Davey returned for other grenades and again attacked the enemy gun, whose crew had by now been reinforced. Davey killed the crew of eight, captured the gun and mounted it in a new post. From here he repelled a counter-attack but was severely wounded. Davey's act of valour took place 300 metres due west of modern Merris.

Merris - The 10th Battalion's Attack

AIF activity around Merris was intense in July 1918. Platoons of the 10th Battalion captured the place on 30 July. Numerous enemy were killed and four officers and 175 others were captured, more than there were Australians in the attack. Forty were taken in one strongpoint at Gerbedoen Farm, near where the Merris hospital now stands. Nine others were found a few days later in the cellars of Merris. The British Inspector-General of Training is said to have described this attack as 'the best show ever done by a battalion in France'.

Meteren

The town of Meteren was the German's first objective in their attack on Hazebrouck in April 1918. The AIF 1st Division was hurried in to recapture the place on 22 April but the German defences were formidable. On the south and the north, the battalions of the 3rd Brigade moved against one fortified farmhouse after another in a series of fierce actions, some times at close quarters. By the 24th the Australians had suffered a sharp repulse at a cost of 200 casualties. The 1st Division renewed the attack between 1-12 May and much fighting took place around Meteren Becque, the stream which runs in a north-west/south-east direction south of Meteren. A principal objective was Meteren baths, south of the town centre, which had become an enemy strongpoint. The Australians burnt it down on the night of 12 May. The division captured a large part of Meteren but part of it remained in German hands until 19-20 July. At this time, the division made an improvised advance, without artillery support, and captured an additional mile of territory, taking ninety-seven prisoners and sixteen machine-guns.A remarkable incident took place near Meteren on 19 July. Lieutenant J. P. Tunn of the 11th Battalion was passing through a wire entanglement with his platoon when one of his men tripped, dropping a grenade out of the cup-discharger attached to his rifle. Tunn dived and caught the grenade but then himself tripped on the wire and dropped the grenade. With only two seconds to spare, Tunn managed to get at it again and held it on the ground. As it exploded it blew off his hand and wounded him in the head. Because of his action nobody else was injured. During the war at least two VCs were awarded to British soldiers for almost identical acts of courage. Tunn, from Red Hill, Queensland, received no award.

Directions

Meteren is reached from Ieper via Bailleul. It is now considerably bigger than it was in 1918 and a large part of the area then fought over is settled. Meteren Becque still runs through the farm fields which the Diggers knew.

Mont de Merris

With a height above sea level of about 50 metres, the Mont de Merris lies 1 kilometre south-east of Strazeele. The Germans held it in strength and as it was one of the few areas of high ground in this flat region it had to be captured from them. The task fell to the 11th Battalion of the 3rd Brigade under Lieutenant-Colonel J. Newman. Officers and men first studied aerial photographs of the position as well as a model on the ground and the battalion carried out a night practice at Pradelles, 2 kilometres west of Strazeele.

On the night of 2 June 1918 the battalion lined up at their jumping-off tape across a line of 1000 metres. The Australian artillery and mortar barrage began at 1 a.m. and the troops, wearing white armbands to distinguish them in the dark, moved ahead in sections. To guide the Diggers in the dark the artillery fired an incendiary shell every few minutes. With practised ease, the 11th Battalion men captured one enemy post after another. The success signal, a rocket bursting into red, green and red, was fired at 1.47 a.m. Meanwhile, the flanking battalions, the 10th and 12th, also advanced their positions. The 3rd Brigade suffered about 100 casualties, chiefly in the 11th Battalion. About 200 Germans were killed; five officers and 253 other ranks were taken prisoner. War booty amounted to twenty-seven machine-guns and seventeen trench mortars, all of which were quickly put into use by the Australians against the Germans. The brief, small-scale battle was a brilliant success. The Germans had lost their view over the Australian lines and their artillery officers were much hampered by the loss of the Mont.

Directions
From Strazeele, take the Vieux-Berquin road for 0.5 kilometre and turn into the first road, Rue Neuve, on the left and opposite a factory. Rue Neuve was part of the 11th Battalion's forming-up line. After 0.5 kilometre, turn right into a minor road which actually runs across Mont de Merris. Australian infantry swarmed across these gentle slopes on the night of 2–3 June 1918.

Nieppe Forest

This 30 square kilometre forest was well known to units of the 1st Division. During the German push of April–May 1918 the 2nd Brigade was dug in along the eastern edge, only 1 kilometre from the village of Vieux-Berquin. The support line was in the forest itself, where the trees provided both concealment and protection. La Motte au Bois village, on the main Hazebrouck-Merville road through the forest, was untouched by shellfire when the Australians arrived on 13 April 1918. The great Château de la Grange became a brigade HQ. The village was still inhabited but when German guns opened on it the villagers were evacuated. They left pigs, rabbits and poultry for the troops, who lived well for the next several weeks. Three canals meet in the centre of La Motte au Bois and Australian soldiers often fished there, according to local people to whom I spoke in the 1960s. Nieppe Forest can be reached easily from Hazebrouck, Vieux-Berquin, or Merville.

Strazeele

Only 7 kilometres from Hazebrouck, Strazeele was just behind the British-Australian front line and would have fallen to the Germans in their offensive of April–May 1918 but for the 1st Division's vigorous work in blocking them. The town was badly damaged by enemy gunfire but several AIF HQs stayed in the ruins. Some estaminets remained in business and battalions billeted their men in farms near the town.

St Venant and Robecq

These villages, south of Nieppe Forest and just 2 kilometres apart, have a brief but interesting AIF 'memory'. In mid-April 1918 Australian Field Artillery batteries were coming under fire from German guns. Scout planes could not spot the enemy guns and as they moved frequently in their advance they were causing casualties among the Australians without being in danger of attack themselves. Lieutenant-Colonel H. W. Lloyd, the local AIF artillery commander, sent some men into the spire tops of Robecq and St Venant churches. Here the gunners crouched uncomfortably, with a telephone wire linking the two churches, while they observed enemy gunflashes. The resulting intersections of the two viewpoints were telephoned to British heavy artillery which at once brought shellfire on to the German guns. The Australians established a third spotter station and handed over their successful set-up to a field survey (mapping) company.

Directions
Robecq is best reached from Merville, by driving 5 kilometres along the D23 and then by taking the D68 at Calonne-sur-la-Lys. St Venant is nearby on the D937. Both churches stand out clearly.

Vieux-Berquin

This village, on the D947 between Strazeele and Neuf-Berquin, entered Australian history during the German attempt to break through to the Channel ports in April 1918. What the 7th and 8th Battalions achieved through their steadfast courage greatly helped to stem the enemy push. A plaque on the street wall of the town hall commemorates the feat of arms. The action began on 12 April when the 7th Battalion, which had been rushed up from the Somme to steady the collapsing British line in Flanders, actually held by itself about 9 kilometres of vitally important front. Nearby is the great Nieppe Forest where AIF units were also engaged.

The plaque at Vieux-Berquin, French Flanders, commemorates the 7th Battalion's remarkable stand. In April 1918 the Diggers blocked a potentially disastrous German breakthrough.

When other 1st Division battalions moved into position, the 7th and 8th Battalions with a combined strength of about 1000 men, held a front of 14 kilometres, a distance which normally would have been held by two divisions. It was a remarkable performance.

Outstanding at Vieux-Berquin was Lieutenant H. Fenton of the 8th Battalion. Fenton became the sole survivor of his platoon and then, with accurate rifle fire, held off a large party of Germans. His platoon sergeant, A. C. Robertson, though wounded, covered Fenton's eventual retirement by operating a captured German machine-gun until he fell.

It was also at Vieux-Berquin that a famous episode occurred. Lieutenant L. C. McGinn and his platoon were holding up the enemy advance along the Vieux-Berquin — Strazeele roads when into his tiny HQ stumbled the CO, Adjutant and Intelligence Officer of the 1st Battalion Lancashire Fusiliers, a unit which had practically ceased to exist. The colonel said to McGinn: 'Boy, is this your post?' 'Yes, sir', said McGinn. 'Well,' the colonel said, 'give me a rifle, I am one of your men.' He jumped into the trench and helped hold off the Germans.

Fenton, McGinn and Robertson were members of D Company 8th Battalion, commanded by Lieutenant W. D. Joynt, later a VC winner. Joynt recommended Robertson for the VC and the two officers for an award. Only McGinn was recognised. The positions held by Fenton and McGinn were within 100 metres of Vieux-Berquin Square. The junction of the 7th Battalion with the 8th was close to the main road which runs through Vieux-Berquin and is not more than 150 metres from the town hall. The square outside the church, which is close to the town hall, had an Australian trench running across it at right angles to the main road.

Chapter 4

Cemeteries in French Flanders of Australian Interest

Anzac Cemetery, Sailly-sur-la-Lys

Sailly-sur-la-Lys village is 8 kilometres south-west of Armentières on the N345 to Estaires and Bethune. Anzac cemetery lies 0.5 kilometre south-west of the village on the D945 and on the way to Estaires. It was commenced by Australian field ambulance units immediately before the attack on Fromelles in July 1916 and many of 111 AIF men buried here were killed in that battle. Another nineteen Australians lie in the Canadian cemetery on the other side of the road. Captain Norman Gibbins of the 55th Battalion, one of the most outstanding leaders in the Fromelles battle, is buried in Anzac Cemetery.

Directions
From the crossroads in Sailly-sur-la-Lys, take the D945 towards Estaires and Bethune. After 0.5 kilometre, the cemetery is on the right.

Anzac Cemetery, at Sailly-sur-la-Lys, contains the graves of many AIF men killed at Fromelles in July 1916.

Aubers Ridge British Cemetery

This cemetery is related to the Australian attack at Fromelles on 19–20 July 1916. It stands on Aubers Ridge, the low plateau on which Fromelles also is situated. The objective of repeated British attacks, the ridge was not captured until October 1918, so the cemetery was made after the Armistice. War graves officers concentrated into it graves from smaller burial grounds and from the battlefields on all sides of Aubers. Plot 1 consists almost entirely of the graves of unidentified Australians killed at Fromelles. In a total of 918 graves, 445 are unidentified. Australian graves total 124 but only sixteen Diggers could be identified so long after the battle. Of these, fourteen are men of the 59th Battalion, which was on the extreme right of the Australian line and thus closer to Aubers than the other battalions. The remains of all the Diggers at Aubers were picked up from where they fell except for a few who had been buried by the Germans.

Directions
From Fromelles village, turn right on to the D141 for Aubers, but do not enter Aubers. At the first crossroads, turn right into the D41, signposted Herlies. The cemetery is on the left within 0.5 kilometre.

Bailleul Communal Cemetery Extension

A commonly heard expression among soldiers was 'Bailleul, Boulogne and Blighty'. Bailleul was a great depot and transit centre, Boulogne was the major Channel port and Blighty was Britain and leave. The trinity loomed large in soldiers' minds. Many hospitals were situated around Bailleul, which even

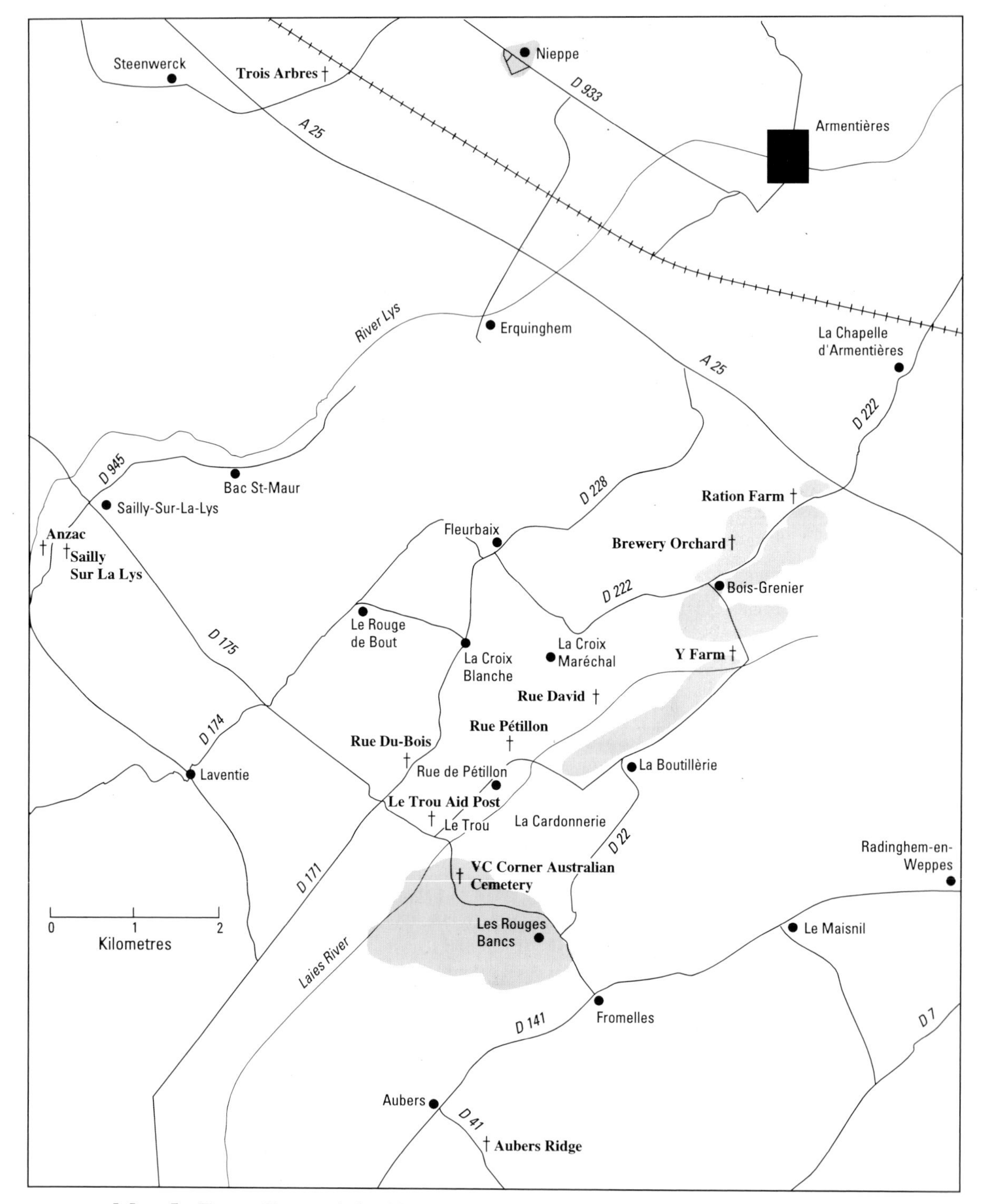

Map 5. Fromelles and the Nursery: Cemeteries and Battlefields (Shaded)

during the war was a big town. It was important enough to be the site of various Corps HQ. Until July 1917 it was fairly safe but the Germans then severely bombed and shelled it and in their spring offensive of 1918 they nearly captured it.

The military cemetery attached to the communal one is very large, with 4384 Allied burials, including 396 Australians. Many of the men buried here died of wounds but some are unidentified. Unusually, in some graves two soldiers are buried together with a joint headstone. For instance, an Australian and New Zealand soldier lie together because their remains could not be separately identified. In this case, their respective army emblems, the rising sun and the fernleaf, are intertwined. The burials at Bailleul span the three years of Australians' presence on the Western Front. Private S. J. Cole, aged 25, of the 15th Battalion, was killed on 1 July 1917. His inscription reads: 'Somewhere in France he sleeps in peace'. The epitaph indicates that to his family the place-name Bailleul meant nothing; their son had died in the enormous graveyard that was France.

Directions
Bailleul is best reached from Ieper, where it is signposted (sometimes as Belle). Approaching the outskirts of Bailleul on the D23, pass a large hospital complex — Centre Hospitalier Specialisé — on the left. At the T-junction turn right. After 200 metres turn left to the war cemetery, which is signposted.

Brewery Orchard Cemetery, Bois-Grenier

The brewery, which is in the village of Bois-Grenier, was taken over by the army and its cellar was used as an Advanced Dressing Station. Traffic to the ADS was concealed from enemy observation by ruined houses. Soldiers who died in the ADS were buried in the orchard nearby. This cemetery is significant in AIF history for in Plot IV Row C are buried twenty-seven soldiers of the 20th Battalion and the 5th Machine-Gun Company and one member of the 5th Trench-Mortar Battery, who were caught by shellfire on 5 May 1916 while on the march. It was a terrible occasion, on an open road without cover, and the enemy salvo left numerous other men wounded. The cemetery is near the village crossroads and easily found.

Douai Communal Cemetery

Douai, an old garrison town and a railway junction on the main line from Paris to Brussels, was captured by the Germans on 1 October 1914 and remained in their hands until 17 October 1918. The Germans used the communal cemetery to bury British, French, Romanian and Italian soldiers who died while in their hands, as well as their own casualties. Seven AIF men are among the burials. They include one of the AIF's most distinguished young officers, Captain Charles Arblaster of the 53rd Battalion. Aged 21, and a Duntroon graduate, Arblaster was cool, resourceful and gallant during the battle of Fromelles, 20 July 1916. Seriously wounded, he fell into German hands and died on 24 July. AIF records record that he died of wounds, CWGC records that he died of sickness. In fact, an illness brought on by his dreadful wounds killed him (Grave D.6).

Also in this cemetery is the grave of Second Lieutenant Trevor Langwill of the 60th Squadron Royal Flying Corps. Langwill came from Newcastle, NSW, and died of wounds received on 17 April 1917 during a dogfight with a German pilot.

Directions
From Douai, take the N43, signposted Auberchicourt. The communal cemetery is signposted off this road, only a few hundred metres after the N43 leaves the ring road. The best way to reach Douai is by the Paris motorway from Lille. At Noyelles, take the N43 exit to Douai.

Hersin Communal Cemetery Extension

This is one of the most interesting cemeteries containing Australian graves because fifty-four of the fifty-five AIF men interred here were members of the 3rd Australian Tunnelling Company. The 55th Digger in Hersin belonged to the Australian Mining and Boring Company. All the Australian tunnelling companies deserve much more prominence than they have received and Hersin Communal Cemetery Extension is, in effect, a tunnellers' cemetery. Twenty of these Diggers were killed in a single enemy explosion on 27 November 1916. One of them, Sergeant John Brockley, was 50 years old. Another was the very brave Sergeant Macklain Kerby, DCM. Sergeant

The graves of Australian military tunnellers in an extension of Hersin Communal Cemetery, northern France.

James Berry MM, another old soldier and aged 46, was killed on 31 July 1916. The 26-year-old CO of the unit, Major Leslie Coulter DSO, was killed on 28 June 1917 and is buried among his men. Lieutenant Hugh Russel MC, aged 45, died of wounds on 23 January 1917. The last Australian burial at Hersin was Sapper Harry Williams who died of wounds on 1 July 1918.

Directions

From Bethune, take the N37, signposted Arras, to the town of Noeux-les-Mines. In the centre of town, at a bend in the long main street, turn right on to the D85, signposted Hersin, a distance of 4.5 kilometres. When you reach traffic lights, turn left into Rue Emile Basly. At the Renault garage, note the sign 'Cimitiére Militaire' to the left. The British military cemetery is at the far end of the large communal cemetery.

Le Trou Aid Post Cemetery, Fleurbaix

The hamlet of Le Trou was prominent in the battle of Fromelles, for here Brigadier-General Elliott, commanding the 15th Brigade, had his HQ during the battle. Le Trou Aid Post had been established early in the war and the cemetery was begun in October 1914. Wounded Diggers were treated here as they came in from the fields of Fromelles. The cemetery contained 123 graves at the Armistice and was then enlarged by the concentration of 230 graves from the battlefields. It now contains the graves of fifty-six Australians, 288 British soldiers, seven Canadians and two Frenchmen. The unnamed graves number 207. Only four Australians could be identified, two from the 54th Battalion, two from the 32nd.

The cemetery is entirely surrounded by an old moat spanned by a concrete bridge. Planted with willows and poplars, it is a particularly beautiful burial ground.

Directions
As for Rue-Petillon Military Cemetery. Le Trou Aid Post is in the same street but closer to Fromelles.

Meteren Military Cemetery

Much fighting took place in and around Meteren at various times during the war before it was finally retaken by the British in July 1918. The cemetery was made in 1919 by the French authorities, who concentrated from neighbouring battlefields the bodies of 749 British and Dominion soldiers, 118 French and 210 German. The Germans and some of the French were later removed, leaving 104 Australians, 583 British, thirty-one South Africans, twenty-two New Zealanders, fifteen Indians, five Canadians and one Newfoundlander, with 181 unnamed graves.

The majority of the Australians were killed during the Battle of the Lys in April 1918; 23–25 April were bad days for the 3rd Brigade (9th, 10th, 11th and 12th Battalions.) All four battalions suffered at Meteren as they advanced along the axis of the main road from the west. The 12th Battalion lost a brave and resourceful leader here, Lieutenant William Sayer (Grave IV.B.576).

In May and June 1918 other Diggers died around Meteren, mostly 1st Brigade men involved in 'peaceful penetration'.

Directions
From Ieper, as for Bailleul Communal Cemetery Extension. Take the D933 signposted Meteren, for 2 kilometres. Here take the second main road to the right, D18. The cemetery is within 200 metres.

Ration Farm Military Cemetery, La Chapelle-D'Armentières

An industrial suburb on the south of modern Armentières, at the time of the war La Chapelle d'Armentières was a mere hamlet. 'Ration Farm' was the name given to a building on the south-east side of the road to Bois-Grenier at a farm known as La Guernerie. For the greater part of the war the farm was about 2 kilometres from the British front line and at the end of a communication trench. Rations for the frontline troops were brought to the farm and then distributed forward. On their return journey the ration parties brought dead soldiers back down the trench and a cemetery was started on the north-west side of the road, opposite the farm. As it was close beside farm buildings, in April 1923 the graves were moved into Plot VI of the present Ration Farm Cemetery. Many bodies buried in isolated places were brought in after the Armistice, including a large number of 5th Division men killed at Fromelles. Of 1308 British and Dominion burials, 260 are Australian but of these 142 are unknown by name. However, their nationality was beyond doubt and they were buried together, mostly in Plots VI, VII and VIII.

Directions
From Bois-Grenier crossroads, taken the D222 for 1 kilometre towards Armentières. After 0.5 kilometre, La Guernerie farm is on the right and after another 0.5 kilometre Ration Farm Cemetery is on the left.

Rue-David Military Cemetery, Fleurbaix

Rue-David, or Rue-des-Davids, is the local name of the road running between the hamlets of La Croix-Marachel and La Boutillerie. The latter place was a key featuring the Battle of Fromelles. The cemetery is on the north-east side of the road and only 750 metres south-east of Fleurbaix. At the Armistice it contained the graves of 220 soldiers but after the war many remains were gathered from small cemeteries and from the fields. Five of the Australians brought in at this time had been buried at Abbey Wall Cemetery, La Boutillerie, under the north wall of the ruined Chartreux Abbey. Now, 353 AIF men, including 256 unknown by name, lie in Rue-David Cemetery, out of a total of 893 graves. The cemetery should be visited in conjunction with a visit to the battlefield of Fromelles. However, not all the Australians buried here were killed in that battle, 19-20 July 1916. Private Thomas Doran of the 23rd Battalion was killed during a patrol on 19 April 1916, one of the earliest AIF actions on the Western Front (Grave I.D.26).

Rue-du-Bois Military Cemetery, Fleurbaix

Fleurbaix village is 5 kilometres south-west of Armentières on the Bethune road. Confusingly, the Fleurbaix-Bethune road is known along most of its course as the Rue-du-Bois but at Tilleloy and Picantin it becomes the Rue-Tilleloy. It is a long, flat road running between farms and orchards over numerous dykes. The Rue-du-Bois Cemetery is on the north-west side of the road, 1.5 kilometres south-west of Fleurbaix village and close to the hamlet of Petillon. Before the Armistice the majority of graves were Australian and Plot 1, Row 8, contained the graves of twenty-seven men of the 5th Division killed at Fromelles. About the time of the Armistice, the remains of more 5th Division men were brought from the battlefields, together with dead of the British Buckinghamshire Battalion. They were put, in two groups, into two big graves of Plot II, Row A. The Australian grave is believed to contain twenty-two bodies. The cemetery has 832 graves, including 242 Australians. Among them is Major Geoffrey McCrae, the highly regarded 26-year-old CO of the 60th Battalion, and a member of a well-known Victorian literary and artistic family. Some of the AIF men in this cemetery were killed in raids in August 1916 (Grave I.F.33). They include Private Leslie Inglefinger of the 57th Battalion, who died at the age of 18 on 27 August (Grave I.G.27). Only twenty-seven Australians buried in Rue-du-Bois are unknown by name.

Rue-Petillon Military Cemetery

This cemetery is one of the many containing Australian dead from the Battle of Fromelles and as such is a significant place. Petillon is a hamlet 2 kilometres to the south of Fleurbaix on the Rue-du-Bois. The Rue-Petillon is a short local road, running parallel to the Rue-du-Bois and about 1 kilometre

Many Australian soldiers killed in the Battle of Fromelles now lie in trench graves in Rue-Petillon Cemetery, close behind the battlefield. The cemetery lies in the middle of farm fields.

Rue-Petillon Cemetery, Fromelles. 291 of the Australians killed in the battle of 19–20 July 1916 are buried here.

south-east of it. The cemetery was begun in December 1914 and the first AIF burials were made in June 1916. Now, 291 Australians lie there out of a total of 1507 burials. Twenty-two of the AIF men are unidentified. The known include the gallant Chaplain Spencer Maxted of the 54th Battalion, killed while stretcher-bearing during the Fromelles slaughter (Grave I.K.2). The most senior AIF officer buried in this cemetery is Major Roy Harrison of the 54th Battalion (Grave I.D.20). Rue-Petillon is one of the most attractive cemeteries with weeping willows at the entrance, mountain ash and other trees.

Directions
From VC Corner Australian Cemetery, take the Rue Delvas right — that is, away from Fromelles — and turn right at the first corner. After passing Le Trou Aid Post Cemetery, Rue-Petillon Cemetery is on the right after 1 kilometre.

VC Corner Australian Cemetery, Fromelles

During the war VC Corner was the name given to the crossing of the Rue Delvas and the Rue-du-Bois, 3 kilometres north-west of Fromelles and within the British lines. The name had nothing to do with any VC-winning exploit. The cemetery, which was made after the Armistice, is nearly halfway along Rue Delvas towards Fromelles. It stands in the middle of the battlefield, actually where the greatest carnage of the Battle of Fromelles, 19–20 July 1916, took place and it contains the bodies of 410 Australians who fell and whose remains were found after the war. No site could be more appropriate. The passage of two and a half years meant that not a single body could be identified. An enterprising and sensitive decision was made by the Commonwealth War Graves Commission to record on a screen wall the names of all 1299 Australian soldiers who fell in the battle and whose graves are not known. By unit, they are as follows: 60th Battalion, 314; 59th, 241; 53rd, 190; 32nd, 163; other infantry battalions, 373; Australian Machine-Gun Corps, 11; Australian Engineers, 6.

The 410 bodies recovered in 1918–19 and a few others found later are buried under the two areas with an outline of the cross. Uniquely, therefore, no headstones are to be seen in the cemetery. It is an area of lawns, with a shrubbery and rubble wall. The Great Cross stands on a stone terrace flanked by two stone shelters, and behind the cross is the screen wall with the inscriptions:

In honour of the 410 unknown Australian soldiers here buried, who were among the 1,299 Officers, Non-Commissioned Officers and Men of the Australian Imperial Force, killed in the Attack on Fromelles, July 19th and 20th, 1916.

At that time the action was officially known as 'the Attack on Fromelles'. The appellation Battle of Fromelles came into use in the 1930s.

Among those commemorated on the memorial is Second Lieutenant John Lees of the 30th Battalion who left Australia as an NCO and was one of the first to be commissioned. A splendid leader, during the battle he quickly had his men digging a trench. He was first shot in the leg, then in the body but kept on until a bullet through the head killed him.

The cemetery is planted with hornbeam and scarlet thorns. The surrounding country is open farming land and it is in these fields that the 'missing' Diggers lie. From time to time, bones are found, especially after the ploughing season. The CWGC gardeners bury them near the cemetery. (*See* **Battle of Fromelles**.)

Other French Flanders Cemeteries with AIF Graves from the Battle of Fromelles

The slaughter at Fromelles was so great that army burial parties could not cope with the need for graves. For this reason, Australians were buried in various cemeteries, some a considerable distance from the battlefield. Those who died of wounds in hospital might also have been buried some way behind the fighting lines.

• Cabaret Rouge British Cemetery, Souchez
115 AIF out of 7551 burials. This cemetery is 10 kilometres north of Arras and 1.5 kilometres south of Souchez on the Arras-Bethune road. Cabaret Rouge is 40 kilometres south-west from the Fromelles battlefield. About half the Diggers buried here were still alive when removed from the battlefield but died so soon after that they were listed as killed in action.

• Laventie Military Cemetery
Four AIF out of 417 burials. The cemetery is 10 kilometres south-west of Armentières and is signposted from the D171.

• Sailly-sur-la-Lys Canadian Cemetery
Nineteen AIF out of 313 burials. The cemetery is across the road from Anzac cemetery.

• Y Farm Military Cemetery, Bois-Grenier
163 AIF out of 818 burials. The cemetery is 1.2 kilometres south of the village on the D22.

Trois Arbres Cemetery, Steenwerck

The site of Trois Arbres (three trees) Cemetery was chosen for the 2nd Australian Casualty Clearing Station in July 1916. The 2nd CCS used the original cemetery (Plot 1 and the earlier rows of Plot II) until April 1918. It contained 948 graves, of which 466 were Australian. Trois Arbres was captured by the Germans in April 1918 and after the Germans retired at the end of 1918 some other burials were made in it. Following the Armistice 732 bodies were brought into it from the battlefields of Steenwerck, Nieppe, Bailleul and Neuve-Eglise (Nieuwkerke). There are now 470 AIF burials in a total of 1694. This cemetery contains the grave of the most senior AIF officer killed in action on the Western Front: that of Major-General William Holmes, GOC of the 4th Division. Aged 55, he was killed in action near Messines on 2 July 1917 (Grave I.Y.42). Another particularly fine Australian soldier is buried here, Major Harold Howden MC and Bar, of the 48th Battalion, killed three days after General Holmes (Grave U.U.17). Many of the Diggers buried at Trois Arbres died of wounds in the CCS.

Directions

Steenwerck lies between Bailleul and Armentières, close to the Belgian border. From Steenwerck, take the D77, signposted Ploegsteert, 2 kilometres to the hamlet of Rue des Meuniers. Turn right on to a minor road for 1 kilometre. The cemetery is on the railway line opposite the Ferme (farm) Devos.

Chapter 5

Australian Battlefields and Administrative Centres North of the Somme River: Amiens to Bapaume and Sailly-Laurette

The Somme is the name of an important river and of a French *département*, the equivalent of an English county. Most frequently, the name given to the area as a theatre of war is 'the Somme', though much of the fighting took place many miles from the river. The AIF fought two battles of the Somme. Officially, the first lasted from 1 July 1916 until 18 November 1916 but the fighting was certainly not over for the troops at that date. The Second Battle of the Somme was fought between 21 March and 5 April 1918. These dates, however, do not take into account the many battles which took place north and south of the Somme for several months. The AIF was not finished with the Somme until its capture of Peronne in September 1918.

It is convenient to describe Australian activities under the general divisions 'North of the Somme' and 'South of the Somme'. It is also more convenient for visitors to travel the battlefields in this way. Albert is the best centre to use as a base for touring the northern Somme. For touring south of the river and eastwards into the Aisne in the steps of the AIF, Peronne is the most convenient centre.

The First Battle of the Somme began on 1 July with the British attacking on a front of 30 kilometres, from Gommecourt on the left or northern flank, to Maricourt on the right, or south. The French army, on the right of the British line, made its attack south of the Somme River. On the first day the British lost 20 000 dead and 40 000 wounded and with such appalling loses the battle soon deteriorated into one of attrition. By the time the AIF became involved the fighting had been raging for three weeks. The 1st Division marched into Albert, 4 kilometres behind the fighting line, on the night of 19 July and was soon followed by the 2nd and 4th Divisions.

The Diggers already knew something of Flanders and they found the Somme quite unlike it. Much of the Somme region is an undulating plateau (125–170 metres elevation) which descends in a series of hills, separated by deep depressions, to the valleys of the rivers Somme, Ancre and Tortille. Some river valleys have such steep sides that in places along the Somme they are virtual escarpments. The higher parts of the plateau form a ridge, one of whose tapering ends rests on the Thiepval Heights above the Ancre. Running west to east, the ridge crosses the Albert-Bapaume road at Pozières and runs on to Ginchy.

In the summer of 1916 the Germans held the high ground everywhere and they had made intelligent use of it, with thousands of machine-guns covering every possible approach by the British and Dominion troops. Their field and heavy artillery guns were pre-registered on the same approaches and on the positions which the attackers would occupy, if they could. The German trenches were solidly made, with deep concrete shelters. In these, on 1 July, they had weathered the British artillery bombardment without heavy loss. After the bombardment, as the British and Dominion infantry approached, the machine-gunners and riflemen emerged to slaughter the heavily equipped, slow-moving and very visible troops. The Newfoundland Regiment was annihilated, almost to a man.

As the Australians found, the Somme during a war in summer was a hot and evil place in which to fight and after rain the ground became a miry, clinging bog. Many Diggers said that the Somme mud was even more foul and overwhelming than that of the Ypres Salient. Winters were long and bitterly cold and the winter of 1916–17, when the Diggers were fighting there, was one of the worst on record.

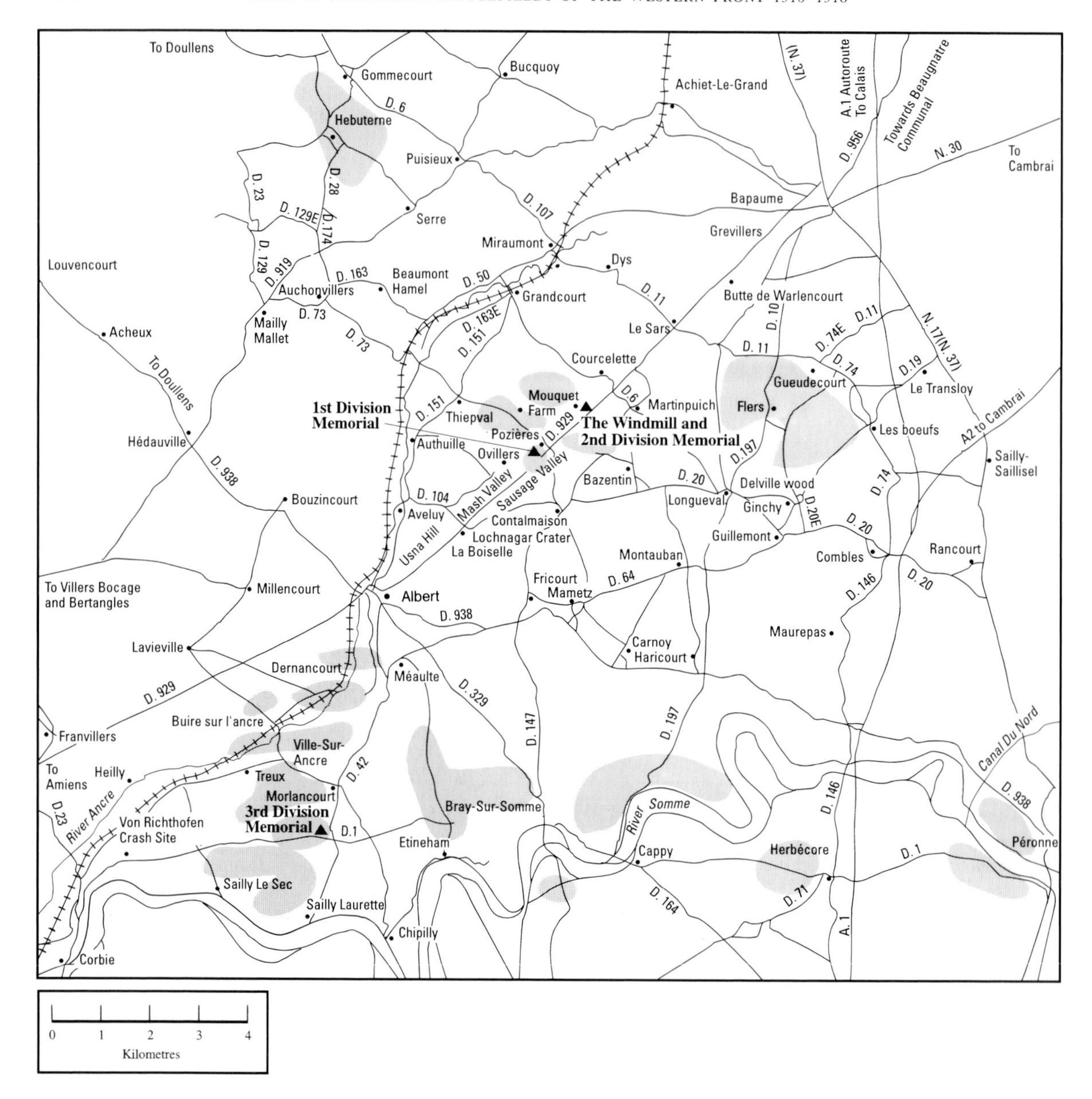

Map 6. The Somme: Battlefields (Shaded)

A quiet and attractive place for the modern visitor — and in places beautiful — in 1916 the Somme was an ugly death trap, a killing field. Many of its place-names have become both famous and infamous in Australian history; famous for heroic endeavour and stubborn fortitude, infamous for the slaughter and suffering. The whole region of the Somme, north and south of the river — from Amiens in the west to Peronne in the east — was one great battlefield where many separate battles were fought. More Australians spent longer periods there than they did in the Ypres Salient and French Flanders together. Casualties, however, were incurred about equally in both the major sectors.

Active service on the Somme had a traumatic effect on Australian soldiers partly because there seemed to be no possibility of survival. Soldierly skill could play only a limited part in bringing a man

Unexploded shells found in a Somme farm field. Those with narrow driving bands (just above the base) are German. The two at right, with the driving bands removed, are British.

through sustained enemy shellfire or the vicious rain of machine-gun bullets. Many units were repeatedly thrust into violent battle and each time they suffered heavy casualties. The survivors were withdrawn for brief rest and reinforcement by drafts of men from the training camps, and sent into the line again. Sometimes British generals visited a camp to praise and encourage a unit that had been in battle. Most of these officers did not seem to realise that they were largely speaking to reinforcements who had just joined the unit and had no real comprehension of what the visiting general was talking about. Many, and sometimes most of the men to whom they were referring, were dead or absent from the unit in hospital with wounds.

The Somme is an area rich in Australian spirit and sacrifice. The Diggers speak from the farm fields that were once battlefields, from the woods, from the stones of the villages and most eloquently of all, from the beautiful cemeteries in which so many of them finally found sanctuary.

Albert

A major military town throughout the war, Albert was virtually taken over by the British in March 1916 and was always called 'Bert' by the soldiers. From early July the AIF had small HQ staffs in the battered town but most Diggers did not see the place until later that month when they arrived from Flanders. As they approached the town they saw the golden Virgin which had stood on the tower of the Basilica, leaning out head-down from the tower. This was the famous 'Leaning Virgin', dislodged from her ancient position by German shelling in January 1915. One of the most famous legends of the war was that when the Virgin fell the war would end. The Germans swept into Albert in March 1918 and the town came under British shellfire. The Virgin crashed to the ground on 16 April — and the war went on.

The British recaptured Albert in August. Virtually every Australian who fought on the Somme in 1916-17 passed through Albert on his way to the front. Many dead and wounded were carried through it in the other direction. In various war cemeteries around Albert are buried thousands of Australians. Two kilometres east of Albert, towards Pozières, the road rises to a hill which obscured Albert from the Germans at Pozières. This was known as Tara Hill on the right of the road and Usna Hill on the left. From these slopes curious and apprehensive Diggers, newly arrived on the Somme front, watched the thunderous bombardment over the trench lines a few kilometres ahead of them — knowing that they would soon be thrown into the fighting.

Albert had a population of 9 000 before 1914; it

Albert Cathedral, with its famous 'Leaning Virgin', as the Diggers saw it in 1916. It was said that when the golden figure fell to the ground the war would end. It fell—but the war went on.

now has 25 000. While it is bigger than when the Diggers knew it, the town's central section around the cathedral square is much the same as in 1916–18. A town of supermarkets and many shops, it serves the district which the Australians knew so well. It is the natural base for visitors to visit Pozières, Thiepval, Le Sars, Flers, Dernancourt, Morlancourt, Ville-sur-Ancre, Henencourt, Millencourt, Hebuterne, Heilly, Ribemont-sur-Ancre, Buire-sur-Ancre, Mericourt-l'Abbé, Treux, Sailly-le-Sec, Sailly-Laurette, Corbie, Chipilly, Etinehem, Warloy-Baillon, Allonville, Bertangles, Querrieu, Daours, Bussy-les-Daours, Bapaume, Amiens and other towns and villages.

The village of Allonville, between Albert and Amiens, which gave its name to the 'Allonville Disaster'.

Allonville

North of the Amiens-Albert road, the small village of Allonville has a stronger connection with Australian war history than most Australians know. It is the site of the AIF's 'The Allonville Disaster'. Early in May 1918 the Germans captured some British and Australian prisoners who disclosed under clever interrogation that the HQ of the AIF 3rd Division was at Allonville, an Australian rest and training village and area. These careless soldiers also disclosed that a brigade HQ was at La Houssoye and another at Franvillers.

On the night of 30 May, by which time the 4th Division had replaced the 3rd, German artillery fired high-bursting shrapnel shells over Allonville. An enemy scout plane hovering overhead observed the explosions and when the gunners had their range precise the pilot dropped flares to indicate that the guns were on target. About 1 a.m. in the morning an enemy gun fired high-explosive shells into the village at the rate of one every five minutes. The third shell hit one of the two large barns in which two companies of the 14th Battalion were sleeping and brought down the roof and walls. The explosion and wreckage killed thirteen men and wounded fifty-six. It is thought to have been the most costly single shellburst in AIF history. The next shell smashed through the roof of the other barn and exploded on the floor, killing five men and wounding twelve. The wounded showed great courage. One soldier, with both legs cut off above the knees, said to his rescuers: 'I'm all right — get the badly wounded boys out first'.

Allonville has other AIF memories. On 31 July 1918 the 4th Division held a famous race meeting

The farm barns at Allonville in which 13 Australians were killed and many wounded by unexpected night-time shelling.

on the aerodrome. About twenty pilots from Nos 2 and 4 Australian Flying Corps squadrons based further north flew in to bet on the events, which included the Polygon Wood Jump, Pozières Stakes and Mule Sprint and Steeple. As a climax to the exciting afternoon one of the fliers gave a breath-taking flying exhibition.

The 8th Brigade had a training school at Allonville which was said to be one of the most efficient in the whole of the AIF.

Directions

When I located the rebuilt barns I found that the people of Allonville had no knowledge of the presence of Australians in their village. However, one elderly woman recalled 'men in large hats' when she was a young girl. From Albert, take the D929 towards Amiens. Immediately after passing through

Querrieu, turn right to Allonville, signposted. If travelling from Amiens, take the same road and turn left at Petit Camon. In Allonville, ask for the château farm which is in the Voirie Neuve and only 150 metres from the centre of the village. Ask for Mr Patrick Van De Kerchoue, owner of the farm, who will show you the barns. *See* **Allonville Communal Cemetery**.

Amiens

The 'capital' of Picardy, Amiens is the largest centre of the Western Front with direct AIF connection. The French garrisoned Amiens until 1916, when the British took over. It became an important supply, medical, recreation and route centre for the army. Trains from Le Havre brought in men and supplies and took wounded out. When the Germans launched their great offensive in March 1918 Amiens was threatened and only the thin Allied line at Villers-Bretonneux protected the city. In two battles here the AIF was largely responsible for saving Amiens. The city later acknowledged this with a commemorative plaque on a pillar in the cathedral. The New Zealand Division was similarly honoured. Thousands of Diggers visited the cathedral during the war. After the war, one of them, Rowley Goddard, established the Anzac Hotel. He continued to be an unofficial guide for Australian and New Zealand visitors until his death in 1968. The hotel no longer has any Australian connection. Amiens is now a large redeveloped city and, away from the cathedral square, the Diggers would not recognise the place.

Despite its large size and prominence, Amiens is inferior to Albert as a centre for Australians visiting the old battlefields.

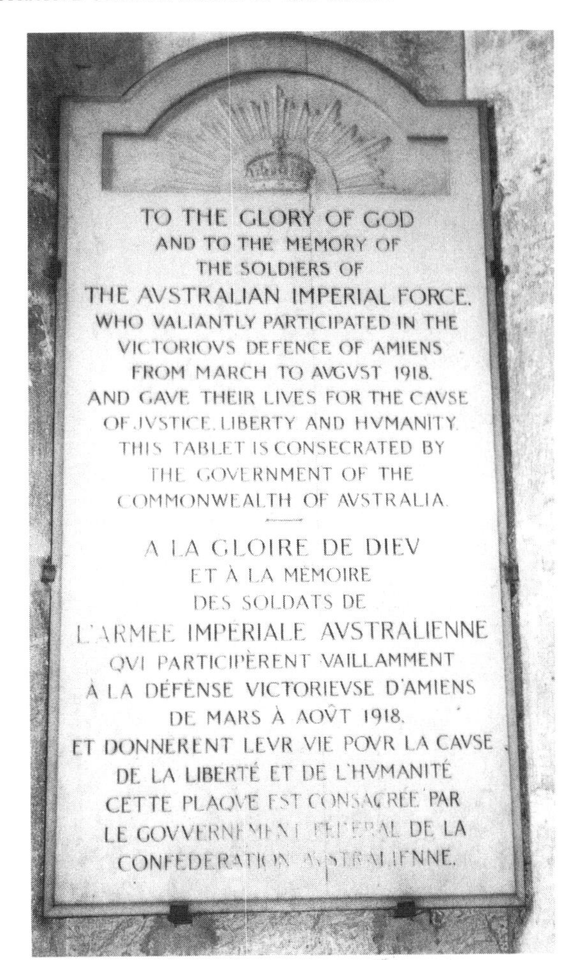

This plaque, in the great cathedral at Amiens, pays tribute to the 'saving' of Amiens by the AIF in 1918. A similar tablet praises the New Zealanders.

Bapaume

During the Battle of the Somme, July–November 1916, Bapaume was the main British objective. However, it was not reached and tremendous casualties, the onset of winter and stubborn German pressure brought the Somme campaign to an end. Following a German strategic withdrawal, the AIF 2nd Division occupied Bapaume from the west and south-west on 17 March 1917. Lieutenant A. C. White of the 30th Battalion was the first to enter the town. He was followed by other soldiers, staff officers, war correspondents and official photographers. They found that the Germans had systematically destroyed the town and then set fire to much of it. The buildings around the main square, including the town hall, were the only ones in reasonably sound condition.

The cellars were searched and a mine was found in the town hall and removed. On the night of 25 March a second mine, better hidden and operated by a chemical fuse, exploded. Sleeping in the town hall were about thirty Diggers, including those who ran the Australian Comfort Fund's battlefield coffee stall, and two French parliamentary deputies. The rescuers, who dug through the rubble all that night and next day, could save only six of the thirty. Some are buried in the Bapaume Australian Cemetery.

Bapaume remained an AIF HQ town for three months after its capture.

Directions

Bapaume is 16 kilometres east of Albert along the D929 road, originally a Roman road and very straight. Many of the sites described in this section are reached off this D929. When driving from Albert to Bapaume you are, in effect, advancing with the British and Dominion troops. In the opposite direction, you see the battlefield from the German perspective.

Bertangles

Eight kilometres north of Amiens, the village of Bertangles possessed a great 18th century château and many associated outbuildings. It was an obvious choice for a major military HQ and in 1918 it became the Australian Army Corps HQ. Before the five AIF divisions were brought under one command at the end of May 1918, General Sir William Birdwood, the British general in command of the Australians, and his brilliant Australian Chief-of-Staff, Major-General Cyril Brudenell White, had their HQ in Bertangles château, and here Lieutenant-General John Monash took over the Australian Army Corps. Major-General Charles Rosenthal, GOC 2nd Division, conferred with Monash at Bertangles on the Villers-Bretonneux operations of April-May 1918. The Commander-in-Chief, Field-Marshal Haig, called on Monash at Bertangles on 29 July to discuss the Allied August 1918 offensive. At Bertangles, on the château steps, King George V knighted Monash on 12 August. It was a splendid occasion, with Australian troops and captured German guns lining the drive from the great ornate gates to the château forecourt.

In the small cemetery along the lane to the west of the village, Baron von Richthofen was buried on 22 April, with an AIF firing party in attendance. The AIF connection with Bertangles remained until the end of the war because of an Australian flying squadron which used an airfield next to the château. However, Army Corps HQ moved on 13 August to

The gates of Bertangles Château, north of Amiens, which was for a time the HQ of the Australian Corps.

Part of the farm within the grounds of Bertangles Château. In 1918 this area was a hive of AIF activity.

Glisy, on 31 August to Mericourt Château and on 11 September to Belloy, as the AIF pushed the Germans back.

Directions

From Amiens, take the N25 road north. Bertangles is on this road, just before Villers Bocage, where Australians were billeted for much of 1918. If travelling from Albert, take the D929 to Rivery, from where a motorway loop connects with the N25. The château and its surroundings have changed little since 1918 though the main gates are kept locked. At weekends between July and September the château may be visited, though nothing remains to indicate AIF occupation. A painting by the Australian official war artist A. Henry Fullwood shows Bertangles as it was in mid-1918, with a sentry at the main gates and, in the courtyard, despatch riders and other troops. The courtyard is approached by the street in the village next to that which goes direct to the château's secondary gate.

After the war Baron von Richthofen's body was removed from Bertangles to the German military cemetery at Fricourt, near Albert. In 1925 it was taken to Berlin and in 1975 it was removed to the family vault in Weisbaden, East Germany. The empty grave site is still visible in Bertangles village cemetery.

Bray-sur-Somme

The village of Bray came into AIF history in March 1918, at the time of the German offensive. Bray was then held by the Germans and became a 3rd Division objective. The first Diggers to reach Bray did so as prisoners. Two of these men, Corporal C. W. Lane and Private R. C. Ruschpler, both of the 24th Machine-Gun Company, escaped when an Australian shell blew a hole in the barbed wire of the prisoners' compound in Bray.

The village became a battle objective on

22 August. Bray lies in a steep valley, which made it difficult for the artillery to arrange a barrage to cover the whole of an awkward front. Major-General John Gellibrand, GOC 3rd Division, decided to attack north of Bray, which would then be captured by encirclement. First attempts to take the place were stopped by brave German machine-gunners. After extraordinarily difficult fighting against the stubborn defenders, Bray was entered by the 40th Battalion in the early hours of 25 August. The Diggers found Bray railway yard full of enemy stores, loaded on to trains. Elsewhere huge dumps of stores had been mined but not blown.

After capturing Bray, the AIF turned it into a base for Australian operations towards Peronne and further east. As much of the place had not been destroyed, it was also a billeting centre. Villagers soon returned to their homes and the estaminets reopened. Many Diggers came to like Bray more than any other place on the river.

Directions
From Corbie, take the D1 — the famous Corbie-Bray road. An alternative route is to take the D233 from Corbie. This road follows the river and passes through Vaux-sur-Somme, Sailly-le-Sec, Sailly-Laurette, Chipilly and Etinehem. The Diggers who entered Bray did so from the north, where much of the fighting had taken place. For several days the 3rd Pioneer Battalion was in position on the hills immediately west of Bray.

Bussy-les-Daours

Five kilometres west of Corbie, Bussy was HQ of the 4th Division during the summer of 1918 and it had many camps around it. The pioneers had a large one on the edge of the village and an Army Service Corps depot and horse lines were established there. After the great Australian triumph in the Battle of Hamel in July, the French President, 'Tiger' Clemenceau, went to Bussy to congratulate the 4th Division men who had taken part in the fighting and to thank all Australian soldiers. Major-General Sinclair-MacLagan, GOC 4th Division, did not receive much notice of this important visit but an AIF guard-of-honour was ready to receive the 77-year-old President at Bussy Château. The Diggers formed a ring around Clemenceau and he spoke to them extemporaneously in English. He said:

> When the Australians came to France, the French people expected a great deal of you. We knew that you would fight a very real fight, but we did not know that from the very beginning you would astonish the whole continent. I shall go back tomorrow and say to my countrymen, 'I have seen the Australians. I have looked in their faces. I know that these men will fight alongside of us again until the cause for which we are fighting is safe for us and for our children'.

The Diggers gave Clemenceau a great ovation.

Directions
From Albert, take the D929 to Querrieu and turn left to Bussy, signposted.

Chipilly

The hamlet of Chipilly lies on some terraced meadows between the Somme River and a steep ridge. Australian soldiers were in this settlement in August 1918, mostly passing through on the north bank of the Somme or crossing to the south bank towards Villers-Bretonneux. Two of them remained in Chipilly, in the communal cemetery extension. They are Company Sergeant-Major G. C. Brodie DCM, of the Australian Engineers who died of wounds on 26 August 1918. At the time he was directing repairs on Chipilly bridge when a German shell exploded near him. The other Digger is Private W. B. Henderson, 3rd Battalion Machine-Gun Corps, who died of wounds 25 August. The communal cemetery is on the ridge, practically in the middle of Chipilly, from where there are superb views of the Somme valley, uplands and woods. This alone makes Chipilly worth a visit. The British 29th Division has a memorial near the town hall, a soldier comforting a wounded horse.

Directions
From Albert, take the D42 through Meaulte and Morlancourt. At the crossroads with the D1 Bray-Corbie road, turn left for 400 metres and then right, signposted Chipilly.

Corbie

Tens of thousands of Australian soldiers knew the small town of Corbie in 1918. Only a few kilometres behind the front line, it was badly battered by German shellfire but its ancient fortifications, some

The town hall in Corbie on the Somme River. The town was an important base and depot for the AIF during the 1918 campaigns.

of them going back to the 8th century, withstood the bombardment. The town's position, behind hills to the east and north, also gave it some protection. Despite the shells, a broad-gauge railway was maintained to Corbie, thus making the place an important railhead for supplying the troops at the front.

Many AIF brigades had extensive bivouacs at or close to Corbie in July and August 1918 and AIF gun batteries had positions just behind Corbie. Before the major Allied attack of 8-9 August 1918, the 2nd Brigade's HQ was at the abbey in Corbie and after the battle the 1st 4th and 5th Divisions used the town and its surrounds as a rest area. Bathing in the Somme was a popular pastime that hot summer. The 4th Division went into reserve at Corbie on 24 August and stayed there for some days.

At certain periods as many as 20 000 Australians were in and around Corbie, which became so busy as an army town that it had field bakeries, clothing stores, hospitals and a major military post office.

An attractive town, Corbie is larger than it was before the war but it is not much busier. Officials at the unusually impressive town hall welcome Australian visitors. The presence of Australian soldiers in the town in 1918 is well known to older inhabitants.

Directions

From Albert, take the D42 through Meaulte as far as the D1, which runs all the way to Corbie, 14 kilometres away. (*See* **Corbie-Bray Road**.)

Corbie-Bray Road

This road, now the D1, was one of the AIF's main lines of advance, north of the Somme and heading east, against the Germans. It climbs sharply out of Corbie, with the Somme valley on the right of the road. Within 1 kilometre of Corbie the north side of the valley is at its steepest, in places almost sheer. From a height of 110 metres, the Diggers had a view south over the river, lagoons and the canal which had been built through them. On the slopes and on the plateau above them were scores of machine-gun posts, with the guns mounted for firing at the enemy aircraft which daily spotted for their artillery. Two kilometres after leaving Corbie, on the left, there is an old brickworks with a tall chimney. It was near here on 21 April 1918 that the Fokker of Baron von Richthofen, the 'Red Knight of Germany', was brought down. Von Richthofen had become the leading air ace of the war with a tally of eighty victims.

During a dogfight on that morning, von Richthofen attacked a Canadian pilot of 209 Squadron RAF. Captain Roy Brown, the Canadian ace who commanded the squadron, dived his Sopwith Camel to the rescue and fired a burst into the Fokker. However, for a full minute the German continued to follow his prey and shoot at it before he himself crashed by the side of the Corbie-Bray road. From their posts by the Somme canal, several AIF gunners had fired at the red Fokker. One was Sergeant Cedric Popkin of the 24th Machine-Gun Company, 4th Division. After Brown fired and turned away, Popkin fired eighty rounds at von Richthofen as the Fokker flew only 18 metres above him. Soon after, anti-aircraft Lewis gunners of 53rd Field Artillery Battery, Gunners Snowy Evans and Robert Buie, opened up. Buie was sure he had hit the pilot but Popkin was quietly certain that his fire had brought down the Fokker.

Two autopsies were carried out on von Richthofen. The first group of surgeons said that a bullet had hit him in the back and penetrated his heart; the bullet could not have come from the ground. At the second autopsy, the surgeons insisted that the bullet had come from the ground. With a bullet through the heart it is unlikely that the pilot could have controlled his aircraft and fired his guns for a full minute before he crashed. Soldiers had fired at the plane from all directions during this time.

The AIF official war artist A. Henry Fullwood produced a watercolour with pen and charcoal which shows Australian soldiers carrying the body of von Richthofen from his crashed plane. This was before the souvenir hunters got busy with the wreck. In a note on the sketch, Fullwood credits the death of the German to Gunner W. J. Evans and Gunner R. Buie. However, Fullwood had nothing more than hearsay to guide him when he made the sketch.

The strongest evidence, including testimony offered decades later by Captain Brown, suggests that Popkin's bullet brought down the aerial scourge of the Western Front, the 'Red Baron' as the troops called him.

Pieces of his aircraft were souvenired before a guard could be placed on it and nothing whatever can be found there now. I know, because I have searched. It is interesting to walk round the area and reflect that here one of the most sensational incidents of the war took place. I place the spot of the crash 30 metres on the Corbie side of the brickworks and 10 metres from the edge of the road (*See* **Bertangles**).

Dernancourt

A few kilometres south of Albert, the village of Dernancourt on the Ancre River was captured by the Germans in their breakthrough offensive of March 1918. Dernancourt was a strong position because the Germans held the protective railway embankment which ran parallel to the river. The AIF 4th Division opposed the Germans on Lavieville Heights, 2 kilometres behind the railway, though forward infantry posts were much further down the slope towards the enemy. The railway embankment posed a strange problem for both Germans and Australians. The Germans were dug into the top of the rear side of the bank in one-man slits, while Australians were on the other side. Nightly, Diggers of the 4th Pioneer Battalion tunnelled under the embankment and Australian patrols ventured into Dernancourt's streets.

On the night of 27 March 1918 a platoon of the 47th Battalion was guarding a cutting near a level crossing used by farm carts and commanding a key position was Sergeant Stanley McDougall, the scout sergeant. A German attack developed and McDougall saw large numbers of enemy advancing along the whole front in the half-light of early morning. A 47th Lewis gun post was hit by a bomb and McDougall, taking the gun, advanced well ahead of his platoon and killed two German machine-gun teams. He also shot several other Germans who tried to cross the battalion defensive line and this act broke up the German attack. Meanwhile, about fifty Germans from an earlier wave had crossed the railway. McDougall took them on before they could get behind his battalion. He badly blistered his hand on the hot gun casing but he was still able to grab a rifle and bayonet to charge and shoot a German officer who was aiming his pistol at two 47th Battalion sergeants. For these exploits he was awarded the VC and eight days later he won the MM for further remarkable bravery at the same place.

In early April German bombardments were frequent. The 46th Battalion had fifty-one casualties on the night of 3 April. The Germans again heavily shelled the Australian positions on 5 April and the

45th Battalion lost four officers and forty other ranks. Meanwhile, the Germans assembled for attack and a fierce fight took place along the railway, especially near the railway bridge across a road. The Germans brought up field guns and blew the Australians out of their posts and by noon some of the Diggers' positions were also under fire from the rear. The 47th Battalion was particularly hard hit and some Diggers were taken prisoner. At one time, Captain W. Kennedy was fighting Germans to his north and east while other Australians, back to back with him, faced the enemy south of them.

That evening (5 April) remnants of the 45th, 46th and 48th Battalions under Colonel J. S. Denton made one of the finest counter-attacks ever carried out by Australian troops. The Diggers went into a whirlwind of fire but by 6.30 p.m. the Germans were in flight, helped on their way by some of the 27 588 shells fired by the Australian artillery in the battle. Australian casualties were 580 in the 12th Brigade, 500 in the 13th Brigade and 153 in the field artillery units. The 47th Battalion suffered most heavily, with eight officers and 261 men hit.

Directions

From Albert, take the D52 for 2 kilometres south to Dernancourt. The battle took place along the railway for 1 kilometre on either side of where the Lavieville road passes underneath the railway. Various actions were fought in the fields within 300 metres of the railway on the northern side of the railway. About 1 kilometre along the Lavieville road, on the right, is a small wood. An AIF HQ was sited here throughout the battle. The Australians kept their prisoners in a POW cage within 150 metres of the railway line, 500 metres right of the road under the railway line. No fewer than 418 Australians are buried in the Dernancourt Communal Cemetery Extension, which is 150 metres from the railway bridge. Stan McDougall's VC and MM exploits took place about 500 metres right of this bridge, towards Albert.

Flers

The Australian divisions, except for the 3rd Division, were ordered back to the Somme from the Ypres sector in October 1916 and took over the Flers front. According to the historian Bean, they were about 'to plunge into the hardest trial that ever came to them'. He was referring to the dreadful conditions of cold, rain and mud. Flers was not shelled as frequently as neighbouring Gueudecourt and some other places but several units reported it to be too dangerous for occupation.

Nevertheless, AIF infantry used Flers as a HQ and sometimes reserve troops were sheltered in the ruins. On 30 October a brigade commander in the front trenches reported that his men remained cheerful but were worn out with exposure and that their rifles were covered with mud, despite all efforts to keep them clean. German and British troops, he said, were equally exhausted, hungry and cold and were walking about exposed on the parapets looking at each other. General J. W. McKay, GOC 5th Division, reported that a supporting artillery barrage, advancing at the slow rate of 50 yards a minute, would still be too fast for the infantry in this hopeless quagmire.

Early on 2 November at Flers, the AIF lost one of its finest young commanders, 26-year-old Lieutenant-Colonel Owen Howell-Price of the 3rd Battalion. He was advising soldiers about the siting of a machine-gun in the front trench when killed by a bullet through the brain.

Conditions steadily deteriorated and men waiting to make an attack were lying in mud and rain. On the night of 4 November three waves of Australian attackers were using a trench at the same time. The first wave of men arched their bodies over the trench to make room for their mates beneath them and lay there strained and uncomfortable in the rain. On the morning of 5 November, short-shooting heavy British or Australian batteries killed ten men of the 3rd Battalion and wounded seventeen others. The gunners had been asked to fire during a gale and the wind affected the flight of the shells.

In the confused and sometimes desperate fighting the 7th Brigade, which was the most heavily involved formation, lost 819 officers and men. Four attempts to advance in this sector had failed but Fourth Army HQ ordered yet another assault. The earliest it could be made was 14 November and as winter wore on life became even harder. Heavily burdened, the soldiers reached the trenches exhausted. The mud was so sticky that men had to be dragged out by mules or horses. A rescue party broke the back of an officer whom they were trying to haul from the mud. It was not unusual for wounded men to be left lying in the mud for twelve hours because not enough bearers were available to carry them out. The trenches were nothing more than muddy drains where the men stood and shivered and waited for their two days in the firing line to pass. After that they spent two days in the support line where life was a little safer but no less uncomfortable.

The attack of 14–15 November was only partly successful and led to the usual German counter-attack. It cost the Australian battalions — 19th, 20th, 25th and 26th — 901 casualties. Apart from battle casualties, men were being steadily evacuated with illness, trench feet and sheer exhaustion. One soldier of the 24th Battalion shot himself dead rather than face another spell in the front trench. Some men suffering from trench feet crawled back to the dressing station to allow the stretcher-bearers to carry men in greater need than themselves. The First Battle of the Somme ended on 18 November.

Directions

The Australian front during this winter of dreadful suffering was forward of Flers and between Gueudecourt and Le Sars. All the fields for an area of 4 square kilometres comprised a sector of prodigious effort and stubborn endurance. From Albert, proceed to Flers. Here, take the D197 towards Bapaume. After 1 kilometre, turn right at the crossroads. After 300 metres there is a track to the AIF Burial Ground, which was in the middle of the Australian battlefield. From the cemetery return to the road and turn right for Gueudecourt, 0.5 kilometre away.

Gueudecourt

The AIF 1st, 2nd, 4th and 5th Divisions were all in the front line south of Gueudecourt in January and February 1917. The weather was often bitterly cold but sometimes not cold enough to freeze the mud, which made operations difficult. The Germans fired a single 5.9 inch shell punctually at the rate of one a minute, night and day, into the ruins of Gueudecourt. This continued throughout the winter of 1916–17. The object was to prevent the British and Dominion troops from using cellars and dugouts in the village, and the tactic succeeded.

On the night of 4 February the 13th Battalion was ordered to attack from Gueudecourt towards German-held Stormy Trench, which lay on a neck of land in a spur leading to the wide, shallow valley before Bapaume. More than 12 000 grenades were carried forward to the jumping-off trench and another 8000 were stored at battalion HQ. The men wore greatcoats against the cold and their large pockets were filled with grenades.

The attack was launched across the frozen snow of No Man's Land. In command of the right company was Captain Harry Murray. He led his men into Stormy Trench, but short of the position intended. As he consolidated the Germans put down a barrage and made a counter-attack. Private M. D. Robertson DCM fired rifle grenades at the enemy, giving Murray time to gather his own bombers and organise a brilliant charge. The fight went on all night and repeatedly Murray rallied his men, led bayonet charges and bombing attacks and somehow found time to carry wounded men to safety. His leadership led to Stormy Trench being held. Murray was awarded the VC for his superb action, which ranks as one of the most outstanding of the war. Even so, the 13th Battalion lost seven officers and 226 men that night and a company of the 14th Battalion, in support, lost ninety-five of 120.

Directions

From Albert, take the Bapaume road for 0.5 kilometre beyond Le Sars. Turn right and pass a large mound on the left (Butte de Warlencourt) to Gueudecourt. From Gueudecourt, take the D74E towards Beaulencourt. Murray's exploit took place roughly 400 metres into the fields opposite the Newfoundland memorial along this road.

Hébuterne

Fifty kilometres west of Bapaume, the town of Hébuterne came under German pressure in March 1918 during the great breakthrough. The 4th Brigade of the 4th Division was rushed there on 25 March and while moving through the back area found the people packing their wagons for flight. As columns of lorries carrying the Diggers rolled into town the people called to one another 'Les Australiens!' and unloaded their wagons. An AIF officer asked why they had decided to stay rather than flee. They said, 'Pas necessaire maintenant, vous les tiendrez'. ('Not necessary now; you'll hold them.')

The Diggers had arrived at Hébuterne too late to encourage villagers who had already fled. The soldiers helped themselves to the remains of meals, to fowls and rabbits in the yards and to wine in the cellars. The battle for Hébuterne, some of them said, looked like being a picnic. But it wasn't. The battalions had barely taken up their battle positions when, on 27 March, the Germans made their first attack. That day brigade HQ distributed an order that 'no retirement was permissible'. Under enemy artillery fire for most of the time, the brigade repelled one attack after another without giving an inch. On 1 April two captains of the 16th Battalion, D. S. Aarons and C. Ahrens, led an attack which advanced the front 350 metres and captured seventy-one prisoners and four machine-guns. The 4th Brigade performed so well that the British corps commander refused to allow it to be relieved.

Directions

Hébuterne can be reached from Amiens, Doullens, Bapaume or Arras. The 4th Brigade's area of operations was east and south-east of Hébuterne, actually on the edge of the present village. The right flank of the right battalion was at the quarry south of the settlement. Australian casualties from the Hébuterne fighting are buried in Gommecourt British Cemetery, Hébuterne (twenty-six burials), Gommecourt Wood New Cemetery, Foncquevillers (one), and Foncquevillers Military Cemetery (six).

Heilly

Australians were in this Ancre River village from July 1916 and again in the spring and summer of 1918 when Heilly Château was HQ of the 15th Brigade of the 5th Division. An Australian official war artist, A. Henry Fullwood, painted a scene at the inner entrance to the château. This entrance is extant but the château has fallen into ruin. The 27th CCS of the Fourth Army, attached to 1st Anzac Corps, was in Heilly from August 1916 to March 1917. Its tents and huts were erected on the green opposite the château gates. Soldiers were billeted in every building in the town.

Directions

From Albert, take the D52 for 8 kilometres. The walls of the old château are on the left of the road, just after passing the turn-off to Franvillers.

Lochnagar Crater near the village of La Boiselle was blown by 27 000 kilograms of ammonal on 1 July 1916, the first day of the Battle of the Somme. From the air, these fields still show the chalk which was brought to the surface by mining, shelling and trench-digging. The road through La Boiselle travels, right,to Pozières, 2 kilometres distant. Photograph courtesy of *After the Battle Magazine*.

Lochnagar Crater

By dimension, this is the largest mine crater on the Western Front although the charge was less than that used at Spanbroekmolen. Lochnagar was one of nineteen blown on 1 July 1916 at the beginning of the Battle of the Somme. AIF troops were not in the Somme region at the time but most Diggers saw the crater and it is in an area where, from 23 July, the divisions had guns, dumps and shelters. It is well worth seeing. Lochnagar was blown by 27 216 kilograms of ammonal, all laboriously put into place under enemy positions by tunnellers working from 600 metres distant. Today the crater has a diameter of 200 metres and a depth of 30 metres. From the lip — the spoil thrown out of the explosion — there are good views of Sausage Valley. The Germans had machine-gun posts in the slopes but when they were pushed out of the valley it became a thoroughfare for troops and their transport. In 1979 the crater was bought by an Englishman, Richard Dunning, to save it from being ploughed under as farmland.

Directions
From Albert, take the D929 to the hamlet of La Boiselle and at the crossroads turn right, near the Tyneside Scottish and Tyneside Irish Memorial, on to the Contalmaison road. After 200 metres turn right and almost immediately fork left. The crater is on the right within 300 metres.

Millencourt

This village lies on high ground only a few kilometres west of Albert. In March 1918 the German onslaught swept over Albert and the defence situation became critical. Two brigades of the 4th Division were rushed into the line, occupying the valley between Millencourt and Henencourt and were kept in close reserve. Brigadier-General John Gellibrand, commanding the 12th Brigade, established his HQ in the beautiful Henencourt Château. The 24th Battalion, which had been billeted in Millencourt in 1916 and 1917, had made friends of the villagers, who now, as the Germans approached, were refugees.

The Diggers salvaged many loads of furniture, potatoes, oats and other goods under shellfire and handed the lot over to the French Mission for distribution to the refugees. Some of the battalion bandsmen rescued a piano, left in the village by a family of girls whom the Diggers had known. One April night they hauled it out on a cart and with much difficulty took it to the rear and ensured that the girls received it.

Between March and May 1918 the area around Millencourt was an Australian 'island' and alive with military activity. On 5 April — the day of the battle of Dernancourt — the 45th Battalion was caught in a violent bombardment near Millencourt and lost four officers and forty men. Among those who died of wounds was the battalion medical officer, Major W. S. Garnett. Also on that day, the 10th and 11th Field Artillery Brigades lost twelve officers and seventy-seven others. Both brigades had their HQs in Millencourt village. Here, Captain A. F. Martin, while dressing a wound received by Lieutenant R. D. Buttercase, was hit by a shell which killed both officers.

Directions
From Albert, leave to the west on the D91, signposted Millencourt 3 kilometres. Every building in the village was occupied by Australians and their front line was at the eastern edge of the present village, facing towards Albert. As late as 1960 villagers remembered the Australians and even now a folk memory exists. The story of the piano is recalled, though with many variations. Fifty Diggers lie in Millencourt Communal Cemetery Extension, all killed either in March or April 1918. To reach the cemetery continue out of Millencourt on the D91. The cemetery is within 100 metres, along a track to the right.

Morlancourt

At the end of March 1918 the Germans, triumphantly advancing, held a strong line on the Albert front. One of the principal hubs of their defensive system north of the Somme River was the village of Morlancourt. They also held the high ground east of the place, from where their artillery could fire accurately at the Australians who would have to cross exposed slopes to the west of the village.

On the afternoon of 28 March Major-General John Monash ordered an advance by the whole line of his 3rd Division. The 10th and 11th Brigades made separate and largely unco-ordinated advances, telephone communications were poor and as a result casualties were heavy for the first stage of the advance. Several officers of the 40th Battalion were hit.

During the night (a very dark one), the 44th Battalion tried to capture Sailly-Laurette, south of Morlancourt. Under the muzzles of enemy machine-guns, it suffered heavy casualties and withdrew. Patrol action continued next day and on 30 March Australian infantry stopped a German counter-offensive. The Germans lost as heavily as the Australians had on 28 March. Also on that day, the 3rd Division's guns played havoc in the enemy lines, despite losses of their own. By the end of the day the Australian battalions had attained their objectives, with a loss of 500 men. German losses were never accurately assessed but are now believed to have been 1000 men.

No fighting took place in Morlancourt nor did the Australians occupy it at that time, so the name given to the fighting, the Battle of Morlancourt, is misleading. The most serious fighting took place on the slopes between Treux and Sailly-Laurette, 2 kilometres west of Morlancourt. The 39th Battalion was engaged in Treux Wood.

One of the greatest successes of 'peaceful penetration' took place on the Morlancourt front. On 17 May, while making his rounds, Lieutenant A. W. Irvine, Intelligence Officer of the 17th battalion, found all the Australians manning a length of trench asleep in the sun. Even the sentry was only half awake. Irvine reckoned that the Germans would also be sleepy on a warm day and on 18 May he led a party of eighteen men in a silent noontime raid. A grenade thrown into a dugout killed four Germans and the other twenty-two in the position surrendered. Irvine's raid, achieved without casualties to the raiders, took only ten minutes.

The fighting from Morlancourt was renewed on 8 August, the first day of the British counter-offensive, and the Australians captured it the following day.

Directions

From Albert, take the D52 south through Dernancourt and Buire-sur-Ancre to Treux. The Bois de Treux, where the 39th Battalion was engaged, is 200 metres south of the village on the road to Sailly-Laurette. This road then runs across the fields of 'the Battle of Morlancourt'. From Morlancourt, the hills on which the battle took place can be seen to the west. The natural strength of Morlancourt as a German bastion can also be appreciated. To reach Morlancourt from Treux it is possible to drive cross-country, but the safest route is to head towards Sailly-Laurette. Turn left on to the D1 at the crossroads. After 1 kilometre turn left again to Morlancourt.

The position of Lieutenant Irvine's raid can be fixed fairly precisely but needs a short walk. From Morlancourt, take the D42, signposted Sailly-Laurette, to the crossroads with the D1, signposted Corbie. Turn towards Corbie and drive approximately 400 metres to the first semi-formed road on the right. This road marked the German front line. On foot, proceed along this road for 700 metres to a farmland crossroads with a small reservoir. Irvine's trench raid took place here.

Battle of Pozières

In Australian Western Front history, Pozières is one of the seven most important names. (The others are Fromelles, Bullecourt, Passchendaele, Messines, Villers-Bretonneux and Mont St Quentin-Peronne). For Australian visitors, there is so much to see at Pozières that after a general description, the sites have been described individually, except for cemeteries which are listed separately.

Situated on the ridge of a broad plateau, Pozières commands the road east to Bapaume and the approaches to Thiepval, on high ground to the north. During 1915 and 1916 the Germans had turned Pozières into an immensely strong position, virtually a great fortress. From their trenches and machine-gun posts they had a clear, gently graded field of fire over all possible lines of British advance. Between 13–17 July 1916 British infantry had made four vain and terribly costly attacks against Pozières, the final one after a sustained bombardment that reduced the already ruined village to rubble.

The AIF 1st Division (Major-General A. S. Walker) was ordered to attack Pozières from the south on 23 July. Lieutenant A. S. Blackburn, 10th Battalion, was sent with fifty men to capture a German machine-gun post. He made two attacks with four men and on each occasion all four were killed. On the third attempt, he captured an enemy trench and in a fourth movement he gained and finally held 250 metres of trench, which he clung to with twenty men, the only survivors.

Private John Leak, 9th Battalion, leapt from a trench under close-range machine-gun fire and threw three grenades into an enemy bombing post. Then he jumped into the post and bayoneted three unwounded enemy bombers. German reinforcements drove the Australians back from

The 'windmill site' at Pozières. The wreckage of the windmill lay on the rough mound on the right and was the scene of much fighting. The inscription on the bench memorial notes that more 'Australian blood was spilled at Pozières than anywhere in the world—23 000 casualties in six weeks'. The Bastiaan plaque is to the rear of the bench. In the distance, left, is Thiepval Memorial.

trench to trench and on each occasion Leak was the last to withdraw, all the time throwing grenades. Captain E. E. Herrod and Lieutenant W. L. Waterhouse of the 2nd Battalion, with about fifteen men, captured the strongpoint known to the British as Gibraltar, such was its apparent impregnability. Leak and Blackburn were awarded the VC.

The task of moving through the village positions was given to the 8th Battalion on 24 July. In desperate fighting, Private Thomas Cooke was ordered to take his Lewis gun and team to a dangerous part of the line. He was seen to do fine work but came under very heavy fire from artillery and machine-guns. After a time Cooke was the only man left. He stuck to his post and continued to fire his gun. Soldiers sent to help him found him dead beside it. He was awarded a VC, the citation for which noted that he 'set a splendid example of determination and devotion to duty'. Many such episodes occurred at Pozières but very often nobody survived to tell of gallantry displayed. In a way, Cooke's posthumous VC was for all the other Diggers who deserved special decoration but did not receive it. Cooke has no known grave but the trench in which he died was somewhere on the north-east side of the village.

German artillery fire was incessant and in three days the 1st Division lost 5285 officers and men, the rest were exhausted and the division was replaced by the 2nd Division. During the afternoon and night of 26 July, in great heat, the 5th Brigade's battalions threw 15 000 grenades in fierce close-quarter fighting. The 24th Battalion had a company wiped out by shell fire and many 28th Battalion men were hit as they tried to force their way through uncut enemy barbed wire. The 4th Pioneer Battalion lost eight officers and 222 men in ten days while keeping open just one section of communication trench. The 2nd Division was spent after ten days and had lost 6848 officers and men. It was replaced by the 4th Division.

On 7 August there occurred one of the most dramatic episodes of the Pozières saga. As dawn was breaking, German infantry stormed across the shell holes and craters on a 400-metre front. They recaptured some of their positions and took some Australians prisoner. A serious breakthrough was imminent. In one dugout was Lieutenant Albert Jacka VC, with his platoon of the 14th Battalion. The enemy raiders threw bombs into his dugout, causing casualties, and left a sentry at the entrance. Jacka shot him with his revolver and led eight men in a rush up the stairway. Above ground, with his men in line, he charged the advancing Germans from behind.

Inspired by Jacka's ferocious assault, other Australians joined in. Jacka dived into an enemy-held shell hole, killing and capturing a number of

Germans. He himself suffered seven wounds before he collapsed. Because of his leadership and example, the captured Australians were freed, many German prisoners were taken and the lost ground was recovered, together with even more territory. C. E. W. Bean considered that Jacka's counter-attack was 'the most dramatic and effective act of individual audacity in the history of the AIF'. Jacka was awarded the MC but throughout the AIF it was believed that he should have been given another VC. (It is my opinion also.)

The 4th Division pressed northwards along the ridge to capture Mouquet Farm — 'Mucky Farm' or 'Moo-cow Farm' to the Australians. The only evidence of any former building was scattered bricks but the Germans had strong positions in and under the ruins. Captain Harry Murray, of the 13th Battalion, captured 200 metres of Fabeck Graben trench and on 7–8 August the 16th Battalion captured Point 78. Under appalling conditions, Private Martin O'Meara became almost solely responsible for the carriage of water, supplies and care of the wounded. Four times he went out through the barrage with supplies, on one occasion taking a party with him. Then he brought out all the wounded of his battalion. His outstanding courage earned him the VC.

When the 4th Division was exhausted the 1st was brought back into the ghastly shambles of churned up earth. Its job was to capture the Mouquet Farm defences on 21 August. The Diggers made some gains at a cost of ninety-two officers and 2558 men. With the 1st Division now virtually destroyed, the 2nd Division was brought back from behind Albert. In four days' fighting it lost 1268 men and the 4th Division took its place again. The Australians made their last attack at Pozières on 3 September. In wild fighting, posts were captured, lost and taken again. Two companies of the 21st Battalion, about 160 men in all, were surrounded and not seen again. Eight years later, officers of the War Graves Commission found their remains in a trench beyond Mouquet Farm. The 13th Brigade lost forty-one officers and 1305 men.

As each division had become exhausted it was withdrawn, rested and then put in again. As a result of these attacks, the Australians had captured, step by step, the crest of the main ridge and Pozières windmill. Then, turning north, they progressed to the ruins of Mouquet Farm. As intended, they got behind the Germans but in so doing they themselves presented a salient quite as exposed as those they forced on the Germans.

On seven occasions the AIF had been used as a battering ram at Pozières and it had lost 23 000 officers and men, 50 per cent of the four divisions' fighting strength.

1st Division Memorial

The obelisk monument is 100 metres off the Albert-Bapaume road, on the Albert side of Pozières village. It was erected here at the request of the division's leaders because the Pozières fighting had cost it more lives than any other action. Also, an important enemy trench ran across the lawn on which the

The battle honours plaque of the 1st Division Memorial at Pozières. Although the rising sun badge carries the title 'Australian Imperial Force' (AIF), the badge worn by the troops bore the words Australian Commonwealth Military Forces.

monument stands, actually just in front of it. The Division's battle honours are shown on a plaque: Pozières, Mouquet Farm, Le Barque, Tilloy, Boursies, Demicourt, Hermies, Lagnicourt, Bullecourt, Third Battle of Ypres, Menin Road, Broodseinde Ridge, Passchendaele, Battle of the Lys, Second Battle of the Somme, Lihons, Chuignolles, Hindenburg Line.

Gibraltar

Known to the Germans as Panzersturm (armour-post), this blockhouse of reinforced concrete was the most feared single enemy position in the Pozières sector. It is just across the side street from the gate to the 1st Division Memorial. Originally much higher and of greater extent, Gibraltar could now easily be passed by as a scrub-covered mound. However, on examination its angular shape can be made out. A blocked-off entrance was opened up in 1992 and I hope the entire position will be uncovered. Men of the 1st Division's 2nd Battalion captured Gibraltar on 23 July 1916.

The Church

No church existed by the time the Australians saw Pozières; it had been pounded to powder. It was rebuilt in the 1920s and is now in parlous state from water damage and neglect. Inside there is an Australian flag on a staff. The key is obtainable from the house facing the front door of the church, which is in the street leading to Thiepval.

Mouquet Farm

After the war, the Vanderdriessche family built a new farmhouse about 200 metres closer to the Albert-Bapaume road than the rubble of the old one. The only visible surviving remnant of the old farm is a block of concrete and bricks in the field which faces the farm's iron gates. Near the gate is a pile of shrapnel shell cases and other debris from the battlefield. Between the farm and the Pozières-Thiepval road is an old quarry, ringed by trees. It was a strong German post in 1916 and was captured on 14–15 August by men of the 50th Battalion. In 1988 I found an Australian rising sun collar badge in Mouquet's fields. Martin O'Meara won his VC

Above: The author at the only piece of the original Mouquet Farm which remains. Hundreds of Australians were killed around this spot.

Below: Cut into a stone slab, these words express the tragedy of the 'heights' of Pozières. In six weeks' fighting the AIF suffered 23 000 casualties.

THE RUIN OF POZIERES WINDMILL
WHICH LIES HERE WAS THE CENTRE
OF THE STRUGGLE IN THIS PART OF
THE SOMME BATTLEFIELD IN JULY
AND AUGUST 1916 IT WAS CAPTURED
ON AUGUST 4TH BY AUSTRALIAN
TROOPS WHO FELL MORE THICKLY ON
THIS RIDGE THAN ON ANY OTHER
BATTLEFIELD OF THE WAR

The Australian memorial at the windmill site on Pozières Ridge, Somme. The windmill, which stood on the mound, was the site of ferocious fighting in July-August 1916.

for his bravery in the fields between Mouquet Farm and the modern Pozières village.

The Windmill and 2nd Division Memorial

By the side of the Albert-Bapaume road, on the east side of Pozières, this site is less obvious than the striking British tank memorial on the opposite side of the road. However, the windmill site is one of the most significant of AIF landmarks. An engraved inscription on a raised stone slab emphasises the importance of the ridge to Australia, not merely to the 2nd Division (see photograph). In fact, there is nothing at the memorial site to indicate that it 'belongs' to the 2nd Division, whose principal monument is at Mont St Quentin. The old windmill stood on the mound just behind the memorial and the entire piece of ground is owned by Australia. A small party of the 27th and 28th Battalions, led by Captain Maitland Foss, captured the windmill site on 5 August 1916.

Site of Albert Jacka's 'VC Stunt'

Jacka's famous exploit — for which he was *not* awarded a VC — took place in a field near the Australian memorial plot and the 2nd Division memorial at the old windmill site. The German dugout from which Jacka began his furious attack was about 100 metres from the north-east corner of this fenced-off plot and in a north-easterly direction. The general fight which followed his intervention in the German counter-attack raged over this part of the battlefield in all directions from the dugout. A little exercise of the imagination is needed to see the present flat and ordered agricultural land as an area torn and gouged by shellfire and crossed by trenches. For his audacious feat Jacka received the MC.

Leak and Blackburn VC Exploits

Pozières Trench was the Germans' front line protecting their complex positions against the Australian attack from the south. Arc-shaped, it cut the Albert-Bapaume road near where the Contalmaison road now joins it and looped south and then east. At its furthest it was 600 metres south of the Albert-Bapaume road, the D929. The machine-gun post which Private Leak captured on 23 July 1916 was at the junction of a trench just beyond Pozières Trench and a communications trench. Turn off the D929 south towards Bazentin on the D73. After 400 metres the site of Leak's exploit is just off this road in the fields to the left.

Lieutenant Blackburn's activities on the same day were further into these same fields and closer to the D929. As he made seven separate movements and captured 400 metres of enemy trenches he covered a lot of ground around where Pozières Trench crossed the 'O.G. Lines' at right angles. At one time he passed under the Pozières–Bazentin road through a German tunnel. Forty of the seventy men he commanded during the day were killed or wounded during his eight hours of sustained effort, which greatly helped in the taking of Pozières. Blackburn ranged so far during his operations that perhaps we should know the area as 'Blackburn's Battlefield'.

Pozières — Sausage Valley

A large depression rather than an obvious valley, in 1916 this area was constantly busy with wagons, gun teams, and marching men. Many posts, depots and dumps were stationed here. From the comparative shelter of Sausage Valley — sometimes called a gully on Australian maps — units moved up to the firing line at Pozières.

Directions

From Albert, take the Bapaume road and after 3 kilometres reach La Boiselle crossroads. Turn right towards Contalmaison and after 100 metres right again to La Crête (the crater). This is Lochnagar Crater, blown by the British on 1 July 1916. Drive past the crater 100 metres and you are on the slopes of Sausage Valley. The Albert-Pozières road is on the skyline, left, and halfway up the slope is Gordon Dump Cemetery.

Pozières — Mash Valley

The natural twin of Sausage Valley, Mash in on the north side of the Albert-Bapaume road. Rather deeper than Sausage, it runs from La Boiselle, only 3 kilometres from Albert, towards Pozières Ridge. From the front line at the head of Mash Valley, Australian infantry moved off to attack German positions in the quarry at Mouquet Farm. Some places in Mash were protected from enemy fire by sharply rising banks and here casualty clearing stations were set up.

Directions

For the best view of Mash drive from Albert, turn left at La Boiselle, drive 300 metres and look right.

Becourt Wood (Bois de Becourt)

Two kilometres east of Albert, Becourt Wood was a haven for artillery wagon lines but against aggressive German fliers the trees were not always the cover which soldiers believed. On the morning of 21 August 1916 six enemy aircraft flew low over the back area and dropped seven bombs on the wagon lines of the 7th Battery Australian Field Artillery. The results were devastating. Nine men were killed and the commander, Lieutenant H. E. Moody, and thirty-eight men were wounded. Fifteen horses were killed and thirty-eight others wounded. The battery's lines were on the left of the road at the entrance to the village of Becourt. Some of the victims of the bombing are buried in Becourt Military Cemetery. C. E. W. Bean set up his camp on the eastern edge of Becourt Wood on 31 July 1916 and worked from there for five weeks.

Directions

From Albert, leave by the D938 Becordel-Becourt road, which breaks off from the D329 Bray-sur-Somme road. After 500 metres, at the crossroads, turn left for 500 metres to another crossroads. Here, turn right for Becourt, 1.5 kilometres.

Ribemont-sur-Ancre

On the banks of the Ancre River, opposite Mericourt-l'Abbé, Ribemont was yet another billeting town for the AIF in 1918. During the German breakthrough in March, Ribemont formed a bastion of defence, with the 9th Brigade of the 3rd Division in occupation. On 30 March, in the fields around Ribemont, a couple of Australian horsemen rounded up cows and got them away out of German shellfire. Although looting occurred in Ribemont and elsewhere it was seldom proved to be the fault of Australians. The French Mission thanked General Monash for his 3rd Division's work in recovering property. For instance, the 3rd Division's transport saved ninety-six tonnes of wool from Ribemont mill. It also saved wheat, cattlefood, wine and other property valued by the French Mission at £94 472 stg. The division collected from homes and handed to the Mission more than sixty cases of clocks, tableware, linen, curtains and furniture. Much of this came from Ribemont, some from Bonnay and other villages.

Ribemont seemed a happy place to the Diggers but on 19 May this outlook changed. As a company of the 22nd Battalion was leaving the village for the front line a single shellburst in the village square hit fifteen men. On 24 May the Germans gas-shelled Ribemont and caused some further casualties. Ribemont Communal Cemetery Extension contains 178 Australians in a total of 483 burials.

Directions
From Albert, take the D52 through Dernancourt and Buire. The Diggers not only occupied the whole of Ribemont but were also camped in the woods between that village and Heilly. The cemetery is on the D179E, signposted Baizieux, at the five-ways on entering Ribemont from Buire.

The 3rd Division memorial on the plateau above Sailly-le-Sec, on the Somme River. The memorial faces an area of once intense Australian activity.

St Pol

For the British and Dominion armies, St Pol was a billeting centre and hospital town and a major route junction. On 28 March 1918 the 15th Brigade of the 5th Division was en route by train from Flanders to take up a position further south during the German breakthrough. That afternoon, the troop train carrying the 58th Battalion had just cleared St Pol station when a German 14-inch shell hit it. The explosion killed sixteen Diggers, including the whole of the quartermaster's staff of the battalion. Another nine soldiers were wounded. The officers' carriage and four trucks were derailed and eight horses were killed. Most of the 58th Battalion casualties were buried in St Pol British Cemetery and a few in St Pol Communal Cemetery Extension.

Directions
St Pol is 34 kilometres west of Arras and 15 kilometres north of Doullens. It can be reached from Albert via Doullens, a total distance of 45 kilometres.

Sailly-le-Sec

The Australian soldiers, especially those of the 3rd Division, knew this Somme-side village well in 1918. The surrounding country, virtually all of it battlefield, was the scene of numerous actions in which the AIF participated. Also, the 3rd carried out some of its most daring acts of 'peaceful penetration' here. The division held the high ground between the Ancre and the Somme and during April 1918 captured Germans on three days out of every five, a remarkable record. In the sunken roads, the copses and the hedges, they gave the enemy no peace.

When the time came after the war to find a site for a memorial the 3rd Division seriously considered Messines Ridge, where its men had fought so well and successfully, but finally decided on the northern Somme heights above Sailly-le-Sec. The monument was built at the crossroads of the D1 Bray-Corbie road and the Sailly-le-Sec—Mericourt L'Abbé road. The tall obelisk faces towards the Somme and has views in every direction, symbolising the all-encompassing sweep of the 3rd Division's operations. The bronze plaque shows these battle honours: Messines 1917, The Windmill, Third Battle of Ypres, Broodseinde, Passchendaele, Morlancourt, Treux, Hamel, 8th August, Proyart, Suzanne, Bray-sur-Somme, Curlu, Clery-sur-Somme, Bouchavesnes, Roisel, Hindenburg Line. From all these triumphs the 3rd Division, which was commanded by John Monash for most of the war, chose to place its memorial on the Somme heights. The selection reveals much about the Diggers' feelings concerning the Somme.

Directions
From Albert, the easiest of several routes is the D42 to Meaulte and Morlancourt and 1.5 kilometres further to its junction with the D1. Turn right and drive 4 kilometres to the monument, by the side of the D1. This route takes the visitor across territory fought over by the 3rd Division.

Sailly-Laurette, Somme

The village of Sailly-Laurette, 1.5 kilometres east of Sailly-le-Sec, on the northern bank of the Somme, was another place of battle for the AIF, especially the 3rd Division. Its involvement followed the German offensive of March 1918. The 42nd, 43rd and 44th Battalions of the 11th Brigade, the units immediately involved, were rushed forward to form an emergency front line between Sailly-le-Sec and Sailly-Laurette. Sailly-Laurette was held in strength by the Germans.

On the night of 28–29 March two companies of the 44th stumbled upon the German outposts at Sailly-Laurette and suffered rather badly. However, the Germans had greater casualties on 30 March when they launched a fullblown attack. Not a single enemy soldier passed the Australians' outpost line. The attack later developed along the Bray-Corbie road, still on the 11th Brigade's front but 2 kilometres north of the river, and again it was stopped. Much Australian 'peaceful penetration' took place along the entire AIF front during April.

In No Man's Land on the night of 4 May Brigadier-General Charles Rosenthal and Lieutenant-Colonel H. W. White, CO of the 33rd Battalion, overcame and captured some scouting Germans in the sunken Sailly-Laurette—Treux road. Meanwhile Lieutenant H. W. Lilja of the 34th Battalion was on patrol in the dark and his Lewis-gunner, hearing noises in the sunken road, was about to open up when a German flare illuminated No Man's Land. Fortunately for Rosenthal, he was a very large man and his bulky shape was well known to his men. Lieutenant Lilja stayed the gunner's trigger finger.

Generally, the 35th Battalion's outpost line ran along the Sailly-Laurette—Treux road. Two of its companies were north of the Corbie-Bray road and two south of it. From the outpost line the Australians attacked the Germans on the night of 5–6 May. One of the main objectives was the highest point in the area, known as 'Brick Beacon', 1 kilometre east. In fact, such was the stubbornness of German resistance that it was not taken until the night of 8–9 August. Sailly-Laurette fell at the same time. Many casualties from this period of fighting are buried in Beacon Cemetery, Sailly-Laurette. Of 668 burials, 195 are Australians.

Directions

From Albert, leave by the D42 south through Meaulte and Morlancourt, from where Sailly-Laurette is signposted, 3 kilometres. For Beacon Cemetery, turn right at the D42—D1 crossroads and the cemetery is on the left within 0.5 kilometre. For the Sailly-Laurette—Treux road, which ran through the centre of No Man's Land and was later the Australian front line, drive through Sailly-Laurette towards Sailly-le-Sec and turn right on the edge of the village. Dive Copse Cemetery is en route.

Ville-sur-Ancre

On 26 March 1918 the German offensive broke through the British line from Albert south to Bray, a breach 15 kilometres wide. The principal captures by the Germans were the settlements of Ville-sur-Ancre, Morlancourt and Dernancourt. The AIF 3rd Division and the 4th Division (except for the 4th Brigade, which was at Hébuterne) were rushed south from Flanders to plug the gap. As both the Allies and the Germans had suffered heavy losses and much disorganisation during the German offensive the front became relatively quiet, apart from Australian raids.

It was essential for the British High Command to recapture Ville-sur-Ancre, which was vital to the Germans for their defence of Morlancourt. The task of capturing it was given to the 6th Brigade, which attacked on the night of 19 May. The plan called for an advance on a front of 1400 metres, penetration to the same depth and capture of high ground south of the village. The attack frontage was a wide one, with up to 20 metres between men. The objective included sunken roads, code-named Big Caterpillar and Little Caterpillar. Both were defended by outposts and machine-guns.

During the advance Captain W. R. Hunter's company of the 22nd Battalion suffered casualties and he himself was severely wounded. Sergeant William Ruthven took charge of company HQ and rallied the Australian line as close-range machine-gun fire blocked the advance to Big Caterpillar. With bomb and bayonet, Ruthven rushed the enemy post and captured it. Then he attacked a group of enemy coming out of a post. Having handed over the surviving prisoners to an escort, Ruthven re-organised the men in his vicinity and established a post in Little Caterpillar. Seeing enemy movement in another part of the sunken road, he went over the top alone and, armed only with a revolver, rushed and captured an enemy post, taking prisoner thirty-

At the entrance to French military cemeteries a weatherproof noticeboard gives details of French battlefields and memorials in the district.

two Germans. Largely because of Ruthven's example and success, the Australian line took the objectives and advanced to the crest of the slope overlooking Morlancourt. Ruthven was awarded the VC for his exploit, one of the most daring of all Australian VC actions.

Directions

From Albert, take the D42 road south, signposted Meaulte, to Ville-sur-Ancre. In Ville, take the road to Treux. To reach Big Caterpillar, turn into the unnamed road with a public telephone cabinet on the corner. Just 100 metres along this road Big Caterpillar sunken road begins. After inspecting Big Caterpillar, return to the Treux road, turn left and continue to the communal cemetery. Turn left into the road beside the cemetery. This becomes Little Caterpillar sunken road. The 6th Brigade's operation was eastwards, across the sunken roads towards the heights beyond. However, the Australian attack, which began at the railway line, encompassed the whole of the village. Four Australians are buried in Ville-sur-Ancre Communal Cemetery.

Chapter 6

Cemeteries in the Northern Somme Area of Australian Interest

All the cemeteries described here are north of the Somme River.

Abbeville Communal Cemetery Extension

For the greater part of the war Abbeville was the HQ of the British lines of communication. Three military hospitals, including at one time the 3rd Australian General Hospital, were stationed in Abbeville from 1915 to 1919. Ten Diggers are buried in the Abbeville Communal Cemetery and 227 Diggers, in a total of 1352 soldiers of the British and Dominion armies, in the Cemetery Extension. Most of the Australians died of wounds during the Pozières fighting of summer 1916. Others died of disease in 1917 or 1918. As is to be expected of burials in a base town, many units are represented. Occasionally in military cemeteries an Australian is to be found who served in the British Army. In the Abbeville cemetery is Lance-Corporal Kenneth McDonald, born at Gundy, NSW, who served in the 1st Battalion King's Royal Rifle Corps and was killed on 7 August 1916.

Albert Communal Cemetery Extension

The extension was used by fighting units and field ambulances from August 1915 to November 1916, especially in and after September when many field ambulances were posted in the vicinity. Thirty-nine Diggers are buried here among 822 other British and Dominion troops. For some years a wooden memorial erected by the 2nd Field Company Australian Engineers stood in the cemetery but it eventually rotted. Several engineers are buried in the cemetery. One of the earliest Pozières casualties, Captain Hermann Hubbe, adjutant of the 1st Pioneer Battalion, lies here. He was killed on 23 July 1916 near Contalmaison while his unit was moving into its attack position (Grave I.K.28). Most of the Australians are July 1916 casualties but a few died of wounds suffered in February 1917. These include 19-year old Second Lieutenant Lovell Wright, 23rd Battalion (Grave I.N.60).

Directions
The cemetery is in the township of Albert, at the junction of the roads to Fricourt and Meaulte. Take the Fricourt road.

AIF Burial Ground, Grass Lane, Flers

This is a significant cemetery for Australians, since it is in the middle of the Flers battlefield of November 1916 to February 1917. It was an AIF sector and the cemetery was begun by Australian medical units stationed in neighbouring chalk caves which gave the site the local name Aux Cavées. These original graves are in Plot 1, Rows A and B. After the Armistice, the cemetery was greatly enlarged by the concentration of many graves from various killing fields of the Somme. It now contains 3450 graves of which 402 are Australian. A special memorial commemorates fifteen Diggers known or believed to be somewhere in the cemetery. Among the Australians are two particularly fine junior leaders. They are Second Lieutenant Frederick Matthews

DCM, 6th Company Australian Machine-Gun Corps, killed on 8 November 1916, and Captain Walter Sheen MC of the 56th Battalion, killed on 22 October 1916. Both were aged 26 and both had been noted as future senior officers.

Directions

See **Flers**. Grass Lane was the army name for the track on which the cemetery is situated. It is indeed grassy in summer but it turns into a quagmire with the first winter rains.

Allonville Communal Cemetery

The military section of this cemetery is largely an AIF burial ground since it contains the graves of forty Australian soldiers. The other thirty-eight are British

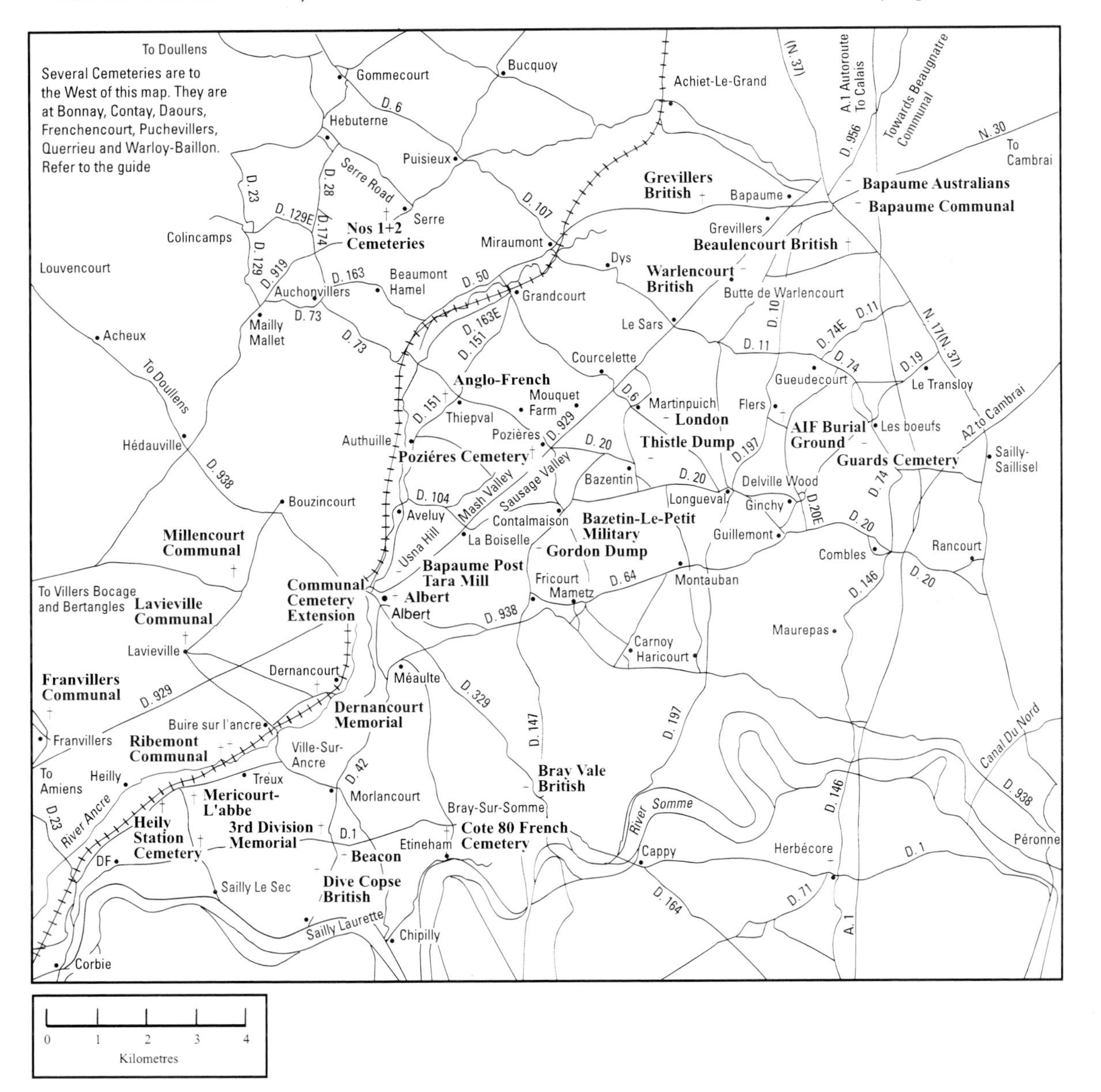

Map 7. The Somme Cemeteries

AIF Burial Ground, Grass Lane, Flers contains the graves of 402 Australians killed during the Somme fighting in the dreadful winter of 1916–17. This is the only cemetery in which the acronym AIF appears.

soldiers. Here are buried the eighteen victims of 'the Allonville disaster' of May 1918. All were members of the 14th Battalion, a Victorian unit. Several of the other Australians buried here died of sickness, three of them from meningitis. They are Gunner Ivo Davidson, Private Robert Dunnicliffe of 8th Light Trench Mortar Battery and Bombardier Gordon Stooks. None of the sick men ever reached hospital; they died in the 39th Casualty Clearing Station in Allonville. Lieutenant Herbert Masters, of the rarely heard of 1st Anzac Wireless Section Australian Engineers, died of accidental injuries on 15 April 1918, and is also buried at Allonville. *See* **Allonville**.

Bapaume Australian Cemetery

This cemetery is Australian in the number of burials as well as in name. Of the eighty-eight graves, seventy-four are Australians. The cemetery was begun by 3rd Australian Casualty Clearing Station in March 1917 and used until June. There are only twelve British soldiers but twenty-five Germans are also buried here. The first Diggers interred in the cemetery fell on 26 March during fighting at Lagnicourt, east of Bapaume. The majority, however, were wounded during the First Battle of Bullecourt, 11 April 1917, and died in the CCS. The last burial was Driver George Cook of the Australian

Engineers, who died of accidental injuries in a traffic collision (Grave B.37).

Directions
The cemetery is reached from the Bapaume—Cambrai road, just beyond a small park on the corner of this road and the Bapaume—Peronne road. It is 500 metres down local streets and as the CWGC sign is sometimes missing — souvenired perhaps? — it is best to ask for final directions.

Bapaume Communal Cemetery

Twenty Australians, four New Zealanders and two British soldiers are buried in the local cemetery. Three of the Diggers are men of the 23rd Battalion killed on 17 March 1917 during skirmishing before the Australian entry of Bapaume. One, Trooper Joseph Colmo of the 1st Australian Light Horse, was killed while scouting towards the German outpost line on 26 March. Mayor Raymond Pybus, the 26-year-old CO of the 43rd Brigade Australian Field Artillery, was killed on 15 April. His battery, in action on the Ecoust-Vraucourt road, east of Bapaume, was spotted by observers in a German balloon who directed their artillery on to the Australians. A rain of 5.9-inch and 4.2-inch shells hit one Australian gun and the ammunition supplies. The other guns continued to fire despite the inferno around them. A second gun and then a third were hit. Pybus ordered his men to take the wounded and get out. With Lieutenant E. J. R. Clarke, he remained to see that all the survivors were safe. An exploding German shell caught them, killing Clarke outright. Pybus lingered for a few minutes and said to a medical orderly, Private G. W. Freeman, 'Tell my wife I died at my guns'. Freeman took his CO's body on a gun limber to HQ, which until then knew nothing of the incident. I have not been able to locate the battery position. Lieutenant Clarke is buried next to his CO.

Directions
The communal cemetery is on the right of the N37 Bapaume-Arras road on the edge of Bapaume.

Bapaume Post Military Cemetery

In June 1916 the British front line crossed the Albert-Bapaume road between the site of this cemetery and the village of La Boiselle. The attack on La Boiselle on 1 July failed and several days passed before the village was taken. The cemetery was begun almost at once. After the Armistice 257 graves from the battlefields close to the cemetery were brought in. The cemetery now contains 408 graves, 181 of them unnamed. Eighteen Australians are buried here, all of them casualties from Pozières in July and August 1916. Note the grave of Private Harry Maxim, killed on 19 July. He was a member of the Australian Machine-Gun Corps, a highly suitable unit for anybody named Maxim. (The American inventor, Hiram Maxim, gave his name to the first successful portable machine-gun in 1884.) Harry Maxim would have been using a Vickers machine-gun, a variation of the Maxim gun.

Directions
From Albert, take the Bapaume road for 1.5 kilometres. The cemetery, which is on what the army called Tara Hill, is visible from Albert.

Bazentin-le-Petit Military Cemetery

The village of Bazentin was in German hands until 14 July 1916 when British troops captured it. The military cemetery was begun at the end of July and used until May 1917 as a frontline cemetery. Most of the fifty-five Australians buried here were killed in February 1917 during the Battle of Stormy Trench. Many are 2nd Brigade men. The senior Digger in the cemetery is Captain Harold Teague, 11th Battalion, killed on 14 February (Grave G.11).

Directions
From Albert, take the D929 to La Boiselle and turn right to Contalmaison. Two kilometres after Contalmaison, on the Longueval road at the Bazentin sign, turn 90 degrees left on to an unformed road. The cemetery is within 300 metres.

Beacon Cemetery, Sailly-Laurette

The cemetery is named from the 'Brick Beacon' on the summit of the ridge above the north side of the Somme River, and along the ridge runs the Bray-Corbie road. The cemetery was made on 15 August 1918 and then contained only 109 graves. After the

Armistice another 660 graves from the battlefields and small burial grounds were brought into it. Now 195 Australians are buried there, though fifty-eight are unknown. In all, the cemetery has 1315 graves. The AIF 25th Battalion erected a memorial in the cemetery, near the war stone, to their men who had fallen on 10 June 1918, the day of the attack on Morlancourt. The battalion had eleven officers and 167 men hit that day.

Among the Diggers buried here are several members of the 3rd Pioneer Battalion, killed while fighting as infantry in the attack on German machine-gun posts at Bray-sur-Somme on 22 August. One was Lieutenant James McConnell who, at the age of 48, was one of the oldest Australians engaged in frontline fighting (Grave V.J.1).

Directions
From Albert, take the D42 for 7 kilometres through Meaulte and Morlancourt to the D1 Corbie-Bray road. Turn right towards Corbie. The cemetery is within 700 metres.

Beaugnâtre Communal Cemetery

Just ten military graves are in this local cemetery, five Australian and five British soldiers. Three of the Diggers were killed in March 1918 and two in May. The two 14th Battalion men, Corporal W. W. Goodwin and Private Frederick Thorne, were killed while scouting towards the Hindenburg Line at Bullecourt. They were members of a platoon often used by Captain Albert Jacka VC, the battalion's scout officer.

Directions
From Bapaume, leave on the D956 through the suburb of St Aubin. The small village of Beaugnâtre is 2 kilometres distant. Cemetery indicated along a side road.

Beaulencourt British Cemetery, Ligny-Thilloy

The cemetery was made by a number of casualty clearing stations posted in Beaulencourt after mid-September 1918. The original burials are in Plot I, Rows A to D. After the Armistice 531 graves from nearby battlefields and other cemeteries were brought in to make a total of 715 graves. There are fifty-one Australian graves but twenty-two of these are unidentified by name. The majority of the identified Diggers are from the 31st Battalion, killed on the night of 15 March 1917 while on patrol north-east of Bapaume, after the capture of the town.

Directions
From Bapaume, take the N37 Peronne road. After 3 kilometres at Beaulencourt, turn right towards Ligny-Thilloy. The cemetery is on the right after 2 kilometres. The Irish yews, Lombardy poplars and limes make it an attractive cemetery.

Bonnay Communal Cemetery Extension

This cemetery has the only Great Cross dedicated by an Australian Prime Minister, an event which took place in August 1921. There was a good reason for this official blessing since the cemetery contains seventy-five Diggers out of 106 burials. Most of the Australians are from the 3rd and 4th Divisions and nearly all fell during the fighting at Villers-Bretonneux in April and May 1918. Thirty men, mostly from 12th Brigade, died on 24 April. The cemetery is set in the middle of farm fields, 3 kilometres north of Corbie. The Prime Minister concerned was W.M. Hughes.

Directions
From Albert, take the D929 towards Amiens. After 10 kilometres, turn left to Bonnay at the Bonnay-Franvillers crossroads. The cemetery is 150 metres off this road, on the edge of Bonnay.

Bray Vale British Cemetery, Bray-sur-Somme

The Somme village of Bray was well known to Australians. A cemetery was not started there until August 1918, the month in which the AIF 40th Battalion and parts of other units recaptured the village from the Germans. There were then only twenty-five graves but the cemetery was enlarged after the Armistice so that now there are 279 burials, the majority unknown. Seventeen Diggers, thirteen of whom are identified, lie here. Among the Australians is a well-known and highly regarded leader, Captain Harold Dench, 38th Battalion, killed on 24 August 1918. On that day, just north of Bray, Dench was worried that the British line, to his left, was bent back, thus exposing the flank of his battalion. He went out twice, under fire, to bring the British line forward. While organising this movement on the second occasion he was killed by a sniper (Grave II.C.10). Some Diggers in the cemetery were killed by a British airman who dropped a bomb on their position, believing it to be a German post.

Directions
From Albert, take the D329 to Bray, passing the Albert-Bray airfield. The cemetery is on the left within 2 kilometres of the airfield.

Bernafay Wood British Cemetery

This wood is frequently mentioned as an evil place by Australian soldiers writing home. In the middle of the Australian sector of the Somme battlefield of 1916, Bernafay Wood had been heavily fortified by the Germans, and their machine-gunners, concealed by the shelltorn tree stumps, inflicted many casualties.

The cemetery was established on the very edge of the wood and British soldiers were being buried there by 8 July, only a week after the beginning of the British Somme offensive. The first Australian dead, of the 122 Australians now there, were buried in September 1916 and the last in May 1917 but the greatest number arrived there during the dreadful winter of 1916–17. The physical strain at that time is indicated, for example, by the death from 'heart failure', at the age of 39, of Private William Watson, 6th Field Ambulance (Grave J.58).

Private Ernest Buckland, 3rd Battalion, was 44 when he died of wounds on 26 December. His widow, Elizabeth, of Laurel Street, Cabramatta, NSW, named her home 'Bernafay'. It expresses her anguish (Grave J.53).

A splendid soldier and gentle man, Captain Percy Chapman MC, 55th Battalion, who was killed on 12 March 1917, was a survivor of the Battle of Fromelles. He left a poignant description of an incident during that battle when he and Captain Norman Gibbins saw a German crawling towards them in the dark. Gibbins and Chapman led him but when Chapman let go one of his hands, 'The poor mangled brute got up on his knees and started to pray'. 'O cruel, cruel', said Gibbins, as the two officers helped the German along. Gibbins himself was killed later in the battle (Chapman's grave, J.42).

A very young, very brave, very junior leader in Bernafay Wood cemetery is also worthy of mention. He is Lance Corporal Robert Otter, 1st Battalion. A veteran of the Gallipoli campaign, he was only 19 when he was leading patrols at Flers in October 1916. Two shells exploded in the middle of his last patrol and Otter was too severely wounded to be moved to the rear. He died of his wounds on 1 November (Grave G.28).

Directions
From Longueval, east of Pozières, take the Maricourt road and pass a cemetery on the left. After 0.5 kilometre Bernafay Wood cemetery is on the right.

Contay British Cemetery, Somme

Next to this cemetery, 10 kilometres west of Albert, is a quarry which was the site of Casualty Clearing Stations from August 1916 until August 1918. These CCSs chose the burial ground site, now terraced and one of the most beautiful cemeteries in France. Of the 1133 graves only twenty-nine are of Australians. Most were killed around Pozières on 4 September 1916 but two were accidently killed early in 1917 and three others died of wounds in April 1918. I particularly recommend a visit to Contay because of its attractive and peaceful setting.

Directions
From Albert, take the D91 to Warloy-Baillon and continue 1 kilometre to Contay. At the T-Junction, turn left for 0.5 kilometre on to the Franvillers road.

Côte 80 French National Cemetery, Etinehem

Australian soldiers were sometimes buried in French cemeteries during the war but in nearly all cases their bodies were removed to British cemeteries after the Armistice. The French National Cemetery at Etinehem, a village on the north bank of the Somme

River, is an exception. Twenty-nine Diggers still lie here, with 938 French soldiers, nineteen British and one Canadian. Two French Field Ambulances made this cemetery in June-October 1916, which was originally called Point 80 French Military Cemetery. Côte 80 is the name of the nearby crossroads. The village of Etinehem remained in Allied hands until March 1918, when the Germans captured it. The 50th Battalion retook it on 10 August 1918.

The Diggers of Côte 80 are mostly from the 35th Battalion of the 9th Brigade and the 49th Battalion of the 13th Brigade, together with one gunner, one pioneer, one machine-gunner, an engineer, two infantrymen from the 44th Battalion and one from the 34th. The casualties of the 35th and 44th Battalions occurred on the night of 22 August on the Meaulte-Etinehem road, that is, the road on which the cemetery lies.

Australians should visit the Diggers who lie in this cemetery as it is rarely visited by people other than CWGC officials and my wife and I. The cemetery stands on high ground with wide views in all directions except the north.

Directions
The cemetery is only 8 kilometres south of Albert. From Albert, take the D42 to Meaulte and turn into the main street, signposted Becordel-Becourt. In less than 400 metres turn right to Etinehem, signposted. After the second crossroads the cemetery is on the left. There is nothing at the cemetery entrance to suggest that it contains British and Dominion graves. They are at the far end of the long, narrow cemetery and difficult to see from the entrance. After visiting the cemetery continue into the village of Etinehem, on the banks of the Somme.

Dartmoor Cemetery, Becordel-Becourt

Close to Albert, the twin hamlets of Becordel-Becourt were bases for a Corps Main Dressing Station in September 1916. Many of the 758 soldiers lying in Dartmoor Cemetery had passed through this MDS. Seventy-one Australians are buried here and nearly all died of wounds received in the Flers sector in November 1916. One of them is Captain Frederick Fanning of the 56th Battalion, who had been three times mentioned in despatches (Grave II.E.38). Lieutenant Richard Guthrie was one of ten officers of the 27th Battalion hit at Flers on 6 November 1916 (Grave II.E.45). Captain Samuel Morgan, 26th Battalion, killed on the same day as Guthrie, had been through the worst of the fighting on Pozières Heights in August and was mentioned in despatches (Grave II.E.41).

While Australian visitors are naturally more intent on their own dead, they might linger by the adjoining graves of a British father and son killed on the same day. They are Sergeant George Lee, aged 44, and Corporal Robert Lee, aged 19, both of 156th Brigade, Royal Field Artillery. They were killed by the same shell on 5th September 1916 (Graves I.A35 and 36). There is also a British VC winner in this cemetery, Private J. Miller, killed on 30 July 1916.

Directions
From Albert, take the D938, signposted Becordel-Becourt. After 2 kilometres do not enter the village but 300 metres further take the sliproad to the cemetery, which is then visible on the right.

Daours Communal Cemetery Extension

The village of Daours is on the Amiens-Albert railway line, and for this reason it became a site for casualty clearing stations during preparation for the Somme offensive. No fewer than five CCSs were established here in June 1916 and burials took place within a few days of the battle's opening on 1 July. When the British and Dominion troops advanced, the CCS and hospitals went forward too. When the Germans recovered the initiative and recaptured the ground, between April to August 1918, Daours was almost a frontline cemetery. It contains the graves of 1224 soldiers, 458 of them Australian. Nearly all the Diggers died of wounds between May and September 1918 and every man is identified.

Among the officers is Captain James Cartwright MC, one of the most outstanding officers of the 2nd Division's Engineers. During the Battle of Mont St Quentin, September 1918, the Germans wrecked many Somme River bridges which had to be re-opened if Mont St Quentin and Peronne were to be captured. Cartwright was in charge of the work at the Halle Bridge on 1 September when he was mortally wounded. He died the next day (Grave IV.E.24). Corporal Peter Garoni (served as Maroney), a double MM winner of the 6th Battalion, died of wounds on 24 August. Garoni, a Lewis gunner, showed much bravery at the Battle of Lihons on 10 August before being hit by machine-gun fire (Grave VI.A.36).

Private William Irwin, a soldier of mixed European-Aborigine parentage, distinguished himself in an action at Bouchavesnes during the Battle of Mont St Quentin. Irwin, of the 33rd Battalion, was notably courageous and already had a DCM to his credit. At Bouchavesnes on 31 August 1918, he rushed an enemy machine-gun position and fell wounded; he died the next day (Grave VIII.B.32). Captain Leonard Roberts, a medical officer of the Australian Army Medical Corps, was killed by a shellburst while tending wounded at Peronne on 2 September 1918 (Grave IV.E.30). Company Sergeant-Major Henry Todd DCM, of the 9th Battalion, was wounded on 8 August 1918 during fighting at Villers-Bretonneux and died three days later (Grave IV.A.8). In Daours, there is an echo of the VC exploit of Corporal T.L. Axford of the 16th Battalion on 4 July 1918 at Le Hamel. It is the grave (111.D.37) of Captain Frederick Woods, Axford's company commander. When a German machine-gun killed Woods, his sergeant-major, H. G. Blinman, and a Lewis-gun team, Axford attacked the enemy post and killed ten Germans. CSM Blinman is buried next to his company commander.

Daours Communal Cemetery Extension has two distinctions in AIF history. First, it has a greater representation of units than any other Western Front cemetery. Practically every infantry Battalion is there, as well as Army Service Corps, Machine-Gun Corps, Field Artillery, Field Ambulance, Engineers, Pioneers, Trench-Mortar batteries and Light Horse. Second, the dead Diggers come from a greater spread of battles than in any other cemetery: Morlancourt, Ville-sur-Ancre, Hamel, Villers-Bretonneux, Lihons, Chipilly, Proyart, Etinehem, Mont St Quentin, Hindenburg Outpost Line.

Directions

From Albert, take the D929 Amiens road and turn left at Pont-Noyelles to Daours, signposted. The cemetery is on this road on the edge of town.

Dernancourt Communal Cemetery and Extension

Dernancourt is one of the important place-names in Australian war history because of courage, triumph and loss of life. The XV Corps Main Dressing Station was formed at Dernancourt in August 1916 and in that month the Extension was opened. Several Casualty Clearing Stations were there, including the 3rd Australian CCS in March and April 1917. On 26 March 1918 Dernancourt was evacuated by the British and Dominion forces and the Extension remained in enemy hands until its recapture on 9 August. A large cemetery, it has 2130 burials including 418 Australians, forty-eight of them unknown. The 49th Battalion erected two wooden memorials to its officers and men who fell in the neighbourhood in March-April 1918 but they disappeared many years ago.

Australian casualties at the Battle of Dernancourt, 4 April 1918, were 1233; the 49th Battalion lost fourteen officers and 207 other ranks.

The senior Australian officer buried at Dernancourt is Lieutenant-Colonel Allan Leane, CO of the 28th Battalion and a member of the famous Leane military family. Leane, aged 44, had been a brilliant and considerate leader at Pozières. He was walking across the Somme mud on a duckboard track on 4 January 1917 when a shrapnel shell exploded over his head and mortally wounded him (Communal Cemetery, Grave A.5).

Australian casualties in Dernancourt Cemetery are almost equally divided among killed in action and died of wounds. However, Second Lieutenant Henry Dingle MM of the 1st Battalion, died of accidental injuries on 20 February 1917. It is believed that he was killed in a grenade mishap (Grave V.C.21). Also accidentally killed was Corporal Edgar Dyring, 6th Light Trench-Mortar Battery, who died on 1 June 1917. (Grave VI.F.2)

Sergeant Francis Hocking DCM of the 55th Battalion was about to become an officer when he died of wounds on 4 February 1917 (Grave IV.H.27). Second Lieutenant Harold Cornell of 68th Squadron Australian Flying Corps was killed in air combat and crashed on 11 December 1917. His battered body was taken to Dernancourt (Grave III.J.5). Major Karl Friedrichs, 27th Battalion, prominent in the fighting at Lagnicourt in March 1917, was considered to have led a charmed life until killed on 21 April 1918, on the Villers-Bretonneux front (Grave VIII.H.5).

Driver Matthew Lacey, 5th Division Ammunition Column, died of hemiplegia, 15 April 1917, aged 39 years. He is the only AIF man recorded in a cemetery register as having died on active service of hemiplegia (paralysis). Private Cyril Willmott, of the 60th Battalion, aged only 17, died of pneumonia on 5 February 1917 (Grave V.A.7).

Dernancourt Cemetery has a double MM winner, Corporal Dennis McAuliffe, 7th Light Trench-Mortar Battery, who died of wounds on 12 March 1917 (Grave VI.D.1).

Directions

From Albert, take the D52 to Dernancourt, 2 kilometres. Pass under the railway bridge and the cemetery is in sight on the minor road to Lavieville.

Dive Copse British Cemetery, Sailly-le-Sec

The village of Sailly-le-Sec is on the north bank of the Somme and Dive Copse Cemetery is 1.3 kilometres north-east of Sailly Church. In June 1916, before the Somme offensive, an area north of the cemetery was chosen for a concentration of field ambulances, which became the XIV Corps Main Dressing Station. A small wood close by, under the Bray-Corbie road, was known as Dive Copse after the name of the officer commanding the Main Dressing Station. The cemetery was made by these units. Plots I and II were filled in the first three months' fighting and Plot II contains the graves of seventy-seven men who fell in August 1918 when ground captured by the Germans in the spring was retaken. Later, 115 bodies were brought in from scattered graves.

Of the 579 burials, fifty-three are Australians. All the Diggers are buried in Plot III, on the far left of the entrance. Twelve of them are unidentified and another six are commemorated in special memorials to the right of the War Stone. Their whereabouts in the cemetery are unknown. Many of the Australians, especially those of the 18th Battalion, were killed in the Battle of Ville-sur-Ancre on 19 May 1918.

Directions

From Albert, take the D42 successively to Meaulte, Morlancourt and towards Sailly-Laurette. At the crossroads of the D42 and D1 turn right. After 1.8 kilometres turn left to Sailly-Laurette, signposted, through a small wood. Dive Copse Cemetery is 1 kilometre on the left.

Franvillers Communal Cemetery and Extension

Two Australians are buried in the communal cemetery. The Extension was used from April to August 1918 by units and by field ambulances engaged in the defence of Amiens. It contains the graves of 134 Australians, 113 British soldiers and one New Zealander. Among the Diggers is Regimental Quartermaster Sergeant George Brigatti, 20th Battalion, killed 20 May 1918. RQMS Brigatti had gone forward, on the Ville-sur-Ancre front, to inspect the ration arrangements for his battalion and was killed in a shellburst. Several other 28th Battalion men buried here were killed at Morlancourt on 10 June. Lieutenants Percy Blythe MM and Walter Cobbold were among them (Graves I.E.24 and I.F.3).

One of the oldest Australians killed on active service and probably the oldest to be decorated for gallantry in the field lies in Franvillers Cemetery. He is Lance-Corporal Henry Fleischmann DCM, 14th Field Ambulance. Aged 55, he died of wounds received on 21 June 1918 while bravely treating a wounded man under fire. From Laidley, Queensland, Fleischmann was an outstanding Army Medical Corps soldier who, for his own reasons, had resisted promotion to sergeant.

Directions

From Albert, take the D929 Amiens road. After 10 kilometres turn right to Franvillers. The cemetery is on the near edge of the village.

Frechencourt Communal Cemetery

Located 3 kilometres north of Querrieu on the Amiens-Albert road, the D929, Frechencourt local cemetery has fifty-seven military burials, forty-nine of them Australians. It is virtually a gunners' cemetery, since all but two of these men were from artillery units. Sixteen of the gunners were killed on 5 April 1918 during the Battle of Dernancourt. The Germans began the action with a heavy bombardment of Australian gun positions and the 11th Brigade Australian Field Artillery was badly hit. Six other gunners were killed on 24 April during the second Battle of Villers-Bretonneux. The only two AIF men who are not gunners were from the 4th Division Signal Company Australian Engineers, who were working with the artillerymen. One of them is Lieutenant John Harrison, killed on 5 April and mentioned in despatches.

Gordon Dump Cemetery, Ovillers–La Boiselle

Plot I of Gordon Dump Cemetery on the Pozières battlefield, was made by fighting units after 10 July 1916 and closed in September. It had various names, one being Sausage Valley Cemetery from the name given to the broad, shallow valley that runs from the cemetery south to Becourt. After the Armistice, the cemetery was enlarged by bringing in many graves from battlefields, mostly those of men who had been killed in July 1916. The cemetery now contains the graves of 1641 soldiers of whom ninety-five are Australian. While the larger number of Diggers are from infantry units, there are gunners, pioneers, army service corps personnel and field ambulance men in this cemetery.

Directions
From Albert, take the Bapaume road and at La Boiselle turn right to Contalmaison. Gordon Dump is on the right after 1 kilometre.

Grevillers British Cemetery

The Australian 3rd Casualty Clearing Station, together with two British CCS units, began this cemetery in April 1917, soon after Australian troops had occupied Bapaume, 3 kilometres to the east. The CCS continued to use it until March 1918 when they hurriedly left to escape the Germans, who captured Grevillers on 25 March. After the Armistice 200 graves were brought in from south of Grevillers. Among them were nineteen Diggers of the 1st Battalion who were killed on 5 November 1916 and had been buried in Bayonet Trench Cemetery, Gueudecourt. They are among 413 Australian fighting men, out of a total of 2088 burials at Grevillers. Many of the Diggers died of wounds received either during the First Battle of Bullecourt, 11 April 1917, the Battle of Lagnicourt, 13–15 April 1917, or Second Battle of Bullecourt, 3-16 May 1917. Among the soldiers is Lieutenant Douglas Morrison of the Australian Flying Corps, who died on 29 October 1917 of wounds received in air combat (Grave VII.C.19). Twenty AIF burials are unidentified but came from the Somme battlefields of 1916.

Directions
From Bapaume, take the D929 Albert road. Within 100 metres turn right to Grevillers.

Guards' Cemetery, Lesboeufs

The village of Lesboeufs does not figure directly in AIF history, since few of the 202 Australians buried in the Guards' Cemetery actually died in the immediate vicinity. They were gathered in after the Armistice from a number of smaller cemeteries which no longer exist — Flers Dressing Station Cemetery, Flers Road Cemetery, Ginchy ADS Cemetery, Ginchy Royal Field Artillery Cemetery, Needle Dump Cemetery, Windmill Trench Cemetery and, most significantly, from Switch Trench Cemetery, Flers. No fewer than 110 came from there. Switch Trench was part of the Stormy Trench System, where ferocious fighting took place in February and March 1917. In all, Guards' Cemetery contains 3050 war graves, 1642 of them unknown, and of these nineteen are Australian. All the Diggers buried here died between November 1917 and March 1918.

Directions
From Albert, take the Bapaume road 10 kilometres to Le Sars and turn right into the D11. Follow signs to Gueudecourt and Lesboeufs. Guards' Cemetery is 0.7 kilometre south-west of Lesboeufs on the road to Ginchy.

Heilly Station Cemetery, Mericourt-l'Abbé

Just 7 kilometres south-west of Albert, Mericourt-l'Abbé village was well known to Australians because the AIF maintained a transit camp there. Heilly Station Cemetery is 2 kilometres south-west of the village, and across the Ancre River from the cemetery is Heilly, another village where the AIF had a brigade HQ and where soldiers were billeted. The cemetery was begun in May 1916 and used by three casualty clearing stations until April 1917. From March to May 1918 it was used as a battle cemetery by AIF units and in the early autumn for hospital burials. Now it has 2890 graves, 402 of them Australian. The graves of two Diggers and of some other soldiers which cannot now be exactly located are represented by special memorials. Some graves

Above: Private memorials are rare in Commonwealth War Graves Commission cemeteries. Corporal O'Neill was killed during grenade practice and is buried in Heilly Cemetery near Albert.

Left: Brigadier Glasfurd, buried in Heilly Cemetery, near Albert, was the most senior Australian soldier killed in action in France.

contain two soldiers and where they are of different units both regimental badges are shown, intertwined. British regimental badges, numbering 117, are carved on a cloister wall on the north side.

Unusually, two Diggers have private grave markers in addition to their regulation CWGC stones. The 'ever loving sister' of Sapper John Greenan, Australian Engineers, placed a marble memorial against her brother's grave and noted on it that he came from Roma, Queensland. The other is strikingly unusual, being a solid base supporting a column topped by a cross. The inscription reads: 'In loving memory of 1812 Lance-Corporal J. P. O'Neill, 13th Battalion bombers, accidentally killed 4th January 1917. R.I.P. Erected by his comrades.' The accident referred to occurred during bombing practice. It happened on 6th January not the 4th.

The most senior AIF officer killed in France is buried in Heilly Station Cemetery. He is Brigadier-General Duncan Glasfurd, commander of the 12th Infantry Brigade. Aged 43, Glasfurd was wounded on 12 November 1916 while inspecting positions near Flers into which his brigade was about to move. Relays of stretcher bearers laboured strenuously to carry him through the mud to the nearest dressing station. Their journey took ten hours of herculean endeavour but Glasfurd died that night (Grave V.A.17). Another senior officer in this cemetery is Lieutenant-Colonel Owen Howell-Price, CO of the 3rd Battalion. In CWGC records he is shown of having died of wounds on 4 November 1916. In fact, he died instantly from a bullet through the brain but devoted bearers of his own battalion struggled to get him back to medical help in the hope that he would perhaps be saved (Grave V.A.14).

Nearly all the AIF casualties of the winter of 1916–17 died of wounds. Those of the period March to May 1918 were killed in action. Among these men at Heilly is Captain Lawrence Cadle of the 18th Battalion, killed on 14 May during the Battle of

Morlancourt. A schoolmaster, aged 33, Cadle was regarded as one of the 5th Brigade's most conscientious officers (Grave II.H.6).

It is interesting to note the unusual rank of one Digger at Heilly. He is Honorary Lieutenant and Quartermaster Alick Atkinson, 12th Field Ambulance, who died of wounds on 27 January 1917 (Grave VI.D.27). Lieutenant Reg Forward, scout officer of the 27th Battalion, is also buried at Heilly. First wounded during a raid on the Fromelles front in October 1916, he had recovered only to be wounded again at Flers on 17 November. He died from these wounds on 20 November (Grave VI.A.1).

Pause and reflect at the grave of Private Francis Moad on the urge which brought him to France. A country boy, from Orange, NSW, he had enlisted very early in the war (his number was 153) in the 6th Light Horse Regiment. Impatient to see action and believing that he would not see it as a cavalryman, he transferred to the 3rd Battalion. He died on 8 November 1916 from wounds received at Flers (Grave V.F.14).

Directions

From Albert, take the D929 for Amiens but on the edge of Albert divert left on to the D52 for Dernancourt, Buire-sur-Ancre and Heilly. Continue through Heilly, cross the Ancre and the railway, and the large and beautiful cemetery is ahead of you.

Lavieville (Formerly La Vieville) Communal Cemetery

This burial ground is an example of how even a small cemetery in a hamlet can be rich in Australian sacrifice. Seven soldiers are buried here and six of them are Australian. All were killed 23–25 April 1918. Three were from the 22nd Battalion, one from the 21st Battalion and two were signallers attached to Australian Engineers. Apparently, at the time they were killed there was so much pressure on the larger cemeteries that the unit burial officers looked around for space in the smaller communal cemeteries. Lavieville villagers say that the graves of these Diggers 'never' have any English-speaking visitors.

Directions

From Albert, take the D929 Amiens road for 3.5 kilometres to the Buire-Lavieville crossroads. Lavieville is to the right and the cemetery is 300 metres from the centre on the Henencourt road.

London Cemetery and Extension, High Wood, Longueval

Longueval is one of the many Somme villages, while High Wood, so named by the British army, is actually in the commune of Flers. The cemetery is directly opposite High Wood, scene of some of the most desperate and costly fighting of the Somme battles. Australian divisions were not involved in the High Wood operations. The cemetery is the third largest in the Somme, with 3870 burials of which 3114 are unidentified. Most of the 299 Diggers who lie here were brought in from the surrounding fields. Many of them were killed during the Pozières fighting in July and August 1916. Among them was Major Trevor Cunningham of the 27th Battalion who died in action against German positions near the Windmill on 2 August (Grave 4.D.6). Some of the casualties are from the Flers fighting of winter 1916–17 and one, Lance-Corporal Frederick Tindall of the 50th Battalion, died on Anzac Day 1918. His presence in this cemetery, as a 1918 casualty, is a mystery (Grave 10.E.13).

Directions

From Albert, take the D929 Bapaume road and at Courcelette, the village after Pozières, turn right to Martinpuich. From here, follow Longueval signs. The cemetery is on the right. It stands on high ground with extensive views over the battlefields with at least five parish churches in sight. On either side of the Stone of Remembrance is a yew hedge, pierced by arched openings looking on to the graves.

Mericourt-l'Abbé Communal Cemetery Extension

Mericourt was another Ancre River village in which Australians were billeted in the spring of 1918. For the 24th Battalion it was a particularly happy place following the discovery of a cellar of red wine. It was issued in daily rations to the companies. The cemetery lies under the north side of the hills separating the Ancre from the Somme, in pleasant well-wooded country. The military cemetery extension has 419 graves of which 122 are Australian. Some of them are from the 24th Battalion, the unit which had so enjoyed the red wine. Most of the Diggers died of wounds received in the fighting of June and July 1918 to defend the city of Amiens.

The cemetery is remarkable for its number of young officers who were decorated as NCOs and then commissioned. They are: Lieutenant Bert Davies DCM, aged 24, 30th Battalion, killed 22 June (Grave III.D.3); Lieutenant Thomas Eales DCM, aged 22, 21st Battalion, killed 19 June (Grave III.B.4); Second Lieutenant Stephen Facey DCM and Belgian Croix de Guerre, aged 31, 59th Battalion, killed 4 July (Grave III.E.1); and Lieutenant John Moore MC and Bar, MM, aged 29, 60th Battalion, killed 4 July (Grave III.E.3).

Two other officers held the MC while four NCOs had won the MM. Lieutenant Moore was regarded as the most outstanding junior officer of his battalion and Brigadier-General Elliott of the 15th Brigade had specially selected him for transfer to 15th Trench-Mortar Battery, where morale was low following the issue of inferior ammunition. Moore was killed at his post with the battery during the Battle of Hamel. Another trench-mortar officer killed that day was Lieutenant J. R. Ranson of the 8th Battery (Grave III.E.2).

Directions

From Albert, take the D52 through Dernancourt, Buire and Ribemont. Here, cross the Ancre River to Mericourt, from where Treux is signposted. The cemetery is on the edge of Mericourt, on the right of the Treux road.

Millencourt Communal Cemetery Extension

The communal cemetery was used by units and field ambulances from August 1915 to May 1916, and again in April 1918, for the burial of three Australian and sixty-one British soldiers. The extension was used by fighting units, Field Ambulances and III Corps Main Dressing Station in 1916 and by the AIF 4th Division in March and April 1918. Fifty Diggers are buried here out of 340 British and Dominion burials. The great majority of them are 12th Brigade men killed at Dernancourt on 5 April 1918.

Directions

From Albert, take the D91 for 3 kilometres to Millencourt and pass through the village 200 metres towards Henencourt. The cemetery is on the right.

Pozières British Cemetery and Somme Memorial to the Missing of the Fifth Army in 1918

This large cemetery is enclosed by massive marble walls on which are engraved the name of 14 690 British and Dominion soldiers 'missing' while serving with the British Fifth Army in 1918. In effect, the memorial commemorates the men who fell during the retreat which followed the German breakthrough.

The cemetery contains the graves of 2733 British and Dominion soldiers, including 690 Australians. Of the AIF men 250 are unidentified. There is a special memorial to nineteen other Australians known or believed to be buried in the cemetery but whose exact whereabouts are unknown. Twenty-one of the Diggers had first been buried at Casualty Corner Cemetery, Contalmaison, only 2 kilometres south, but all graves there were gathered in to Pozières British Cemetery.

The only VC winner in the cemetery is Sergeant Claude Castleton, 5th Australian Machine-Gun Company. Aged 23, he was killed on 29 July 1916. He was awarded the VC for making two trips into No Man's Land under intense fire, to rescue wounded men. He was bringing in a third casualty when he was killed (Grave IV.L.43).

Directions

From Albert, take the D929 Bapaume road for 3.5 kilometres. The cemetery is unmistakeable by the side of the road, at a place that in 1916 was called Tramway Crossing or Red Cross Corner.

Puchevillers British Cemetery

North-east of Amiens, Puchevillers was close to a station on the railway line between Albert and Doullens. Therefore, in preparations for the Battle of the Somme in July 1916, the village became a suitable place for Casualty Clearing Stations to base themselves. Before the end of March 1917 various CCSs filled Plots I to VI. Plot VII contains many men who fell in the German advance in 1918. Of the 1763 British and Dominion graves 416 are Australian and virtually all died of wounds received in the holocaust of Pozières, July-September 1916. A few others died of disease in 1917.

The only headstone of its type on the Western Front, the grave of Lieut Bert Crowle, 10th Battalion. Records do not show how Bert's widow and brother managed to have this non-standard stone erected. The Commonwealth War Graves Commission steadfastly refuses all requests for private grave markers.

Among the Puchevillers Diggers is Second Lieutenant E. L. A. Butler of the 12th Battalion, a popular Tasmanian cricketer, who was mortally wounded by German shellfire at Mouquet Farm on 23 August (Grave III.A.10). The battalion medical officer, Captain W. W. S. Johnson, went through the barrage to attend to Butler and many others. Buried next to Butler is Second Lieutenant Herbert Crowle of the 10th Battalion, who died of wounds two days later. Crowle, of 'Gunyah', Glen Osmond, S.A., wrote what is, for me, the most eloquent and moving 'last letter' of the war. Bert Crowle's letter to his wife, Beatrice, clearly shows the dreadful conditions of Pozières battlefield:

Dearest Beat and Bill,

Just a line you must be prepared for the worst to happen any day. It is no use trying to hide things. I am in terrible agony. Had I been brought in at once I had a hope. But now gas gangrene has set in and it is so bad that the doctor could not save it [his leg] by taking it off as it had gone too far and the only hope is that the salts they have put on may drain the gangrene out otherwise there is no hope. The pain is much worse today so the doctor gave me some morphia, which has eased me a little but still is awful. Tomorrow I shall know the worst as the dressing was to be left on for 3 days and tomorrow is the third day it smells rotten. I was hit running out to see the other officer who was with me but badly wounded. I ran too far as I was in a hurry and he had passed the word down to return, it kept coming down and there was nothing to do but go up and see what he meant, I got two machine-gun bullets in the thigh another glanced off by my water bottle and another by the periscope I had in my pocket, you will see that they will send my things home. It was during the operations around Mouquet Farm, about 20 days I was in the thick of the attack on Pozières as I had just about done my duty. Even if I get over it I will never go back to the war as they have taken pounds of flesh out of my buttock, my word they look after us well here. I am in the officers ward and can get anything I want to eat or drink but I just drink all day changing the drinks as I take a fancy. The Stretcher Bearers could not get the wounded out any way than over the top and across the open. The had to carry me four miles with a man waving a red cross flag in front and the Germans did not open fire on us. Well dearest I have had a rest, the pain is getting worse and worse. I am very sorry dear, but still you will be well provided for I am easy on that score. So cheer up dear I could write on a lot but I am nearly unconscious. Give my love to dear Bill and yourself, do take care of yourself and him.

Your loving husband
Bert.

Herbert Crowle died the day after he wrote the letter.

In the same row of graves as Butler and Crowle lies Captain Cecil Maitland Foss MC, 28th Battalion, one of the most outstanding officers of the AIF. On 5 June 1916 Foss, a West Australian farmer, led the first trench raid on the Western Front. Foss rehearsed the raid behind his own lines and in a finely timed operation on the south-eastern edge of Armentières, he and his men took some prisoners, killed several Germans and withdrew without loss. Wounded on Pozières Heights on 5 August, Foss died of wounds in a Puchevillers CCS on 11 August (Grave III.A.6).

Directions
From Amiens, take the N25 Doullens road. After 16 kilometres turn right, at Talmas, to Puchevillers, which is signposted. In the small village the cemetery is signposted left.

Querrieu British Cemetery

For much of 1918 Querrieu was virtually an Australian village as the AIF billeted various brigades there. The AIF 3rd Division opened the cemetery at the end of March 1918 and here 102 British and eighty-four Australian solders are buried. All but ten of the Diggers died of wounds, a number of them being hit in April 1918 during the first Battle of Villers-Bretonneux. The most decorated member of any AIF Field Ambulance unit, Sergeant Alexander Wilson DCM, MM and Bar, is buried at Querrieu. From the 10th Field Ambulance, Wilson was killed in action on 20 May 1918 during the Battle of Morlancourt. He was noted for the courageous way in which he frequently risked his life to reach wounded men and evacuate them to safety (Grave A.22). Private Maurice Whelan (Grave C.8) of the 42nd Battalion was drowned in the River Hullue at Querrieu on 16 May 1918.

One young Digger buried at Querrieu has a private grave marker, a large marble base surmounted by a white column, topped by a cross. His inscription reads: 'Well done. Pray for Gunner J. P. Farrell, 9th Battery F. A. AIF. Killed in action 20th May 1918. Aged 20 years. R.I.P.' The marker is identical to that of Lance-Corporal O'Neill's grave, described in the section on Heilly Station Cemetery.

Directions
From Albert, take the Amiens road to Querrieu. Here, turn left on to the Bussy-les-Daours road and the cemetery is on the left within 400 metres. It is one of the many smaller cemeteries which are now part of their local communities, with houses on either side.

The privately erected grave marker of Driver J. P. Farrell in Querrieu Cemetery, between Albert and Amiens. He also has a regulation military headstone.

Ribemont Communal Cemetery Extension

This sector of the Albert front was taken over from the French by the British in 1915 but burials did not begin until the end of March 1918. From then until July, fourteen Australians were buried in the communal cemetery. The extension was used from May to August 1918, when sixty-eight burials were made by units engaged in the defence of Amiens. After the Armistice it was greatly enlarged by the concentration of graves from smaller cemeteries and the battlefields. It now contains the graves of 178 Australians out of 502 British and Dominion soldiers. Seventy-nine of the Australians had originally been buried in Heilly British Cemetery within the grounds of Heilly Château, which was an AIF HQ.

While most of the Australians were killed in action, a few died of wounds. The deaths occurred from March 1918, the Battle of Dernancourt, through to engagements during 'peaceful penetration' of July. Captain Thomas Elliot, 48th Battalion, was killed on 28 March at Dernancourt by a sniper while raising his head to observe (Grave III.J.7). Lieutenant John Whittle, of the same Battalion, was badly hit early in the battle but fought on only to be hit again and killed later in the day (Grave III.J.6). Of the fourteen Diggers in the civil cemetery, five are from the 58th Battalion.

Directions
From Albert, take the D52 for 3 kilometres through Dernancourt and Buire to Ribemont. The cemetery is at the crossroads in Ribemont.

Serre Road No. 1 Cemetery

Serre Road No. 1 Cemetery has 149 Australian burials out of 2424 burials. More than three-quarters of the total are unidentified. Among the Diggers of Serre Road is Captain Francis Barton, one of the two 13th Battalion captains who led the assault on Mouquet Farm on 11 August 1916. He was officially 'missing' until the end of the war, when his remains were found at the farm (Grave VII.D.21). Captain James McNamara, also buried here, was one of nine 52nd Battalion officers killed in yet another attack on Mouquet Farm on 3 September 1916 (Grave VIII.D.20). All the Australians in this cemetery are First Battle of the Somme casualties except one. The exception is Driver Lionel Collings of 26 Battalion, who died of wounds on 1 May 1918. Hit during fighting further north, he was buried here by the

The markers of young Diggers known to be buried in Ribemont Cemetery, near Albert. Their original graves were destroyed by enemy shelling.

CCS in which he died and which was still using Serre Road (Grave IV.H.9).

Directions
From Albert, take the D50 road north to Authuille and continue to Hamel, near Beaumont-Hamel. From here, Serre is signposted. The cemetery is 1.2 kilometres west of the village.

Serre Road Cemetery No. 2

One of the largest cemeteries in France, Serre Road No. 2 has 7133 graves. Of these 699 are Australian but 370 are not identified. All but a few of the Diggers buried in Serre Road are Pozières casualties killed between 23 July and 4 September 1916, and nearly all were interred directly here, rather than having been brought in after the war. In 1916 'Serre Road' was the road leading out of Mailly-Maillet and reaching No Man's Land about 2 kilometres south-west of Serre, which was held by the Germans. One of the few Diggers not killed in the summer of 1916 is Private Frederick Pearson MM of the 49th Battalion, killed on 5 April 1918 during the Battle of Dernancourt (Grave XL.M.12).

Directions
As for Serre Road No. 1 but closer to Serre village.

Thiepval Anglo-French Cemetery, Authuille

Placed at the foot of the Somme memorial and within the park which surrounds it, this cemetery symbolises the joint effort of the British and French Armies, not only in the battles of the Somme but throughout the war. The Somme Memorial, which is more frequently called the Thiepval Memorial, stands in 20 hectares of lawns, gardens and woodland. It commemorates the Allied offensive on the Somme which began on 1 July 1916. On its many facets the memorial carries the names of 73 412 officers and men who fell in the original British Third Army area, from 1915 to March 1918, and whose graves are not known. It was erected by the Imperial (later Commonwealth) War Graves Commission on behalf of the people of the Empire. The unveiling by the Prince of Wales took place on 1 August 1932. The purpose of the memorial is illustrated by the words carved on tablets above its main eastern and western arches: 'Aux Armées Française et Britannique l'Empire Britannique Reconnaissant'.

To stress the French-British union, in the winter of 1931–2 a small mixed cemetery was created. The 600 dead who lie in it represent equally the one million British and Dominion dead and the even greater loss of France and its colonies. Ten Australians are buried here, with four Canadians and one New Zealander. All the British and Dominion bodies were found in December 1931 and January–March 1932. The majority came from the battlefields of July–November 1916 and only sixty-one are identified. Among them are four named AIF men: Private Robert Barbour, 23rd Battalion, killed 10 January 1917, from Ascot Vale, Victoria; Private Matthew Good, 4th Battalion, killed 25 July 1916, from Marrickville, NSW; Private Lewis Grant, 26th Battalion, killed 29 July 1916, from Sydney; Private Edwin Titton, 28th Battalion, killed 29 July 1916, born in Bristol, England.

The cemetery's Cross of Sacrifice carries an inscription in English and French: 'That the world may remember the common sacrifice of two and a half million dead here have been laid side by side soldiers of France and of the British Empire in eternal comradeship'.

Directions
From Albert, take the D929 road and turn left in Pozières, just after the AIF 1st Division memorial. The Somme (Thiepval) Memorial is well signposted and towers above the countryside.

Thistle Dump Cemetery, High Wood, Longueval

This burial ground was begun in August 1916 and was used as a frontline cemetery until February 1917. After the Armistice fifty-six graves were brought in from the battlefields. Of the 192 war graves thirty-six are Australians, most of them casualties from the Battle of Flers in November 1916. Among them is Major Ivan Sherbon MC, 19th Battalion. Sherbon won his MC at Pozières and was killed at Flers at 6.20 a.m. on 14 November while placing his troops in position during the Battle of Flers. On that day eleven officers and 374 other ranks were hit.

Directions
Thistle Dump Cemetery stands in a field about 800 metres south of the southern apex of High Wood.

From Albert, follow the same directions as for Bazentin-le-Petit Military Cemetery, but instead of turning off at Bazentin continue for 0.5 kilometre.

Warlencourt British Cemetery

This large Somme cemetery contains 4588 graves, of which 1823 are of unknown soldiers. Australia is all too well represented, with 461 burials of whom 138 are unidentified. The villages of Warlencourt and Eaucourt, with the Butte de Warlencourt between them, were the scene of very fierce fighting in 1916. The Butte, a Roman mound of excavated chalk once covered with pines, was never captured. The Germans simply left it when they withdrew towards the Hindenburg Line at the end of February 1917.

Among the Diggers is Second Lieutenant William Healy MC, 25th Battalion, who had distinguished himself at Pozières. Near the Windmill, on 4–5 August, command of the entire battalion fell to Healy when he found himself the only officer still standing. He won the MC for his outstanding leadership. With several other 25th Battalion officers, Healy was killed at Flers on 14 November (Grave VI.A.25). The senior officer at Warlencourt is Major Julius Kayser, who had been intelligence officer of the 12th Battalion before becoming its second-in-command. He was killed on 16 February 1917. Without an identifiable grave, Kayser is commemorated on one of Warlencourt's special memorials. Among the rank and file is Corporal Leslie Sneyd DCM, 27th Battalion, yet another Flers casualty 5 November 1916 (Grave II.E.32).

Directions

The cemetery is on the south side of the D939 Albert-Bapaume road, on the Bapaume side of the Butte de Warlencourt, and stands out for several kilometres in any direction.

Warloy-Baillon Communal Cemetery Extension

Only 7 kilometres from Albert, Warloy-Baillon was yet another village which saw the arrival of field ambulance units in June 1916, as they made ready to receive casualties from the great British attack of 1 July. The fighting from that time until November 1916 accounts for the greater number of burials but some resulted from the German attack in the spring of 1918, which pushed the British and Dominion troops back to their former front line. The 1337 British and Dominion burials are the largest number to be buried in a communal cemetery extension. They include 327 Australians, nearly all of whom died of wounds received at Pozières. The relatively few March or April 1918 burials are also Diggers who died of wounds.

Among the Pozières casualties is Lieutenant Henry Dobbie of the 14th Battalion. When Albert Jacka VC of the same battalion carried out his outstanding courageous and daring action at Pozières on 7 August it was Dobbie and his platoon who supported him and routed the Germans. Dobbie was killed later that day (Grave III.D.9). Six graves away from Dobbie's is that of Lieutenant Victor Dridan, 50th Battalion, mortally wounded at Mouquet Farm on 14 August (Grave III.D.3).

Yet another famous 14th Battalion officer, Captain Stewart Hansen MC, is buried in Warloy-Baillon Cemetery. While making plans for the raid on Stormy Trench, 4 February 1917, the CO of the 13th Battalion, Lieutenant-Colonel J. M. Durrant, was told that he could select any company of the 14th Battalion to support him. He at once chose Hansen and his company. One of the AIF's great junior leaders, Hansen was mortally wounded in the fight and died three days later.

A large number of casualties are from the First Battle of Villers-Bretonneux on 4 April 1918. Among the 1918 casualties is Major Terence Garling, OC of the 37th Battery Field Artillery, killed during the Battle of Morlancourt on 5 April 1918. On that day fourteen officers and 139 other ranks of the five artillery brigades supporting the 4th Division were killed by counter-battery fire.

Directions

From Albert, take the D91 west to, successively, Millencourt, Henencourt and Warloy-Baillon. On the edge of Warloy-Baillon, at the T-junction with the D179, turn right for 250 metres. At the next crossroads turn right towards Arras. The cemetery is on the left within 100 metres.

Chapter 7

East of Bapaume; Hindenburg Line Outpost Villages and Bullecourt

After the AIF's occupation of Bapaume in March 1917 the Australians' operations moved east and north-east of that strategic centre. They were following the Germans who had withdrawn from their 'RII Line' and 'RIII Line', which passed north-south close to Bapaume. In no sense had the Germans suffered a defeat. The High Command was simply making some strategic adjustments to position its armies along the Hindenburg Line, which had long before been prepared as the main bastion, both for defensive and offensive action. It was a massively strong line, running the length of the Western Front, consisting of blockhouses, trenches and barbed wire. In addition, it had well-made underground shelters where the garrison was comfortable in all weathers and where they were protected from shellfire. The German leaders believed that the Hindenburg Line was virtually impregnable, but as further protection they fortified and garrisoned many French settlements in front of the Line. They became known to the British and Dominion armies as 'the Outpost Villages'.

It is a military maxim that pursuit of a withdrawing enemy must be immediate. 1 Anzac Corps' part in the pursuit was to use Bapaume as its base and fan out eastwards to capture the villages. During March and April 1917 this campaign brought into Australian history a score of place-names which are mentioned in this section.

There then followed the two great battles of Bullecourt, another place of prodigious Australian valour, effort and sacrifice. The first battle took place on 10–11 April and the second 3–17 May. Second Bullecourt was one of the most brilliant of AIF achievements, especially as it was fought against the most stubborn opposition the Australians faced on the Western Front.

In mid-March, however, Bullecourt was only indirectly in the AIF's sights as it was not really an Outpost Village but effectively part of the Hindenburg Line itself. Brigadier-General John Gellibrand was given command of the 2nd Division's advance guard, on the left of the Australian drive. On the right was Brigadier-General H. E. Elliott, commanding the 5th Division's advance guard. On Elliott's front lay Fremicourt, Beugny, Lebucquière, Velu, Beaumetz, Hermies, Doignies, Morchies, Louverval, Demicourt and Boursies. Ahead of Gellibrand's troops lay Sapignies, Favreuil, Vaulx-Vraucourt, Vraucourt, Lagnicourt, Noreuil and Longatte. Immediately behind the Hindenburg Line were yet more fortified villages, notably Queant, Pronville, Flesquières and Havrincourt.

The operations of March–May 1917 before the Hindenburg Line was reached (and excluding Bullecourt), were unlike anything the Australians had experienced. Since the area had not been the scene of battles of attrition for months on end, as in Flanders and the Somme, the fields were not quagmires and morasses. They were not even scarred by lines of trenches, while barbed wire was in place only around the German-held villages. In the actions to capture the Outpost Villages the rolling ground, with its buildings, sunken roads, walls, trees and hedges, provided an opportunity for what the Diggers called 'real soldiering'. With just a reasonable amount of luck, it was possible for skilled soldiers to survive.

The Australian advance was spirited and one after another the German positions there were captured, though often only after hard fighting; there were many Australian casualties and examples of outstanding leadership and courage.

The Diggers stayed only briefly in the Outpost Villages, just long enough to bury their dead, treat their wounded, snatch some sleep and quickly reorganise before marching on. They were not long enough in any one village to develop a sense of identity with it, as they did in Albert and the villages behind it, and in Flanders. However, the Outpost Villages are still important for modern visitors, if only because they were once the scene of dramatic events involving young Australians.

For instance, at Beaumetz on 23 March, Lieutenant H. A. Harrison of the 29th Battalion, led about ten NSW Light Horsemen, who had only just joined his battalion, in a charge against Germans who were holding a knoll west of the town. After a short bayonet fight, the German survivors fled towards their support troops. In capturing Beaumetz, Brigadier Elliott had twelve men killed, thirty-eight wounded and two captured. For this cost, 50 Germans lay dead in the streets of Beaumetz and eleven others had been take prisoner.

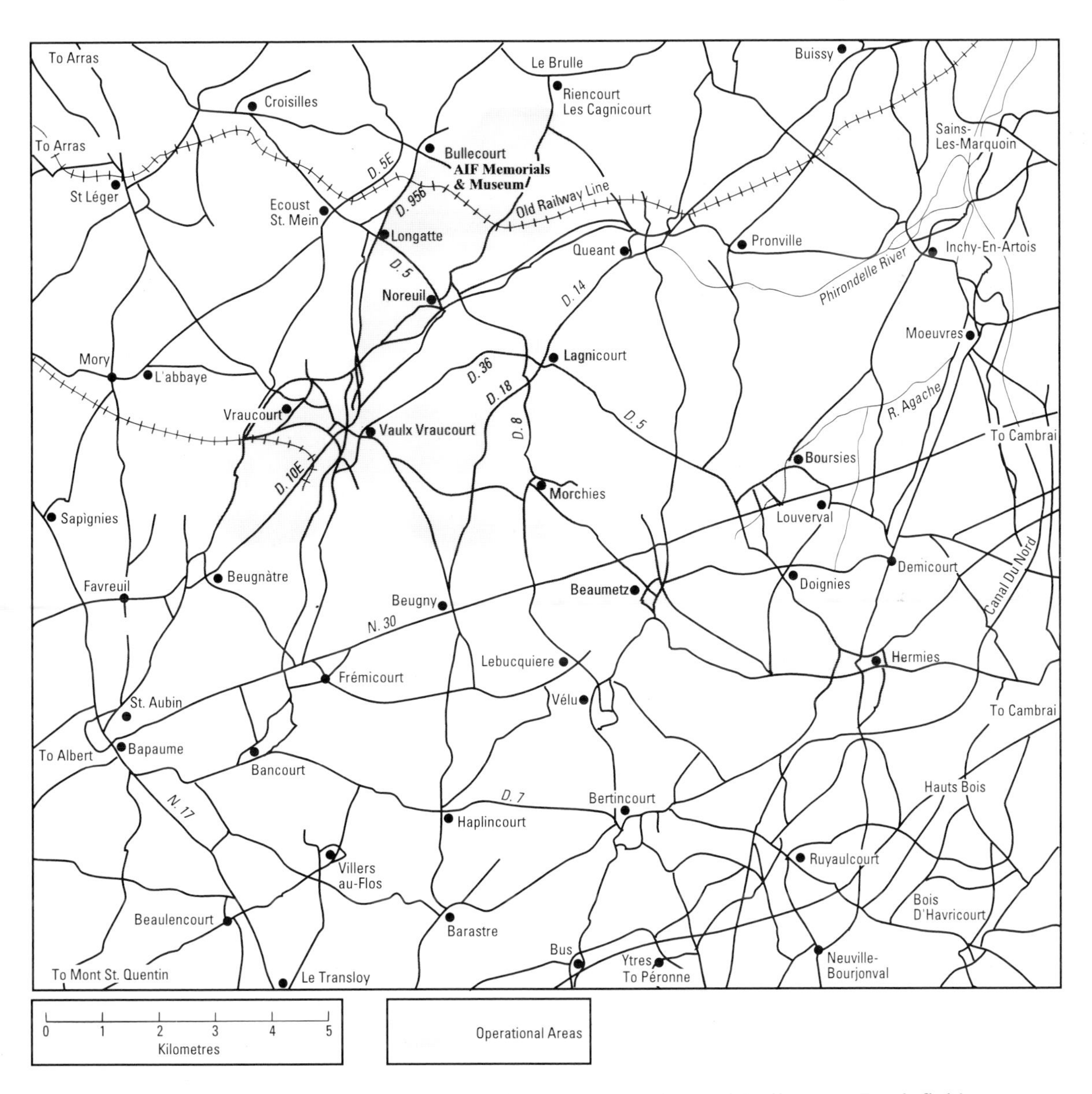

Map 8. East of Bapaume: Hindenburg Outpost Line and Bullecourt: Battlefields

That afternoon the 59th Battalion attacked from Velu to capture a fortified crater at a railway crossing. The Germans fled, only to be caught in the open by the 8th Battery Australian Field Artillery and destroyed. In this and scores of minor operations the Australians pushed the Germans from their strongholds, though the Germans never gave up without a fight and nearly always counter-attacked.

On 26 March the 7th Brigade set out to capture the village of Lagnicourt. Some units encircled the place while the 26th Battalion's task was to enter Lagnicourt, which was held by about 300 enemy. The principal role was given to Captain Percy Cherry and his company, which met sharp resistance as it moved forward. For the attack, Cherry took one part of the company and gave command of the other part to Lieutenant W. F. J. Hamilton, who was wounded soon after the attack began. Cherry captured a fortified farm on the outskirts and went on into the main street where, after a fight in a stable yard, the enemy surrendered. Cherry now found that the centre of the village was a shell crater, strongly defended. Without mortars and impatient when they did not arrive, Cherry rushed the position. Here he found Lieutenant H.H. Bieske, who had taken over from Hamilton and was himself wounded. Having taken the crater, Cherry pushed on through Lagnicourt and after stiff fighting joined up with other Australians already digging in on the east side of the village.

The Germans counter-attacked all day. Restlessly moving from one threatened spot to another, Cherry noticed that German infantry were firing yellow flares to notify their gunners of their positions. He obtained some of these flares, fired them from his own position and was pleased to see that the German gunners moved away from it. However, late that afternoon a single shell killed Cherry and other officers in a sunken road east of the village, as they were planning their next moves. Cherry, who already held the MC, was awarded the VC. His citation mentioned his 'conspicuous bravery, determination and leadership and his wonderful example'. He was one of 377 Australians hit at Lagnicourt on March 26, in what turned out to be only the first of two battles at that place. (*See* **Lagnicourt**.)

On 2 April, a week after the First Battle of Lagnicourt, the 50th and 51st Battalions were given the task of capturing another strongly held village, Noreuil, only a few kilometres north of Lagnicourt. In two waves, the Diggers made for the village under cover of a thin barrage. On the right, along the Lagnicourt-Noreuil road, forty-five enemy behind a massive barricade and armed with machine-guns impeded the advance. Even Stokes mortar bombs could not destroy the post. Rather than leave it intact at the rear of the advance the sergeant in command at that point of the attack ordered a small bombing party of five men to attack the post. Private Jorgen Jensen was one of the party. Alone, and with a bomb in either hand, he rushed the post and threw in a bomb. Then he took a bomb from his pocket and drew the safety pin with his teeth. Menacing the Germans with his two bombs, Jensen told them that they were surrounded and induced them to surrender. Jensen sent one of his prisoners to order another enemy post to surrender, which they did. When these surrendering Germans were fired upon by Australians who did not understand the situation, Jensen jumped on to the barricade, where he risked being shot, and waved his steel helmet to reassure his mates. Finally he sent all of his sixty prisoners back to the Australian lines. Jensen was later awarded the VC for his 'extraordinary bravery and determination'.

The 50th Battalion captured Noreuil after such a severe fight that the unit lost five officers and ninety-four other ranks killed. Total casualties that day were 360.

Meanwhile, on the southern flank of the 1 Anzac Corps front, by early April only three villages in front of the Hindenburg Line remained to be captured: Boursies, Demicourt, and Hermies. The 12th Battalion was given the task of capturing Boursies. At 4 a.m. on 7 April Captain James Newland, commanding the assault company, personally led a bombing attack on an old mill to dislodge the Germans established there. Despite casualties among his own men, Newland occupied the village and next night repelled a strong counter-attack. Throughout the fight, Newland was ably helped by Sergeant John Whittle, in charge of the left platoon. After the bombing capture of the old mill, Whittle commanded a post established beyond it. That night the Germans launched a bomb attack of their own against the Australians and drove in some of their posts. Whittle led a charge against the Germans which stabilised the situation until Newland arrived.

Active at every part of the line and taking many risks, Newland held Boursies until another battalion relieved the 12th. However, on 14 April the 12th Battalion was brought back into the fighting and thrown into breaches made that night by the Germans between Lagnicourt and Noreuil. Again the major responsibility fell to Captain Newland, who found himself being attacked on three sides by a force which outnumbered his by ten to one. Falling back to a sunken road, Newland inspired and directed his men as they fought back on both sides of the road. Sergeant Whittle attacked and captured a machine-gun with which the Germans were about to enfilade the sunken road defenders. The gun could have wiped out Newland's force to the last man. For his various acts of gallantry and leadership, Newland was awarded the VC, as was Whittle, though more for his exploit at Boursies than at Lagnicourt.

The capture of Hermies on 9 April fell to the 2nd and 3rd Battalions. The 2nd was held up by an enemy strongpoint which was inflicting many casualties. Private Bede (actually Thomas) Kenny, braving a hail of machine-gun fire, charged the post by himself, killing a German soldier who tried to stop him. He bombed the strongpoint, killing an officer, wounding the entire gun crew and seizing the gun. The 2nd Battalion's advance continued and Hermies fell in a fight lasting only 65 minutes. Demicourt now lay open to attack and it fell to the 1st Battalion that day. Kenny's exploit won him the VC.

On 10 April the 11th Battalion was given one of the most daunting tasks in the advance to the Hindenburg Line when ordered to establish posts along an extraordinarily long front of 4.5 kilometres in front of the captured village of Louverval. The various commanders were told to hold at all costs. In charge of the strategic centre post on A Company's front was Lieutenant Charles Pope. At 4 a.m. on the morning of 15 April the Germans counter-attacked, first with an intense artillery barrage and then with infantry in overwhelming numbers. Many Germans passed between Pope's post and the post next to him and got behind him. His hard-pressed men were running short of ammunition and Pope sent Private A. G. C. Gledhill for more supplies. Gledhill survived the hazardous journey to HQ but the fifteen men with ammunition sent to help Pope could not get through. Pope organised a charge of all his survivors, to be made as the last rounds were fired. Bayonets fixed, the Diggers charged into the mass of Germans who had surrounded them — and all fell. Round their bodies were later found eighty dead Germans. The 12th Battalion suffered 245 casualties in the Louverval battle, 180 of them posted missing.

The Australians had now captured and were firmly holding all the Hindenburg Outpost Villages on their front.

Carved into the stone of the Louverval Memorial to the Missing, stretcher-bearers evacuate a wounded soldier from a trench. The memorial is east of Bapaume on the Australian front of 1917.

Directions

The wartime Outpost Villages are easily found from Bapaume. For those in the northern sector of the 1 Anzac Corps front, take the DIOE for Vaulx-Vraucourt and from there, the D36 to Lagnicourt-Marcel. Noreuil is less than 2 kilometres north from Lagnicourt by the D5. Similarly, Morchies is the same distance south of Lagnicourt on the D18. The villages of Fremicourt, Beaugny, Lebucquière, Doignies, Louverval, Boursies, Demicourt and Hermies are all on or just off the N30 Bapaume-Cambrai road. All can be visited in a round trip of 50 kilometres.

Specific points of interest

Captain Cherry's exploit

The stable yard in which Cherry fought is opposite the present town hall of Lagnicourt. The fortified crater which he captured was just behind the stable yard. He and his company passed right through the centre of the village from west to east.

Private Jensen's exploit
About 200 metres out of Noreuil on the road to Lagnicourt there is a rise in the road, which is sunken. The German barricade, protected by its Maxim machine-gun, was across the road at this point. Jensen approached it by running along the bank of the road from Lagnicourt.

Captain Newland and Sergeant Whittle
The exploits of these VC winners are closely connected. The windmill they captured at Boursies no longer exists but it stood 100 metres along the first street on the left of the main road, as Boursies is reached from Bapaume. In Lagnicourt, the length of road in which Newland and Whittle carried out their amazing back-to-back fight against overwhelming odds turns towards Bapaume just out of Lagnicourt, on the D36.

Private Kenny's exploit
This site can only be found by seeking directions in Hermies (though the villagers know nothing of the AIF or Bede Kenny). Ask for the Vallée Cochon and follow the unformed road for 300 metres. On the D19 to your left is a large farm, la Raperie Ferme. Just below this, on the floor of the shallow valley, is the vestige of a former chalk pit. The German machine-gun which Kenny captured was in this pit. On the road Kenny's mate, Sergeant A. R. McPhee, had a position from where he gave Kenny covering fire.

Australian Guns at Lagnicourt
In mid-April 1917 Field Artillery batteries were in position in Lagnicourt. One was just out of the village on the Vaulx-Vraucourt road. Another three guns were situated at the first crossroads on this road. Two others were on the very edge of the village on the road south to Beugny. Other guns were in pits at Noreuil, near where the Australian cemetery is now located. The Germans captured twenty-one guns of the 2nd AFA Brigade and held them for two hours but were so busy looting Australian dugouts for food and souvenirs that they failed to destroy the guns, which the Australians then recaptured. In one day, 15 April, the field artillery fired 21 315 shrapnel shells and 13 264 high-explosive shells. Heavy artillery fired 8283 shells. Shell cases and unexploded shells are still found around Lagnicourt. Twelve Australian gunners killed on 15 April are buried in the same row in H.A.C. Cemetery at Ecoust — St Mien, which adjoins Bullecourt.

Lieutenant Pope's grave
Charles Pope VC is buried in Moeuvres Communal Cemetery Extension, not far from Queant Road Cemetery.

Bullecourt

On 9 April 1917 a British officer of tanks told General Sir Hubert Gough's 5th Army HQ that his twelve machines could break down the enemy wire on the Bullecourt front and open the way for infantry. General Birdwood, GOC 1 Anzac Corps and his Chief-of-Staff, Brigadier- General Brudenell White, disliked the idea of using the unproven tanks but Gough swept aside their objections. He ordered Major-General W. Holmes, GOC 4th Division, to attack German positions in the Hindenburg Line at Bullecourt on 10 April. Holmes too, considered the plan foolhardy but ordered the 4th Brigade (Brigadier-General C. H. Brand) and 12th Brigade (Brigadier-General J. C. Robertson) to prepare for immediate attack. Just before midnight Birdwood heard from a patrol that the preliminary bombardment had not damaged the German wire and tried desperately to get Gough to cancel the attack. He was overruled.

Lying out in fresh snow on the night of 10 April, the Australians waited for the dawn and for the roar of the tanks. Held up by bad weather, the tanks did not arrive and the troops were hurried back into cover before the Germans saw them. General Haig now ordered that the attack would be made at dawn on 11 April. This time three tanks reached the battlefield, only to stick fast in the mud. Against all the odds, some Australians fought their way through to occupy a section of the Hindenburg Line. Unsupported by the British artillery and the failed tanks, the Diggers sent up flare after flare asking for shells to be dropped on to the village of Riencourt, 1.5 kilometres from Bullecourt, from where they were coming under machine-gun and rifle fire. The Australian battalions now found themselves cut off from their rear by enemy shells, machine-guns and counter-attacking infantry. There was no option but to retire through the storm of steel. The order to retreat did not reach all the scattered posts and some isolated NCOs wondered if it was a genuine command or one inspired by anxiety and spread by rumour. Corporal J. C. Wheeler, in charge of a small 15th Battalion post, ordered his men to 'Fight it out like Australians'. The battle lasted ten hours and in that time the 4th Brigade, which had sent 3000 officers and men into battle, suffered 2339 casualties. The 12th Brigade had 2000 men actually engaged and suffered 950 casualties. The British battle scheme employed at Bullecourt on 11 April was later used by British instructors as an example of how *not* to plan an attack. In fact, the Australian infantry had performed magnificently in an attack that should never have been made, and despite the total failure of the British guns and tanks.

The Second Battle of Bullecourt, 3–17 May, was much better prepared and was part of a major British assault on a 25-kilometre front. The role of the 2nd Division (Major-General N. M. Smyth) was to attack German positions, known as OG1 and OG2 lines, which ran through Bullecourt and capture some villages well beyond them. Refusing the dubious help of tanks, the Australians went into action with ninety-six Vickers machine-guns, more than had ever been used before for a divisional attack.

Smyth, his brigadiers, R. Smith, 5th Brigade, John Gellibrand, 6th Brigade and E. A. Wisdom, 7th Brigade, and their staffs prepared for every possible contingency, with pioneers, gunners, machine-gunners and engineers all playing a part in a systematic plan of attack. Near the village of Favreuil, 16 kilometres south-west, the staff prepared a piece of land similar to that at Bullecourt, with posts, tapes and wire marking the positions of all with known enemy emplacements, and roads and villages were indicated. Here the assaulting brigades practised their advance and finally held two complete rehearsals. The Diggers knew they would be fighting Wurttembergers, whom they knew as tough opponents, and they were ready to go on practising for the battle.

The 6th Brigade's attack at 3.45 a.m. on 3 May was so vigorous and well led that within an hour the battalions held half their objective in the Hindenburg Line. However, the 5th Brigade's assault broke up in confusion. A few officers and NCOs reorganised the men at some points and attacked again and again. In two assaults, the 18th Battalion lost twelve of its twenty-two officers and sixty-one of its eighty-four NCOs.

That afternoon, the 28th Battalion, a fresh unit of the 7th Brigade, came up on the right where the 5th Brigade should have been. They were led by Lieutenant-Colonel G. A. Read, who twenty-two months earlier had been a private soldier. At nightfall on 3 May, the Australians held what was described as a 'mushroom on a stalk', the stalk being the only avenue for communication and supply and for evacuation of wounded. The first companies of the relieving 1st Division arrived on 4 May. Among them was Corporal George Howell, 1st Battalion, who commanded a post on his battalion's right flank. At 6 a.m. on 6 May Howell sent an urgent message to HQ saying that the battalion on his right was withdrawing. This exposed the 1st's flank to attack and the senior officer, a captain, mustered all batmen, signallers and others to face the oncoming enemy. In the subsequent fight, Howell scrambled out of his trench on to the open parapet and ran along it, throwing bombs on to the Germans in their part of the trench. As they retreated in panic, Howell followed and when he ran out of bombs he jabbed down at the enemy with his bayonet. Shot in several places, he fell into OG1 but his mates were inspired by his example and in fierce close-quarter fighting they retook all the ground lost. Howell survived and was awarded the VC.

The fighting elsewhere on the 25-kilometre front had died down, so that the epic struggle at Bullecourt became the focus of attention everywhere the war was reported. On 10 May, the 2nd Division and 1st Division were exhausted, so the 5th was brought into the fighting.

The second Australian VC at Bullecourt went to Lieutenant Rupert Moon, of the 58th Battalion, 5th Division. On 12 May the 58th was to support the British 7th Division by attacking German positions. Moon's duty was to capture a pillbox and the young officer led a charge of his platoon. Wounded in the face he went on, calling to his platoon, 'Come on boys! Don't turn me down!' Driven out of their strongpoint, the Germans retreated into a trench. Moon brought a Lewis-gun crew to enfilade the trench and forced the Germans back. Now wounded in the shoulder, Moon followed them but enemy bombs compelled him to find shelter. Ordering some of his men to shower the Germans with grenades, he led the others in a charge, during which he was wounded in the leg and foot. The surviving Germans dived into a dugout where Moon's small party kept them at rifle point until more Diggers came up. They captured 186 Germans from these dugouts. With German snipers now active, Moon withdrew a short distance and ordered his men to dig in. As he peered over the edge of a cutting to locate the next enemy position he was again wounded. This time his jaw was broken and his face mutilated. Making light of his injuries, Moon saw his men securely in position

Above: The author seated on one of the Bullecourt battlefield memorials in 1990. This memorial was erected upon the site of German trenches captured by the Diggers.

Left: A rear view of 'Digger Corlett' shows a soldier with his full gear. Unveiled in 1993, 'Digger Corlett' looks across part of the Bullecourt battlefield.

before he allowed himself to be helped to the rear. He was awarded the VC.

The fighting ended on 17 May because both sides were exhausted. The Germans had suffered 6000 casualties, the Australians 7000. Nevertheless, Second Bullecourt was a remarkable achievement. Australian leadership, at all levels, overcame the setback posed by the 5th Brigade's failure. At no time in France did the AIF confront such a resilient enemy as the Wurttembergers yet the 2nd Division held the territory it had taken. The captured German lines remained part of the British front line until March 1918 when the great German spring offensive swept aside almost the entire British front line.

Directions

Bullecourt, though little more than a hamlet, is a major place of pilgrimage for Australians. It can be reached from Arras through Croisilles or from Bapaume through Ecoust St Mein. Outside Bullecourt church is the Australian 'slouch hat memorial'. The soldier's hat atop the stone base was actually a felt one of war vintage which was then bronzed. It was presented by the Australian War Memorial in 1980. Continue through the village and fork right to Riencourt-les-Cagnicourt. On the side of this narrow road is another memorial, roughly on the left centre of the old battlefield and close to the Hindenburg Line. Both these memorials were erected on the initiative of André Coilliot of Arras and a leading member of Souvenir Français (SF), an organisation dedicated to remembrance of sacrifice. The memorials were paid for by Souvenir Français Arras branch.

A new Australian national memorial, built by the Department of Veterans Affairs, was dedicated on Anzac Day 1992, at a ceremony attended by the Minister of Veterans Affairs, Ben Humphreys. On 24 April 1993 a splendid Digger figure, sculpted by Peter Corlett and set atop the 1992 plinth, was unveiled by the Australian ambassador to France, Kim Jones. The memorial is by the side of Rue des Australiens, between Bullecourt and Riencourt.

Bullecourt town hall has a small but very good Australian war museum. In pride of place is a painting presented by the Australian War Memorial, Canberra, showing soldiers led by Major Percy Black of the 13th Battalion breaking through the enemy barbed wire on 11 April 1917. Apply to Mr Jean Letaille who lives at 23 Rue d'Arras, Bullecourt, for inspection.

To see the battlefield as the Diggers saw it, drive 3 kilometres to Noreuil, where the units formed up.

They then advanced north-east, under cover of the gentle hills. Along a track, and still under visual cover, they extended into line and advanced 300 metres to a railway embankment. Most units had their HQ behind this embankment and from here the attack began. The railway has long since disappeared but the embankment remains and can be visited.

From Bullecourt village, take the D956 as if leaving for Longatte and Vaulx-Vraucourt. Pass the water-tower *(château d'eau)* on your left and within 100 metres turn left on to an unmarked farm road. The embankment is then 250 metres on your left. Though covered with scrub and short trees it is clearly recognisable as an embankment. Another farm track to the left takes you directly to the embankment.

Imagine the Germans 2 kilometres ahead of you in Hendecourt-les-Cagnicourt and in Riencourt-les-Cagnicourt. Ninety degrees to your right is Queant, also held by the Germans. The farm fields ahead of you, marked on the left flank by Bullecourt and on the right by the Queant, were the killing fields of Bullecourt for both battles. The Australians had to cross these fields without cover other than some communication trenches they had dug. Visible to the

The Bullecourt memorial with its bronzed slouch hat. The hat is a genuine WWI hat, which has been bronzed so that it will withstand the weather.

enemy and under other small-arms fire from the moment they left the shelter of the embankment, they managed to break into the Hindenburg Line only through sheer stubborn courage.

The VC Exploits

The remarkable series of actions by Lieutenant Rupert Moon culminated close to the Australian memorial in the sunken road — Rue des Australiens — from Bullecourt to Riencourt. They started in the fields which the memorial faces. Corporal Snowy Howell's exploit took place about 400 metres distant, on the right of tbe battlefield, along the line of the farm road which approaches Riencourt from the direction of the old railway embankment and close to Riencourt itself.

Lagnicourt

Lagnicourt has been mentioned previously as a Hindenburg Line Outpost Village. It is also the name given to a battle which took place on 15 April, when units of the 1st Division were holding an inordinately long front of 11.8 kilometres against a German counter-attack. With a thin shield of piquet posts, the Division's responsibility extended from left of Lagnicourt to the right of Hermies. On this day a remarkable amount of isolated fighting took place in the valleys and hills as German parties tried either to encircle Australian posts, bomb them out of existence or take them by frontal attacks. One of the most spirited actions took place along the main Bapaume-Cambrai road, 250 metres east of Boursies, where Lieutenant L. L. Agnew, 4th Battalion, set up a post beside a small chapel with orders to hold out until the last. Agnew was wounded and lay helpless in the open, almost within bomb range of the enemy. Two stretcher bearers tried to reach him but one was killed and the other wounded. Private W. Swanney crawled out and brought in the officer. Under more pressure than any other 4th Battalion piquet, the chapel post held out stubbornly until the German attack was called off.

The most critical phase of the battle occurred on the 1st Division's far left flank, 1.2 kilometres north of Lagnicourt, where the Germans used the darkness to move columns of men behind the Australians. It was here that Captain Newland and Sergeant Whittle largely saved the day for their Division. An Australian counter-attack and sustained shellfire against the Germans resulted in a complete AIF victory. The Battle of Lagnicourt cost the Australians 1050 casualties, including 300 men taken prisoner.

Directions

Parts of this battlefield are scattered from Hermies to Noreuil. The most intense and the most crucial fighting took place between Lagnicourt and Noreuil, much of it in the sunken road where Private Jorgen Jensen had won his VC a few weeks earlier. Other fighting took place along the thin stream which runs through Noreuil, known to the Australians as the Hirondelle River but known locally as la Grande Deuve. The site of Lieutenant Agnew's stand at the chapel in Boursies is easily found, as the chapel is still there, only 200 metres out of the village on the eastern side and on the right of the Boursies-Cambrai road.

Morchies

The first Australian contact with this village was made by accident. On the night of 19 March 1917 Lieutenant M. D. Knight of the 60th Battalion lost his way while making the rounds of his posts and entered a village. He believed it to be Beugny, which he knew was held by AIF troops. While walking down the main street, he heard German voices and realised that the place was occupied by the enemy. After a time he realised that he was in Morchies. He made his way through the German sentry posts and returned to his own lines. Morchies was occupied next day by the 59th Battalion. Lieutenant Knight was killed south of the Somme on 6 July 1918. Morchies is reached by the N30, east of Bapaume.

Chapter 8

Cemeteries East of Bapaume of Australian Interest

Bancourt British Cemetery

A large cemetery, Bancourt contains 248 Australian burials in a total of 2479 graves. Most of the Diggers who lie here were brought in from battlefield graves south-east of Bapaume or died of wounds received during the advance to the Hindenburg Line Outpost Villages in March and April 1918.

Directions
From Bapaume, take the D7 for 5 kilometres east to Bancourt. Enter the village, drive along the only main street and fork right as the settlement ends. The cemetery is then in sight.

H.A.C. Cemetery, Ecoust-St Mien

This large cemetery of 1879 war graves contains 162 (fourteen unknown) Australians, most of them killed either at nearby Bullecourt or Lagnicourt. The AIF 4th Division captured Ecoust on 2 April 1917. After the German counter-attack at Lagnicourt on 15 April, twelve Australian gunners were buried in what is now Row A of Plot I. Some Australians in this cemetery were killed by their own machine-gunners on the morning of 3 April 1917. They were among prisoners taken by the Germans and as they left the German trenches to be marched to the rear, their mates mistook them for Germans and shot them

Morchies Australian Cemetery, east of Bapaume, contains the graves of 20 Diggers killed in March 1917.

Close to the old German blockhouse, a Commonwealth War Graves Commission sign points to Noreuil Cemetery near Bullecourt. Most of the Diggers buried in this cemetery were killed in the fighting at Bullecourt and Lagnicourt. It also contains others killed in an ambush near Noreuil itself.

down. The machine-gunners had no idea of their mistake until the next day.

Directions
From Bullecourt, take the D956 past the water tower for 1 kilometre to Longatte. At the T-junction, turn right for 300 metres and at the cross-roads turn left through Ecoust, still on the D956. After 500 metres, the cemetery is on the right.

Morchies Australian Cemetery

This small cemetery was begun by Australian units in March 1917. It was lost to the Germans on 21 March 1918 and recaptured in September 1918. It contains the graves of twenty Diggers, forty-one British soldiers and two Germans. Many of the Australians were killed during the fighting for Morchies on 20 March 1917. Others, including gunners, were killed at Bullecourt.

Directions
From Bapaume, take the N30 east and turn off to Beugny on the D18 to Morchies. The cemetery is on the right on the outskirts of the village.

Noreuil Australian Cemetery

Noreuil was the scene of fierce fighting between the Australians and Germans, on 2 April 1917 and then on 15 April. The cemetery was started at the beginning of April and used until the following December; four burials were made in September 1918. It contains the graves of 182 Diggers and sixty-two British soldiers but twenty-six of the Australians are unnamed and eighty-two are represented by special memorials. Almost all of these eighty-two belonged to the 50th Battalion, and were killed during the attack in which Jorgen Jensen won his VC. They had been buried in marked graves but the graves were destroyed by German shelling during the battles of Bullecourt.

Buried side by side are the Clayton brothers, Edward, aged 29, and William, aged 42. Both served in the 52nd Battalion and both were killed by machine-gun fire at Bullecourt on 12 April 1917. They came from Dover, Tasmania.

During the Second Battle of Bullecourt there was constant loss of life from shellfire. A victim on 9 May was Captain Archie Ramsay of the 55th Battalion, while on 5 May Lieutenant William Dent Young was killed.

Directions

The cemetery is signposted in the village of Noreuil, off the road leading towards Ecoust and Bullecourt. It is on the edge of the settlement and is obscured by a church and other buildings until you are almost upon it. It is very quiet and we have camped for the night in the farm road next to the cemetery.

Queant Road Cemetery, Buissy

This cemetery was made by the 2nd and 57th Casualty Clearing Stations in October and November 1918 and it then consisted of seventy-one graves. After the Armistice it was greatly enlarged by the concentration of 2226 graves from the battlefields of 1917-18 and from some smaller burial grounds. More Australians (954) are buried here than in any cemetery of the entire region, but 699 of them are unidentified. The number of UK graves is 1323, with three-quarters of them unidentified. A special memorial commemorates forty-three Australian soldiers known or believed to be buried in Queant Road. Most of the AIF casualties are from the battles of Bullecourt and that of Lagnicourt, occurring between March and May 1917.

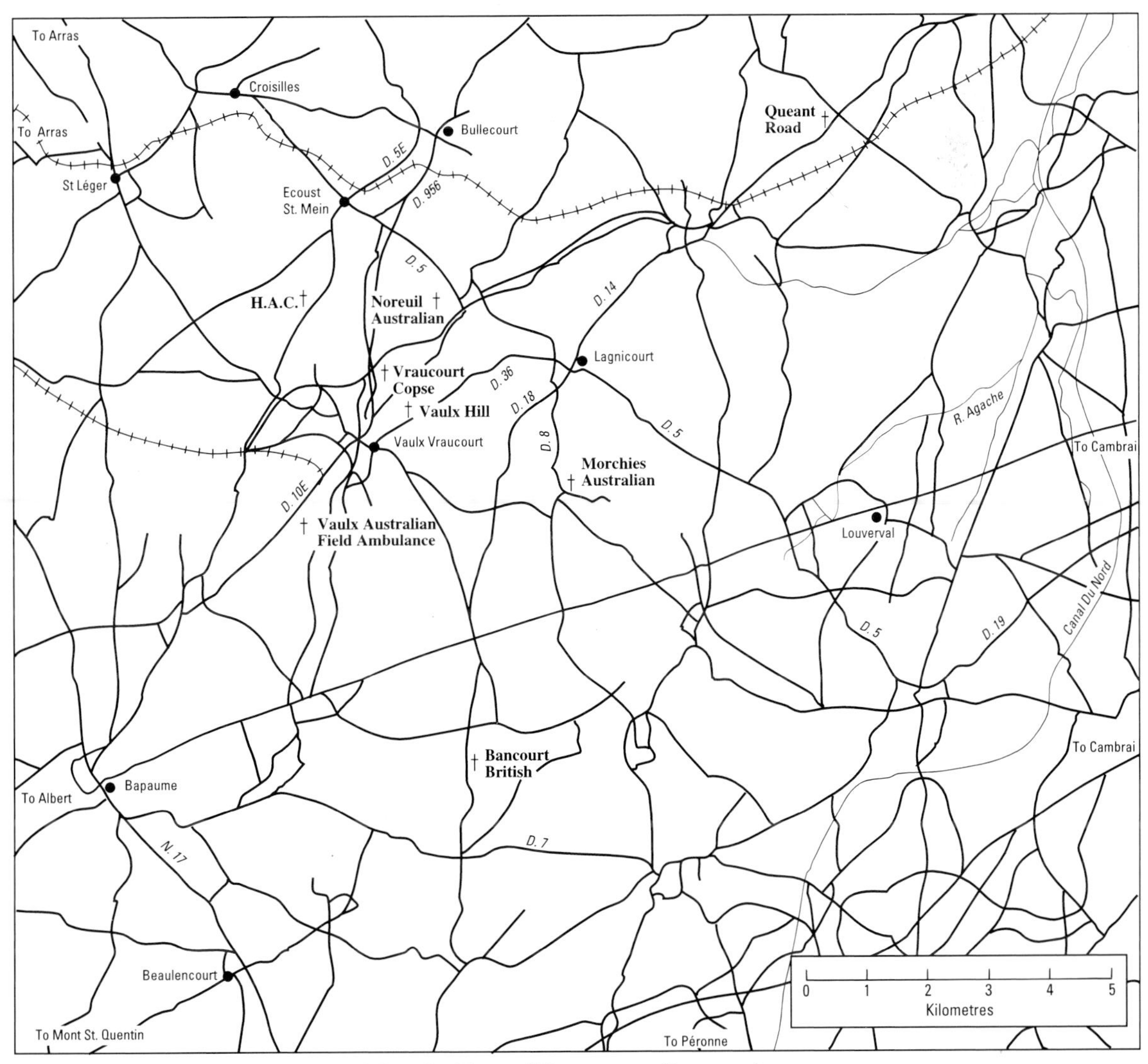

Map 9. East of Bapaume: Cemeteries

The best-known Digger in the cemetery is Captain Percy Cherry VC, MC (Grave VIII.C.10). Equally well-known in the AIF was Major Benjamin Leane of the 48th Battalion (Grave I.C.1). Ben Leane was second-in-command of his brother's battalion, the 48th, which was known to the Diggers as the Joan of Arc Battalion because it was 'made of all Leanes' (Maid of Orleans). Ben Leane was killed by a German barrrage on 10 April 1917 which came down as the Diggers withdrew from their jumping-off line before the projected battle of Bullecourt. Instead, they went into battle the following day. Ben's cousin, Captain A. E. Leane, died of wounds on 2 May 1917 while a prisoner of war. Lieutenant-Colonel Ray Leane, CO of the 48th, was one of the most highly respected battalion commanders in the AIF but Ben was the best loved of the brothers.

Sergeant George Kirkpatrick MM of the 17th Battalion, in a desperate fight at Noreuil on 15 April, killed three Germans in close-quarter combat and was then killed himself (Grave III .E.11). Second Lieutenant Arthur Jerry MM, of the 28th Battalion, fought superbly in the village of Lagnicourt on 26 March only to be hit late in the day. He died in a CCS (Grave VIII.B.12).

The grave of Captain Percy Cherry, one of the AIF's most inspiring young leaders. Killed at Lagnicourt, he is buried with another 953 Diggers in Queant Road Cemetery, near Bullecourt.

Vaulx Australian Field Ambulance Cemetery, set amid peaceful wheat fields on what in 1917, was the Bullecourt front. An Australian Field Ambulance established itself in a farm a few miles behind Bullecourt and buried its dead nearby. The small cemetery is reached by a 150 metre grass path.

Directions

From Queant, take the D14 for 1.2 kilometres towards Buissy. The large cemetery is on the left near the crossroads with the D14E. From Arras, the cemetery can be reached off the Arras-Cambrai road; take the turn-off, right, to Buissy.

Vaulx Australian Field Ambulance Cemetery

This cemetery was begun by Australian units in April 1917 and used until February 1918. The Germans then buried their dead in it and one British burial was made in August. It now contains the graves of thirty-two Diggers, twenty British soldiers and thirty-eight Germans.

Two of the Diggers buried here, Lieutenant Norman Dougall MC and Second Lieutenant Kenneth Wendt, both of the 10th Battalion, had been prominent at Boursies on 15 April when they led an attack to dislodge a party of Germans who had set up a dangerous post within the Australian line. Both were killed at Bullecourt on 6 May. Wendt, a student, was only 18.

Directions

The cemetery is 1.2 kilometres south-west of Vaulx-Vraucourt, along a grassy path 120 metres back from the road to Beaugnâtre and Bapaume. On the bare, cultivated plateau, the cemetery has commanding views of Vaulx-Vraucourt, Beaugnâtre and Fremicourt.

Vaulx Hill Cemetery

About 550 metres east of Vaulx-Vraucourt village, this cemetery contains seventeen graves of September 1918. The rest of the cemetery was formed after the Armistice by the concentration of graves from other cemeteries and from the battlefields in the immediate neighbourhood. Australian burials number 106 out of 822. A special memorial commemorates the names of three Diggers buried in other cemeteries whose graves were destroyed by shellfire.

The bodies of twenty-three Australians came from Sunken Road Cemetery, Beaumetz, which was then declared closed. The bodies of another seven Australians were taken from the Vraucourt Churchyard Extension and reburied here. Among the Diggers on Vaulx Hill is Lieutenant-Colonel Bertram Watts DSO, commander of the 4th Field Artillery Brigade, killed just behind Lagnicourt on 10 April 1917 (Grave l.B.3). Three officers of Watts' staff are buried close to him. They are his medical officer, Captain Brian Mack (Grave II.B.4), Lieutenant Guy Davenport MC and Lieutenant Herbert Harding. These officers are buried together in Grave II.B.6.

Directions

The cemetery is about 550 metres east of Vaulx-Vraucourt village on the Lagnicourt road and in summer has probably the most beautiful gardens of all the CWGC cemeteries in the area.

Vraucourt Copse Cemetery

The copse which gave the cemetery its name is 600 metres to the north. Originally the cemetery contained forty-three British graves of September 1918 but in 1928 Plots II and III were made by the concentration of sixty graves from Vaulx Advanced Dressing Station Cemetery. It contains the graves of thirty-eight Diggers, five of whom are unidentified, and sixty-five British.

Among the Diggers is 20-year-old Second Lieutenant Richmond Howell-Price MC, of the 1st Battalion, who was killed on 3 May at Bullecourt (Grave II.B.7). He was the second of three brothers to be killed on the Western Front. Lieutenant Colonel O. G. Howell-Price was killed at Flers and Major Philip Howell-Price at Broodseinde. The youngest, Richmond, was so named because he had been born at Richmond, NSW.

Two notable soldiers are buried in Vraucourt Copse: Captain James Tyson MC, 3rd Battalion, killed on 3 May 1917 at Second Bullecourt (Grave II.B.11), and Captain Norman Shierlaw MC, 13th Battalion, who died of wounds received on 11 April 1917 during First Bullecourt (Grave II.B.13).

Directions

The cemetery is on the road from Vaulx-Vraucourt, just beyond the fork in the road to Noreuil and on a low cliff. Vaulx ADS Cemetery is nearby on the opposite side of the road.

Chapter 9

South of the Somme River

From the end of March until the beginning of October 1918 the AIF achieved its greatest victories south of the Somme River and ever eastward against the retreating Germans. It was here that Australian senior military leadership proved its qualities, while the Diggers won their reputation as the best fighting troops of any army involved in the war.

The operations of 1918, though still costly in terms of casualties, came almost as a relief after the slaughter of Pozières in 1916, the horrors of the winter of 1916-17, the bludgeoning battles of Bullecourt in early 1917 and the heroic agonies of Flanders and Passchendaele in the latter part of 1917. The rolling, open country south of the Somme provided the Australians with a terrain in which they could exercise their initiative and dash with some expectation of success.

More than this, from 31 May 1918 all five AIF Divisions came under direct Australian High Command. Promoted to Lieutenant General, John Monash took over command of the Australian Corps. In effect, it was the Australian army, but with only five divisions it was not considered a large enough formation to be given this title. For the last six months of the war only some Light Horse, the tunnellers, some artillery units and the air squadrons remained outside the Australian Corps.

The many battles fought by the AIF during 1918 sometimes involved entire divisions but in some actions only a battalion or company was engaged. The list of encounters is impressive and makes it all the more surprising that many British war histories give the Australians scant reference:

30 March - 12 April — Villers-Bretonneux;
9 April — Hangard Wood;
23-27 April — Second Villers-Bretonneux;
28 April - 3 May — Monument Wood;
4 July — Hamel;
5 July - 7 August — 'Peaceful Penetration';
8 August — Amiens, 'the Black Day of the German Army';
9-11 August — Lihons;
10 August — Morcourt;
11-12 August — Mericourt;
12 August — Proyart;
18-23 August — Herleville;
23 August — Chuignolles-Chuigny;
28 August — Curlu;
29 August - 2 September — Mont St Quentin;
29 August - 5 September — Peronne;
18 September — Hargicourt and Le Verguier;
29 September — Bellicourt;
3-4 October — Beaurevoir;
4-5 October — Montbrehain.

In addition, Australians fought at the St Quentin Canal, Bony, Noyon, Epehy, Jeancourt and other places during the operations to capture the Beaurevoir Line.

Battle of Amiens, 8-28 August 1918

The so-called Battle of Amiens was fought nowhere near Amiens but eastwards from Villers-Bretonneux. The AIF was involved in several separate battles to capture places mentioned in this account. The battle began at 4.20 a.m. on 8 August, with 100 000 British and Dominion troops attacking along 20 kilometres of front. The first two AIF divisions involved, 2nd and 3rd, had a front of 3.6 kilometres from Villers-Bretonneux on the right to the Somme at Gailly. In close support were the 4th and 5th Divisions. Without the usual preliminary bombardment the Germans were taken by surprise, and by 7.30 a.m. the offensive had broken the German line so thoroughly that much of their field artillery was overrun and captured. While the men of the 2nd and 3rd Divisions dug in, those of the 4th and 5th leapfrogged over them — as Monash had planned — and at 8.20 a.m. took up the second phase of the attack.

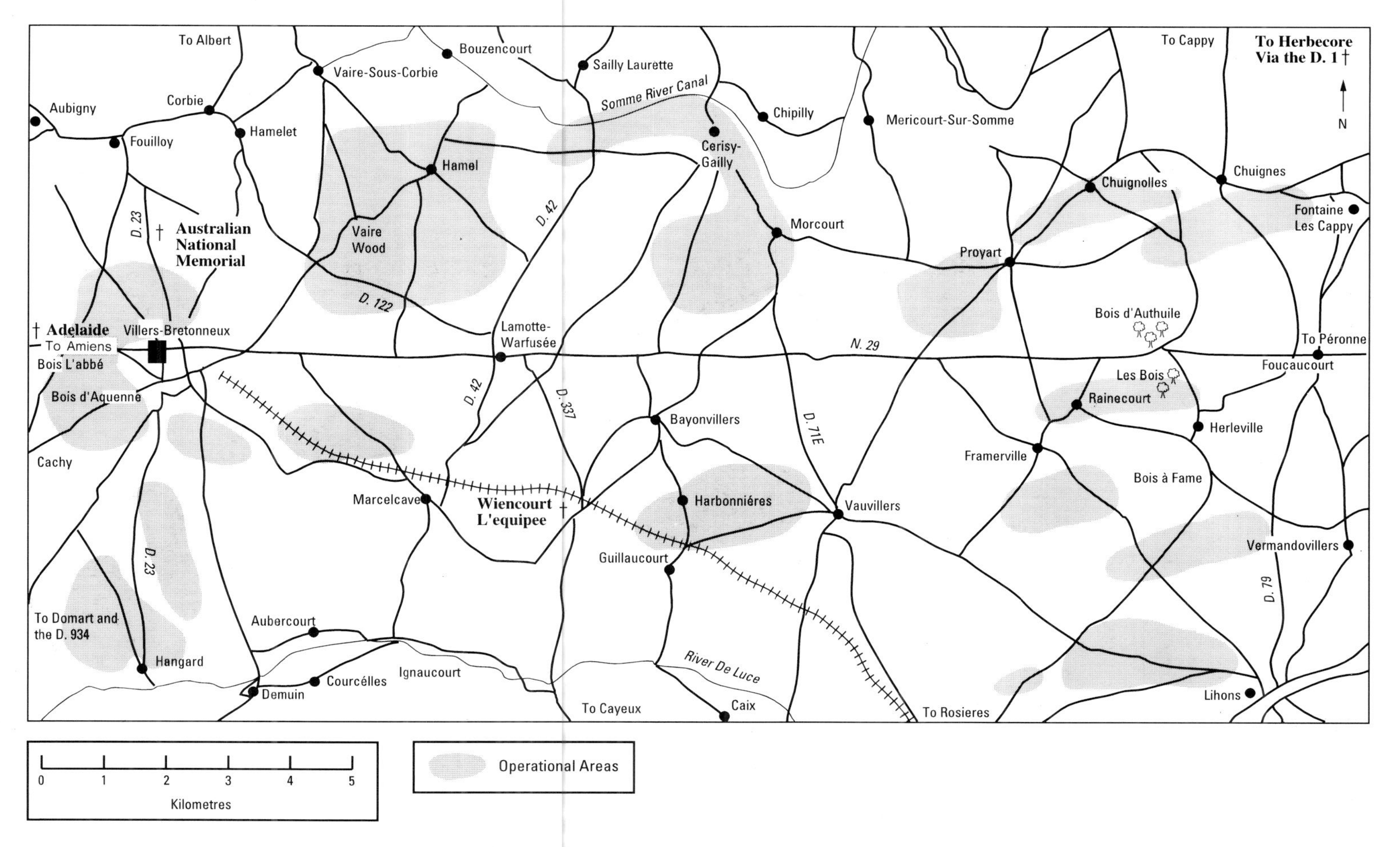

Map 10. South of the Somme: Operational Areas and Battlefields

In Morcourt, the 14th Battalion, helped by tanks, captured hundreds of reserve troops and masses of stores. The 58th captured Bayonvillers while the 59th ran the Germans out of Harbonnières and at 11 a.m. raised the Australian flag on the church tower. The 28th Battalion, advancing from Villers-Bretonneux, were stopped at Card Copse near Marcelcave, where the Germans had left a single gap in their barbed wire defences in the hope that the Australians would funnel through it and be mown down by machine-gun fire. Lieutenant Alfred Gaby rushed the enemy position and disregarding the heavy fire ran along the parapet and emptied his .45 revolver into the garrison. Driving the crews from their guns, he forced the surrender of fifty Germans with four machine-guns. Then he led his company on to its objective.

A patrol of six Diggers of the 1st Battalion, under Company Quartermaster-Sergeant J. C. Hayes and Sergeant H. D. Andrews crossed the river to Chipilly, which was actually part of the British front. They silenced all enemy machine-guns, cleared the village and 2000 metres of ground, captured about 300 prisoners and brought the British front in line with their own. This remarkable performance brought Hayes and Andrews a DCM each.

By the end of 8 August the British and Dominion attack had gathered in 13 000 prisoners and more than 200 guns. Marshal Ludendorff wrote that 8 August was 'the black day of the German Army'. The High Command rushed men and guns from all parts of the front to plug the gap. On 9 August the 4th and 5th Divisions took over the lead and were joined by the 1st Division, just arrived from the north, and they captured the heights of Lihons. For the first time in the war all five Australian divisions were operating together on the one front.

At Rosières, on flat ground east of Villers-Bretonneux, the 8th Battalion was stopped by machine-gun fire until Private Robert Beatham, with Corporal W. G. Nottingham, ran forward to bomb and fight the crews of four enemy machine-guns, killing ten Germans and capturing another ten. The battalion line then swept forward and again Beatham attacked a machine-gun post, only to be riddled with bullets.

Many gallant actions took place along the advancing front and on 11 August Lieutenant Gaby was again conspicuous. However, in this fresh battalion attack he was shot down by a sniper. He and Beatham were awarded the VC, Corporal Nottingham the DCM.

On 12 August, the 37th, 38th, 40th and 42nd Battalions moved against Proyart. Patrols from the 37th and 40th entered the village to find that German troops had abandoned the town so hurriedly that they had left meals on tables. That afternoon the attack was held up in a valley south of the Proyart-Chuignes road. About 6 p.m. the 37th Battalion sent a message saying that it was sending forward a party despite a line of enemy machine-guns stopping them. Sergeant Percy Statton of the 40th Battalion could see these guns and turned his Lewis guns on them but when a party of thirteen men from the 37th made their rush a German gun mowed them down. Statton saw this and leading Corporal W. J. Upchurch, and Privates L. Styles and N. T. Beard, he began a dash across 800 metres of open ground to attack the first gun. The Germans saw him too late and Statton shot two with his revolver while his men killed another three. They raced at the second gun, where Statton shot the crew, except for one man who lunged at him with rifle and bayonet. Statton tore the weapon from the German's hand and bayoneted him. He and his party at once charged the other guns but the terror-stricken crews ran, only to be shot down by the Lewis guns which Statton had earlier positioned. An enemy gun killed Private Styles and wounded Corporal Upchurch but Statton and Beard returned to their lines. That night, Statton ventured out again to bring in his wounded mate and the body of Styles. He was awarded the VC.

On 23 August there occurred one of the most audacious individual exploits of the AIF on the Western Front. C. E. W. Bean regarded it as second only to Albert Jacka's feat of arms at Pozières two years earlier. Close to Madame Wood, just west of Vermandovillers, the 16th and 13th Battalions, together with the 16th Lancashire Fusiliers, were ordered to advance across a kilometre of open ground laced with enemy trenches and push the Germans from their defensive system, known as Courtine Trench. The 16th took its positions as planned but the Fusiliers failed to link up. Lieutenant Lawrence McCarthy, commanding D Company, led a platoon and bombed his way along Courtine Trench until confronted by an earth block, which the Germans were defending with two machine-guns, one of which was firing along the trench held by the 16th Battalion. Setting two British soldiers to dig through the block, McCarthy took Sergeant F. J. Robbins, scrambled around the block and dropped into the enemy trench. Shooting a sentry at another barrier, McCarthy found a machine-gun firing over his head at the Australians. Shooting the gunners, McCarthy raced on and came up behind a German officer giving orders to a crowd of his men. When McCarthy shot the officer the men bolted into another trench. McCarthy and Robbins threw grenades at them until forty shaken Germans filed out in surrender. In 20 minutes of non-stop action, McCarthy had killed twenty Germans, captured fifty more and seized five machine-guns. In addition, he handed over to the Lancashire Fusiliers more than 700 metres of trench which they had been told to capture in the first place. He was awarded the VC for what the men of his battalion called 'a super-VC stunt'.

Also on 23 August, Lieutenant William Joynt of the 8th Battalion won a VC for 'conspicuous bravery and devotion to duty' at Herleville Wood, near Chuignes. In fact, it was entirely due to Joynt's leadership in a series of actions that enemy positions in Herleville Wood and later in Plateau Wood were captured from a demoralised enemy.

During the sweeping advance following the attack of 9 August it was important that the British and Dominion line be kept as straight as possible and some AIF units were sent north of the Somme to stiffen the British. On 27 August the 41st Battalion found itself fighting in difficult country along the banks of the Somme as the Australians headed for Curlu. Enemy posts in Fargny Wood were particularly troublesome until Lance-Corporal Bernard Gordon made several forays against them. Single-handedly he captured two officers and sixty-one other enemy, together with six machine-guns. Curlu was taken the following day after stiff fighting and Gordon was awarded the VC.

Australian casualties between 7–14 August were: 1st Division — 114 officers, 1817 other ranks; 2nd Division — 75 officers, 1220 other ranks; 3rd Division — 52 officers, 1043 other ranks; 4th Division — 44 officers, 740 other ranks; 5th Division — 54 officers, 832 other ranks. Between 15–28 August there were another 600 casualties. The triumph had left streaks of Australian blood across the southern Somme.

Directions

The places between Villers-Bretonneux and the approaches to Peronne, and mentioned in this description, are easily visited by reference to any general map. The specific sites follow.

Albert Gaby's VC exploit

Take the N29 east of Villers-Bretonneux to the first village, Lamotte-Warfusée. Turn right on to the D42. After 0.5 kilometre, Card Copse stood in the field to the right. Gaby is buried in Heath Cemetery at Harbonnières, on the N29.

Robert Beatham's VC exploit

The position is impossible to locate but it was much closer to the hamlet of Vauvillers than to Rosières and was close to the Lihons road, 0.5 kilometre south of Vauvillers. Beatham is buried in Heath Cemetery, Harbonnières, on the N29.

Lawrence McCarthy's VC exploit

What the AIF knew as Madame Wood is actually Bois à Famé (Famous Wood) and it lies 700 metres west of the hamlet of Vermandovillers. From the crossroads in the hamlet, take the minor unnamed road west to the large wood. Courtine Trench, which McCarthy captured, ran along the western edge of the wood.

Percy Statton's VC exploit

Enter Proyart from the Villers-Bretonneux-Vermand N29. Leave on the minor road north-east, signposted Chuignolles. Park on the right of a large German military cemetery. Statton's operations were on the right of this road towards a farm road, partly sunken, 0.5 kilometre east. German posts were in the sunken road.

William Joynt's VC exploit

AIF records describe Herleville Wood and Plateau Wood as being near Chuignes. In fact, they are 2.5 kilometres south of Chuignes. Herleville Wood (army name only), known locally as Les Bois, is between Herleville village and the N29. Plateau Wood (army name) is Bois d'Authuile, 200 metres north across the N29. Joynt established Australian lines on the eastern side of both these woods.

Bernard Gordon's VC exploit

The various actions for which Gordon was decorated took place in Fargny Wood, which is largely unchanged since the war. From Peronne, take the D938 Albert road and turn off left to Curlu. Here, take the minor road — it is the only road — west along the Somme river to the hamlet of Fargny. Gordon penetrated the wood from the 41st Battalion's positions on the western side of the small settlement.

Hamel

Lieutenant-General Monash was eager for a big battle as GOC Australian Corps and he found his opportunity in a plan to capture the village of Hamel and enemy positions around it. North-east of Villers-Bretonneux, Hamel was strongly fortified and a key German defensive position as it protected the area between the Villers-Bretonneux heights and the Somme River.

The new British Mark V tanks had arrived in France and the Tank Corps commander, Major-General H. J. Elles, wanted to redeem the reputation of armour in Australian eyes. Since the tanks' failure at Bullecourt in April 1917 the Diggers had placed no trust in them. Elles invited Monash and his chief-of-staff, Brigadier-General Thomas Blamey, to inspect the new tanks in exercise. They were duly impressed and saw the possibility of using tanks to reduce infantry casualties. This was important, as recruiting in Australia had declined alarmingly and influenza was further reducing AIF ranks.

Entirely under AIF direction, the battle was intelligently and precisely planned. Monash could spare only 7500 men and he allowed 90 minutes, on 4 July, for the battle to be won At 3.10 a.m. the Diggers approached behind the tanks, which were marked with the infantry's own battalion colours. The tanks tore gaps in the enemy wire and their machine-gunners provided steady covering fire for the following infantry. For the first time, ammunition was dropped by parachute, saving carrying parties an immense amount of hard and dangerous work. Hamel and Vaire Woods fell to the 4th Brigade, Hamel village to the 11th. About 2000 Germans were killed or wounded and 1500 were captured, together with a vast quantity of German weapons, including 177 machine-guns. Australian casualties were about 1400. The battle lasted just 93 minutes.

During the battle, the 15th Battalion's task was to capture Pear Trench but the protecting wire was still intact and under heavy fire the attack came to a halt. Private Harry Dalziel, No. 2 on a Lewis gun, charged an enemy machine-gun post and armed only with a revolver killed or captured the entire crew. His trigger finger was shot off and he lost much blood but he made trips over open ground to collect ammunition for his gun until he was shot in the head. He survived the wound and was awarded the VC.

Hamel marked the end of the mainly defensive attitude along the British front. The defeat at Hamel shocked the Germans and after Monash ordered 'vigorous offensive patrolling' they were even more startled. On 6 July on the Hamel front, Corporal Walter Brown of the 20th Battalion stalked a German officer and twelve men and terrorised them into surrender by threatening to throw a grenade at them. His exploit earned him the VC.

Directions

From Villers-Bretonneux, take the N29 east for 0.5 kilometre and turn left into a minor road signposted Le Hamel. After 1.5 kilometres this road skirts Vaire Wood, through which the German front line passed during April–July 1918. It was captured by the 16th Battalion on 4 July 1918 as part of the Hamel Battle. On the right of this road is a steep ridge, captured in the battle. The road continues into Hamel, where other fighting took place. Finally, the Australians captured the high ground 1 kilometre east of Hamel. The forming-up area for the battle was 1 kilometre west of Hamel along a minor road. To reach this road, take the Vaire-sous-Corbie road from Hamel for 1.5 kilometres. Where it forms a three-way junction, turn sharp left. This was the jumping-off road for the infantry and it runs almost dead straight for 2 kilometres. Then it makes a short turn before continuing to Villers-Bretonneux. The tanks formed up 1 kilometre behind the infantry and on a parallel road which starts in the small settlement of Hamelet.

In Vaire Wood (and Hamel Wood) Lance-Corporal Thomas Axford, 16th Battalion, won a VC. To find Pear Trench, where Harry Dalziel won his VC, continue along the road from Vaire Wood towards Hamel. From where the wood ends by the roadside, drive another 0.5 kilometre. Pear Trench was 200 metres in the fields to the left, on a spur of ground.

The site of Wally Brown's exploit is more easily found than that for Dalzeil. From Villers-Bretonneux, take the N29 east for 3.3 kilometres and turn left into a minor road to Le Hamel. Brown made his daring raid 200 metres along this road, then part of a German trench system.

Hangard Wood 7 April 1918

About 3 kilometres south of Villers-Bretonneux, the woods and ravine north-east of Hangard village remained in German hands on 7 April and the 5th Brigade (Brigadier-General Smith) was ordered to recapture the area and so straighten the British line. Companies of the 19th and 20th Battalions formed the spearhead but no barrage fell to support them and they went in without artillery support. Within minutes 25 per cent of Captain C. Wallach's company of 19th Battalion was hit, including Wallach himself. Command fell to Lieutenant Percy Storkey. With Lieutenant F. N. Lipscomb and ten men, Storkey came upon about 100 Germans in trenches firing at Australians in the open. At that moment the Germans had their back to the Australians but one shouted an alarm. Storkey had to act quickly. With himself at one end of the ten men in line and Lieutenant Lipscomb at the other, he led a charge. The Germans nearby put up their hands but those in more distant trenches hesitated. Had they swung around one machine-gun the 19th Battalion men would have been annihilated. Storkey ordered all the Germans to surrender and climb out of their trench and when they hesitated he shot three with his revolver, which then jammed. Some of his men rolled a few grenades into the trenches and about thirty enemy were killed or wounded. Another fifty-three, including three officers, surrendered.

The 5th Brigade carried out its assignment with great spirit but the British general who had ordered it had not understood the complexity of the operation or the difficulties of holding the position. It was considered successful and the German regiment involved suffered 660 casualties between 5–7 April, however, by nightfall on 7 April the survivors of the 19th and 20th Battalions were back in their own lines, having suffered 151 casualties. Storkey was awarded the VC.

Directions
Hangard Wood is 3 kilometres south of Villers-Bretonneux on the Hangard road, which leaves Villers-Bretonneux over the railway bridge. It is impossible to fix the exact position of Storkey's exploit, especially as the shape of the wood has changed since 1918, but it took place roughly 100 metres into the wood from the road and just north of the present limit of Hangard village.

Villers-Bretonneux

The town of Villers-Bretonneux, only 16 kilometres east of Amiens, was the key to the defence of the city. It is on higher ground, at the time had many thick woods around it and it sat astride the railway line. During their offensive of March–April 1918 the Germans were determined to take the town, after which nothing would stand in their way. On 28 March the British 1st Cavalry Division halted the British retreat in front of the village of Hamel, between the Somme River and Villers-Bretonneux and at Villers-Bretonneux itself. The German High Command brought up sixty railway construction companies to restore the battered railway lines and thus bring in a flow of men, guns and ammunition. On 4 April, after heavy bombardment, fifteen German divisions attacked. Their northern thrust was stopped by the British 1st Cavalry and the AIF 33rd Battalion. In Villers-Bretonneux, Lieutenant-Colonel R. A. Goddard, in charge of the 9th Brigade's troops, ordered Lieutenant-Colonel J. A. Milne to counter-attack the enemy with his 36th Battalion. This dramatic and heroic bayonet charge blocked the German advance from Monument Wood, the enemy retreated by more than a kilometre and the front was stabilised. At this time the entire front between Albert and south of Villers-Bretonneux, about 25 kilometres, was being held by Australians.

On 17–18 April, in preparation for a second attempt to capture Villers-Bretonneux, the Germans drenched the woods and valleys behind the town with mustard gas, causing 1000 Australian casualties. Gas was used again on 23 April and at dawn on 24th the Germans attacked behind tanks, which broke through the British battalions. Villers-Bretonneux was captured.

The AIF 13th, 14th and 15th Brigades were hurried into the fight. The 51st and 52nd Battalions were ordered to head for Monument Wood and allow nothing to stop them. In the fight for the wood, Lieutenant Clifford Sadlier of the 52nd won the VC and Sergeant Charlie Stokes the DCM.

Brigadier-General Elliott's 15th Brigade was in action north of the town. Part of the 59th Battalion, supported by the 57th and 60th Battalions, made a ferocious bayonet charge in bright moonlight to rout Germans positioned in orchards. At the same time, on the southern edge of Villers-Bretonneux, the 50th and 51st Battalions drove the Germans out of Abbey Wood. The Diggers spent Anzac Day in street — and house — fighting in the town but it was not fully recaptured until 27 April.

In the second Villers-Bretonneux action, the 8th Brigade suffered 188 casualties, the 14th Brigade 346, the 15th Brigade 455. The 51st Battalion alone lost 365 officers and men.

British and French commanders were generous in their praise for the Australians, especially for their counter-attack made by night across difficult and unknown ground and at a few hours' notice. Brigadier-General G. W. Grogan VC, who saw it, called it 'perhaps the greatest individual feat of the war'. The Allied Supreme Commander, Marshal Foch, referred to the Australians' 'altogether astonishing valiance'. He probably meant valour.

On the night of 2–3 May, Lieutenant-Colonel

Ray Leane led the 48th Battalion to capture a large part of Monument Wood, though twelve officers and 143 men were hit. Monument Wood continued to be an important feature on the Australian front, and on 17-18 July the 25th and 26th Battalions advanced from Monument Wood area to straighten out the Australian line. The railway line divided the area assigned to each battalion, with the 26th south of the line. Lieutenant Albert Borella commanded a platoon at the most critical part of the 26th's operation. Spotting a machine-gun firing through the Australian barrage, Borella ran through the barrage, shot the gunners and captured the gun. He then led his party against the strongly held Jaffa Trench, taking prisoner the thirty Germans who survived. When reinforcements arrived in the trench about dawn, Borella called down artillery fire, which fell on his own men as well as the Germans. Even so, the twenty Australians held their ground to pour fire into the enemy as they assembled to make a counter-attack. When 500 Germans did manage to advance, Borella's steady leadership, together with another request for artillery support, broke up the attack. He was awarded the VC.

Directions
Villers-Bretonneux contains much of interest for Australian visitors and each site is described separately.

Australian National Memorial
This imposing memorial, of a tower rising from a long base, is at the rear of Villers-Bretonneux Military Cemetery, between Villers-Bretonneux and Fouilloy. The names of 10 982 Diggers killed in France (other than at Fromelles) and who have no known grave are inscribed on the screen wall of the memorial. The Villers-Bretonneux monument is classed as a Battle Exploit Memorial, the symbol of the Australian nation in arms. Although the memorial is on a high plateau it cannot be wholly seen from the Villers-Bretonneux-Fouilloy road because of the convex approach to it through the cemetery gardens. It is only after a climb up the slope that the memorial is fully revealed. Anzac Day services are held here.

From the top of the tower there are vast views of the battle area, and an orientation table points to the various sites. The memorial is kept locked for

The Australian National Memorial at Villers-Bretonneux. It is set at the end of a large cemetery. Between the Great Cross and the memorial the Australian and French flags fly perpetually.

security purposes and it is necessary to ask officials at CWGC, in Arras, to open it for inspection. Inside, diagrammatic maps show the position of the AIF's divisional monuments.

On the memorial, note the name of Private Eric Pinches DCM, 5th Company Machine-Gun Corps. He won his DCM at Lagnicourt when he rushed an enemy machine-gun post with bombs and captured the crew. He died on 5 May 1917 of wounds received the previous day at Bullecourt. Private Pinches was aged 16 and I believe him to be the youngest AIF man killed on the Western Front. He came from Ithaca, Brisbane. Strangely, his age is not given in the memorial register, as is the custom.

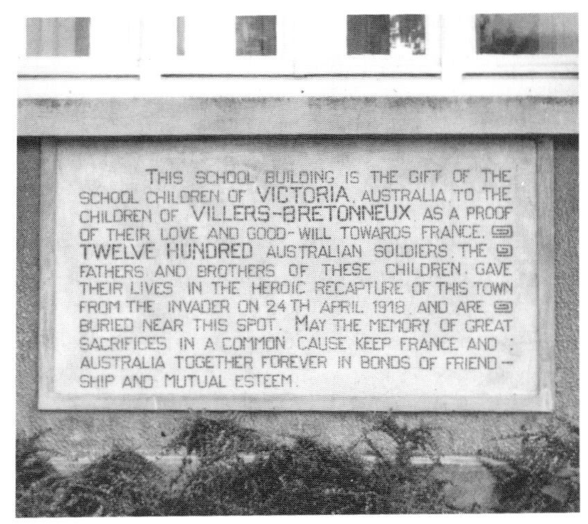

This notice, on the wall of the primary school at Villers-Bretonneux, explains why there is a strong connection between the town and Australia. 1200 Diggers died to save the town, and Victorian schoolchildren paid to have the school rebuilt.

The Town

Villers-Bretonneux was adopted by the City of Melbourne and in 1923 the primary school, which had been destroyed in the fighting, was rebuilt with

The town hall of Villers-Bretonneux, the key town in the defence of Amiens. Villers-Bretonneux is twinned with Robinvale, Victoria.

money raised by Victorian school children. Victorian units were prominent in the Villers-Bretonneux battles. The Town Hall has an Australian Room in which various RSL plaques hang on the walls.

On 5 May 1984 Villers-Bretonneux and the town of Robinvale in Victoria agreed to a 'twinning'. The two have roughly equivalent populations of 3500 and the Robinvale area supplied a large contingent of men to the AIF. The town was named after George Robin Cuttle, an air-gunner, whose plane was shot down at Caix, south of Villers-Bretonneux, on 9 May 1918. The main square in Robinvale is named Place de Caix.

The Anzac Museum

In 1975 the town opened an impressive Anzac Museum of three rooms in the primary school. It houses an interesting collection of war artefacts and AIF memorabilia and is well worth a visit. Apply at the Town Hall for a guide from the Franco-Australian Committee to escort you. A few guides speak some English. No charge is made but a donation to museum funds is appreciated.

36th Battalion's bayonet charge

The unit had been in a sunken road and was taken forward to Hangard Road, which became the jumping-off line. The 36th front began at the railway on their left and extended for 500 metres to the right. Monument Wood no longer exists but in 1918 its nearer edge was about 400 metres from the Hangard road. Having cleared the Germans from the wood, the Diggers pushed on to form a new front line more than 1 kilometre from where they started. Hangard Road begins just after crossing the railway bridge on the town's southern edge.

Abbey Wood and Aquenne Wood

These conjoined woods, west of Villers-Bretonneux, can be reached by taking the road to Cachy on the west side of town. Australians were gassed in these woods in mid-April. They fought in them on 24–25 April 1918 and various units were camped there during April and May.

Australian counter-attack of 24–25 April

Six AIF battalions were in action, three south of the town, three to the north. To the north, the battle took place across the fields on either side of the Fouilloy road and as far east as the road to Hamel. To the south, the action was across the Hangard Road. Thus, on either side of the town and attacking from west to east, the Australians were active in these fields. On 26 April they drove the Germans from the town itself. The six battalions were: north of town — 57th, 59th, 60th (all Victorian); south of town — 50th, 51st, 52nd (from the 'Outer States').

Albert Borella's VC exploit

Monument Wood stood in the fields to the left of Hangard Road, not far from where that road crosses the railway line on the south side of Villers-Bretonneux. About 500 metres east of this bridge is another railway bridge. It marks the position of Jaffa Trench, which Borella attacked. The trench cut across the railway and into the fields either side of it.

Almost lost in a French wheatfield of the Somme valley, the small cemetery of Herbecore British Cemetery is actually Australian by blood; 51 of the 59 soldiers there are Diggers. A wheatfield seems an appropriate resting place for Australians.

Chapter 10

Cemeteries South of the Somme River of Australian Interest

Adelaide Cemetery, Villers-Bretonneux

This cemetery was begun early in June 1918 and used by the 2nd and 3rd Divisions before it acquired the name of 'Adelaide' in July. By the middle of August it was a cemetery of ninety graves and then the great Allied advance of 8 August put an end to its use. After the Armistice 864 graves were brought in from small graveyards and isolated positions, north, west and south of Villers-Bretonneux. Without exception, they were men who fell from March to September 1918. Plot III is almost entirely Australian and Australian graves predominate in the cemetery with a total of 519; another four Diggers have unknown graves.

Thirty-seven of these Diggers had formerly been buried in Embankment Cemetery, which was used by the 2nd and 4th Divisions from the end of April to July 1918. It was a little west of Adelaide Cemetery, beside the railway and behind an Advanced Dressing Station. Another twenty-three came in from White Château Cemetery, between Abbey Wood and the railway, 1.2 kilometres west of Adelaide Cemetery.

There are 365 British servicemen, twenty-two Canadians and forty-eight from unknown units. The 13th Australian Infantry Brigade (49th, 50th, 51st and 52nd Battalions) erected a wooden memorial cross in the cemetery to commemorate its dead in the Villers-Bretonneux actions but it has long since disappeared. It was not in the cemetery in 1956 when I first visited it.

Many of the Diggers who lie in Adelaide Cemetery were killed in street-fighting in Villers-Bretonneux on Anzac Day 1918, but many encounters can be read from the dates of death. For instance, the 48th Battalion had four officers and 148 others killed at Monument Wood on 3 May. Three of the officers are buried in Adelaide Cemetery. They are Lieutenant Angus Ferguson (Grave III.K.2), Lieutenant Hugh Garland DCM (III.R.18) and Second Lieutenant Donovan Leutchford MM (III.K.8). Long ago somebody gave the grave of Private R. T. Simmons of the 34th Battalion a private grave marker, although he had the usual one at III.G.25. I have twice found the private marker leaning against graves in row H and have returned it to row G; on my next visit I found it in row K, propped against the graves of two 31st Battalion men.

Directions
Adelaide Cemetery is on the right side of the Amiens road, just beyond the railway crossing at the west end of Villers-Bretonneux.

Aubigny British Cemetery

This cemetery was made by Australian units, mainly the 54th, 55th, 56th and 57th Battalions, between

The entrance to Adelaide Cemetery, Villers-Bretonneux. It is the resting place of more than 500 Australians, most of them killed in the April–June period of 1918.

April and August 1918. It contains the graves of eighty-eight Diggers, only one of whom is unidentified, and seven British gunners. Early on 9 April 1918 heavy German bombardment hit Australian positions and destroyed the HQ of the 54th Battalion. Among the dead was the adjutant, Captain Norman Lovett MC and Bar, Croix de Guerre (Grave A.17). Also buried here is a soldier of the Australian Cyclist Corps, a unit which receives little mention in records of the war. He is Corporal Edward Callanan, killed on 18 April (Grave B.16). The Cyclist Corps men, actually infantry on wheels, were supposed to be able to move quickly and independently to a threatened part of the front.

Directions
From Villers-Bretonneux, take the Fouilloy road past the Australian National Memorial to Fouilloy village. At the T-junction turn left to Aubigny, 2 kilometres. The cemetery is on the west side of the old Fouilloy-Corbie-Daours road.

Cerisy-Gailly Military Cemetery, Somme

The cemetery was begun in February 1917 and used until March 1918. Following the recapture of the village in August the cemetery was used by AIF units. After the Armistice it was increased by the concentration of 539 graves from Mericourt Military Cemetery and from the battlefields of the Somme. It is the resting place of eighty-one Australians among another 773 British and Dominion servicemen.

The Diggers were killed either in July or August 1918 and twenty-four of them died on 8 August, the first day of the Allied offensive. Most of them were hit in the attack on Morcourt. Another nine were killed on 22 August during the attack on Bray and Etinehem. Among the Diggers is Lieutenant Frederick Appleton, 14th Battalion, and a friend of Albert Jacka VC. Appleton and Jacka were in action together on Pozières Heights (Grave III.E.1). Captain Harold Burke MC, 5th Battalion, also lies at Cerisy-Gailly. Active throughout the advance after 8 August, Burke was to have been left out of battle on 23 August when his battalion was advancing on Proyart. He had pleaded not to be left out and on this day he darted from place to place to keep the advancing troops going under the enemy fire. A drop-short shell from his own artillery killed him (Grave II.A.19).

Another forty-four Australians are buried in the French National Cemetery, next to the British cemetery. All were killed in September 1918 and eight of them, from the 39th Battalion, were killed during a German air attack on 10 September.

Directions
From Albert, proceed to Sailly-le-Sec, passing the 3rd Division Memorial, then to Sailly-Laurette. Cross the Somme by the D42, signposted Lamotte-Warfusée, and at the first crossroads turn right to Cerisy. After 1.1 kilometres, take the second turn left to the cemetery.

Fouilloy Communal Cemetery

Fouilloy was the home of the 28th CCS from September to November 1915, and in April 1918 the No. 53 CCS and No. 41 Stationary Hospital were in the town. The cemetery contains the graves of twenty-five Australians, twelve from the UK and one Canadian. That no soldier had a safe job, even if a member of a non combat unit, is shown by the grave of Major Cyril Seelenmeyer MC, Australian Army Veterinary Corps. Seelenmeyer died of wounds received on 8 August 1918 while attending to some wounded artillery horses. Nearby is Captain Ronald Bingle, 4th Pioneers, who, like Seelenmeyer, was killed by a shellburst. He had been reconnoitring along the Somme riverbank.

Directions
The cemetery is on the edge of Fouilloy on the way to Aubigny. See directions for Aubigny British Cemetery.

Heath Cemetery, Harbonnières

This cemetery was so named because of the wide, flat expanse of country on which it stands, and over which the Australians fought. It was made after the Armistice and soldiers buried on several battlefields between Bray and Harbonnières were gathered into it. There are 985 soldiers and airmen from Australia buried here, as well as 860 British soldiers, nine Canadians, six New Zealanders and two South Africans. The unnamed graves number 369 and

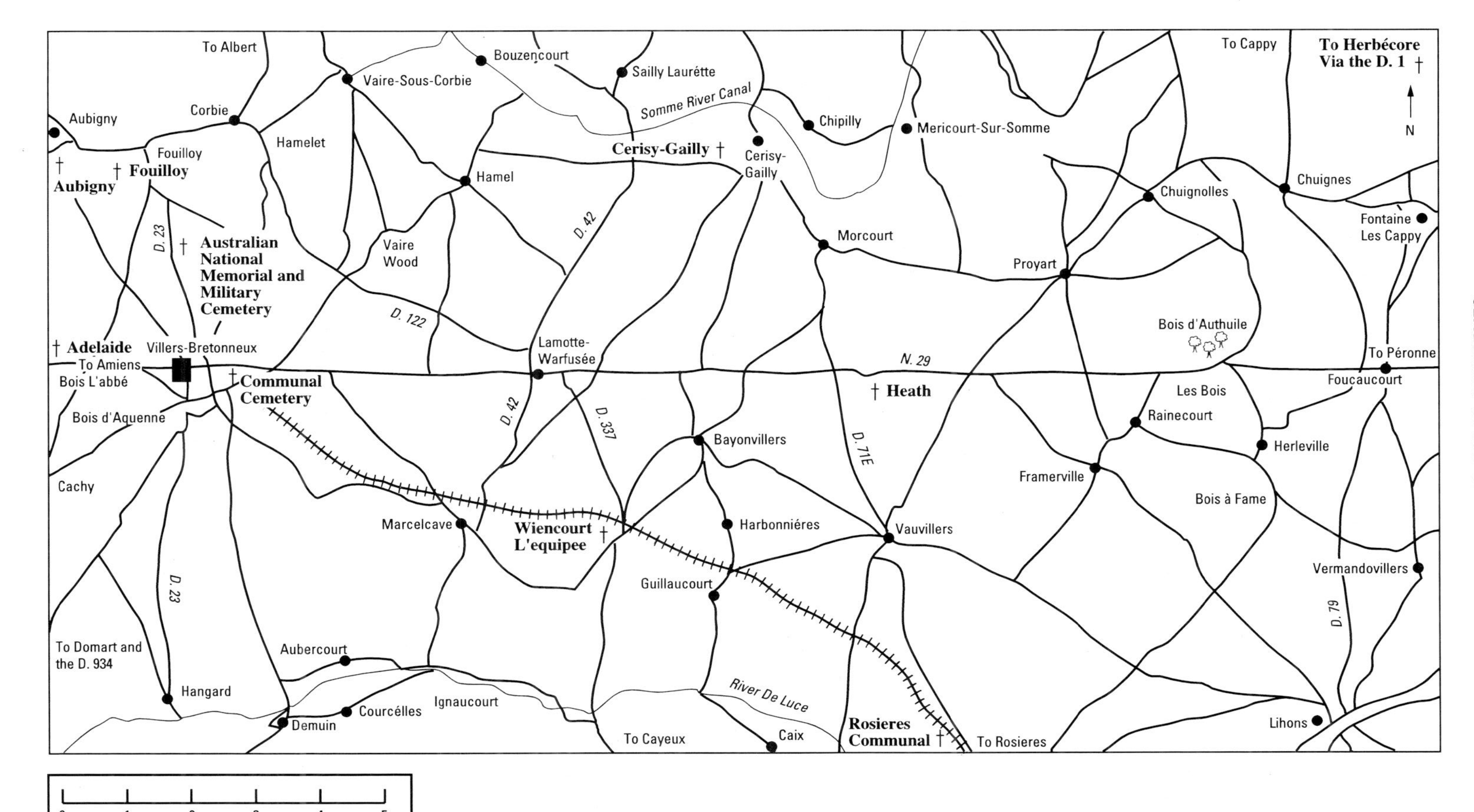

Map 11. South of the Somme: Cemeteries

special memorials commemorate twenty-four Diggers believed to be buried at Heath Cemetery and another two whose graves could not be found.

Australians were brought in from first burial places at Bayonvillers, Rosières, Vauvillers, Herleville, Lone House Cemetery at Harbonnières, Marignolles, Morcourt, Proyart, Lihons and Sailly-Laurette. Some were killed in March-April 1918 but the great majority died in August 1918. They include Private Robert Beatham VC, 15th Battalion (Grave VII.J.13) and Lieutenant Alfred Gaby VC, 28th Battalion (V.E.14).

Many other distinguished Australian soldiers lie in Heath Cemetery. They include the gallant Lieutenant-Colonel John Milne DSO, who as CO of the 36th Battalion was responsible for the famous charge at Villers-Bretonneux on 4 April 1918 (Grave VIII.J.19). Milne's friend, Lieutenant-Colonel Ernest Knox-Knight, CO of the 37th Battalion, is also at Heath. Knox-Knight's battalion led the Australian column along the Villers-Bretonneux — La Flaque road on 10 August in an attack regarded by many officers as 'a mad stunt'. Knox-Knight told a tank commander: 'There'll be a trainload of VCs waiting for us when we get back, if it's a success, but we won't want them if we get through with our lives'. During a night of heavy fighting, he lost his life (Grave V.B.15).

Buried side by side are Lieutenant Edward Bice MC, a pilot, with Lieutenant John Chapman, his observer, both of 3rd Squadron AFC. On 8 August 1918 they were active over the German lines, marking on maps the position of enemy trenches and batteries and the advance of British and Australian units and tanks. They dropped these maps at the HQs of divisions and corps. While engaged in this valuable but dangerous work the Australians were shot down (Grave I.1.12).

Lieutenant C. A. Auchterlonie MC and Bar, 25th Battalion, was a casualty on 10 August. A fine exponent of 'peaceful penetration' techniques, Auchterlonie, aged 22, had attracted much attention by his gallant leadership. On the night of his death he was trying to find another battalion in the dark, just south of Framerville, when killed by a single shot (Grave I.D.12).

An outstanding NCO, Corporal Francis Shaw DCM, 43rd Battalion, had greatly distinguished himself at the Battle of Hamel. A Lewis gunner, Shaw fired his gun from the hip in taking a German strongpoint, enabling his unit's advance to continue. A little later, as the 43rd was entering Hamel, Shaw was even more daring. From a distance of 100

Lieutenant Alfred Gaby VC is buried in Heath Cemetery, east of Villers-Bretonneux. He was killed in another outstanding exploit in an advance made by several AIF battalions as part of the Allied offensive of August 1918.

metres, he advanced, firing from the hip, on another enemy machine-gun post. A German officer, firing a revolver, ran out at the Australian only to be killed. Unscathed, Shaw reached the post and was out of ammunition for his Lewis gun as the last German survivor rushed him. Shaw hit him on the head with his revolver and when he still showed fight, shot him. In the post he had captured were eight dead Germans. Shaw's day was not yet finished. He attacked three enemy machine-gun posts at once, considered the odds a little too unfavourable and hailed a passing tank. While its crew, with machine-guns took on two of the German positions, driving the enemy into a dugout, Shaw captured the third position. He brought out an officer and twenty men. Why Corporal Shaw was awarded the DCM rather than the supreme VC is difficult to understand. Aged

23, he died of wounds on 12 August. He had trekked from a farm on Cape York peninsula to join the AIF and die on the Somme (Grave VII.D.10).

Directions
Heath Cemetery is by the right (south) side of the N29, 6 kilometres from Villers-Bretonneux on the way to Peronne.

Herbécore British Cemetery

This cemetery might be better known as Herbécore Australian Cemetery since fifty-one of the fifty-nine burials are Australian. The British made the first burials in the small village in February and March 1917. Herbécore fell into German hands in March 1918 and the AIF 6th Infantry Brigade recaptured it on 29 August. By September the cemetery was completed. Isolated deep in a wheat field it looks lonely and forgotten, but it is regularly cared for by the CWGC gardeners.

An outstanding young leader, Lieutenant Stanley Colless MC, DCM, 55th Battalion, is buried here. He was killed on 1 September at Mont St Quentin. His close friend, Captain Fred Cotterell MC, was killed next day while reconnoitring at Mont St Quentin. Lieutenant D. McArthur MC, 54th Battalion, was examining a footbridge at Peronne on 1 September when a machine-gun, high on the battlements of the old castle, killed him. Lieutenant Frank Holder of the same battalion was killed by a field gun the same day. Private Robert Bartholomew, a member of that forgotten unit, the Australian Cyclist Corps, is buried here, yet another casualty of 1 September.

Directions
The cemetery is on the D1, the Cappy — Peronne road, at the western edge of the village. If travelling from Peronne, Herbécourt is 0.5 kilometre after you cross the great Autoroute du Nord.

Rosières Communal Cemetery Extension

The town of Rosières was the scene of much fighting in the period 1914–17, before any AIF involvement on the sector. On 9 August 1918, following a stubborn resistance, the place was recaptured by the Canadians and, on their left, the AIF 2nd Brigade, facing Lihons. Most of the sixty-six Australians in the communal cemetery extension were killed in the fighting of 9–10 August. The 8th Battalion lost fourteen men who are buried here and the 5th Battalion eleven men. Private Robert Beatham, 8th Battalion, won his posthumous VC in this battle.

Directions
From Villers-Bretonneux, take the N29 east and turn right on to the D329, signposted Framerville-Rainecourt. From here, Rosières-de Santerre (also known as Rosières-de-Picardie) is signposted. The cemetery is on the edge of town as you approach it.

Villers-Bretonneux Military Cemetery

This cemetery is actually within the neighbouring commune of Fouilloy and was made after the Armistice by the concentration of graves from other burial grounds and from the battlefields. Plot 1 to XX were made by 1920 and contain a majority of Australian graves. Plots IIIA, XIIIA and XVA and some rows in other plots lettered AA were made by 1925 and contain a much larger proportion of unidentified graves. Almost all the graves in Plots I to XX are of the period March–August 1918. The cemetery contains 779 Australians (forty-seven unidentified), 1089 British servicemen, 267 Canadians, four South Africans and two New Zealanders.

Several decorated Diggers lie in this cemetery. They include Lieutenant James Bruce MC, DCM, 34th Battalion (Grave VIII.C.8); Lieutenant Lawrence Brunton MC, Field Artillery, (XIX.F.8); Lance-Corporal William Butler MM, 13th Battalion (XII.A.7); Corporal Leo Campbell DCM, MM, 3rd Battalion (XX.D.7); Sergeant William Dickson DCM, MM, 48th Battalion (XIX.A.2).

The most decorated Digger in Villers-Bretonneux cemetery is Lieutenant Eric Edgerton DSO, MM and Bar. Edgerton, only 21 at the time of his death, was a soldier of outstanding capacity, energy and leadership. He had been at Gallipoli in 1915 and won his first MM there. The DSO, which is rarely awarded to a junior officer, was a reward for his distinguished work at the Battle of Ville-sur-Ancre in May 1918, where he had been largely reponsible for the Australian success. He was killed on 11 August (Grave XX.A.3). A 19-year-old private with the DCM and MM, Richard Nicholls of the 46th Battalion, died of wounds on 11 August (Grave XI.C.1).

Many brave men did not live long enough to be decorated. Lieutenant Culmer Cockrill, 26th Battalion, was making straight for a German machine-gun on 8 August 1918 and was killed just as he reached it (Grave XIII.A.5). Major William Craies, 52nd Battalion, held the line together at Monument Wood on 25 April but was mortally wounded (Grave X.E.9). Lieutenant Hugh McColl, 38th Battalion, after excellent service at Proyart on 12 August 1918, was found dead in a wheatfield. Captain Albert Yates, 35th Battalion and a regular soldier from RMC Duntroon, led the Australians at the most serious part of the fighting at Accroche Wood on 8 August. He was gassed and wounded and after a while was reported missing. When found next day he was dead (Grave XIX.B.2).

Directions

From Villers-Bretonneux, cross the N29 by the D23, signposted Fouilloy and Corbie. After 1 kilometre the cemetery is on the right, with broad marble steps and an imposing entrance. The ground here is convex and the Australian National Memorial beyond the cemetery is not clearly visible from the cemetery entrance.

Villers-Bretonneux Communal Cemetery

Of the twelve soldiers buried here, ten are Australian. Four of them were killed during the First Battle of Villers-Bretonneux. Some of the Diggers died of wounds. The cemetery is on the west side of the town.

The entrance to the tower of the Australian National Memorial at Villers Bretonneux. On either side are screen walls bearing the names, by unit, of the 11 000 Diggers who have no known grave in France. All official ceremonies, such as Anzac Day, are held here.

Chapter 11

Mont St Quentin - Peronne

As a fighting machine, the AIF reached full maturity in the period August to October 1918, the final months of the war for the Corps as a whole though not for certain units. Field-Marshal Haig, having spent the entire war reinforcing failure, considered the results of the fighting between 8 and 21 August, and urged his generals to reinforce success. He told them: 'The most resolute offensive is everywhere desirable', and added: 'Let each one of us act energetically and without hesitation push forward to our objective'. He modified his instructions to General Rawlinson, commanding the Fourth Army and under whose authority came Monash's Australian Corps. The Fourth Army could afford to relax a little after its successes and there was no immediate need to push the Germans from the great bend of the Somme near Peronne.

Monash, convinced that the Australian Corps was invincible, had other ideas. While the 1st and 4th Divisions went into reserve, the others were to press forward, the 3rd north of the river, the 2nd and 5th south of it. Monash wanted a great and wholly Australian achievement, even though all units were much below strength and tanks and guns were in short supply.

His strategic objective was to make the line of the Somme River useless to the Germans as a defensive position and thus hasten their retreat to the Hindenburg Line. The tactic by which he planned to achieve this was an attack on the key position of the whole line, the dominating hill of Mont St Quentin. Lying 1.5 kilometres north of the river town of Peronne, the hill's defences guarded its northern and western approaches. The hill was only 100 metres high but the Germans regarded it as impregnable.

Monash held conferences at each of the three divisions' HQ. On 31 August the 5th Division was to capture the Peronne bridges, then a wooded spur east of the town. 2nd Division was to aim for the bridgehead of Halle, then capture Mont St Quentin. The 3rd Division, operating on the 2nd's left, would seize high ground north-east of Clery and then Bouchavesnes spur. The constant advances of the 3rd Division north of the Somme had already prepared the ground for the 2nd Division to cross from the southern bank.

Marshal Ludendorff and his General Staff were aware of the importance of Mont St Quentin but to make certain of it they sent the 2nd Prussian Guards Division to hold the hill 'to the death'. The garrison of Peronne itself was formed of volunteers, who had scores of machine-guns to mow down any assault. The river flats lying in the angle of the Somme between Clery, Mont St Quentin and Peronne were thick with barbed wire defences. Cover for any attacking force was scant and the few ruins were manned as strongpoints by the Germans.

Bouchavesnes-Bergen

Three kilometres north of Mont St Quentin the village of Bouchavesnes, on the Bapaume road, was the 3rd Division's objective on 30–31 August 1918. After several weeks of combat, the battalions of the 9th and 10th Brigades each had only 300 men fit to fight and they were dazed with exhaustion. Patrols of the 13th Light Horse made reconnaissance patrols into the difficult country around Bouchavesnes and at least saved the infantry this arduous work.

One kilometre south of Bouchavesnes is Bois Madame, known to the Australians as Road Wood. The 33rd Battalion (Lieutenant-Colonel L. J. Morshead) was attacking this wood from the direction of Clery. It was garrisoned by many Germans who had, it was later found, hundreds of machine-guns. At 6.20 a.m. the battalion was held up by what Colonel Morshead described as

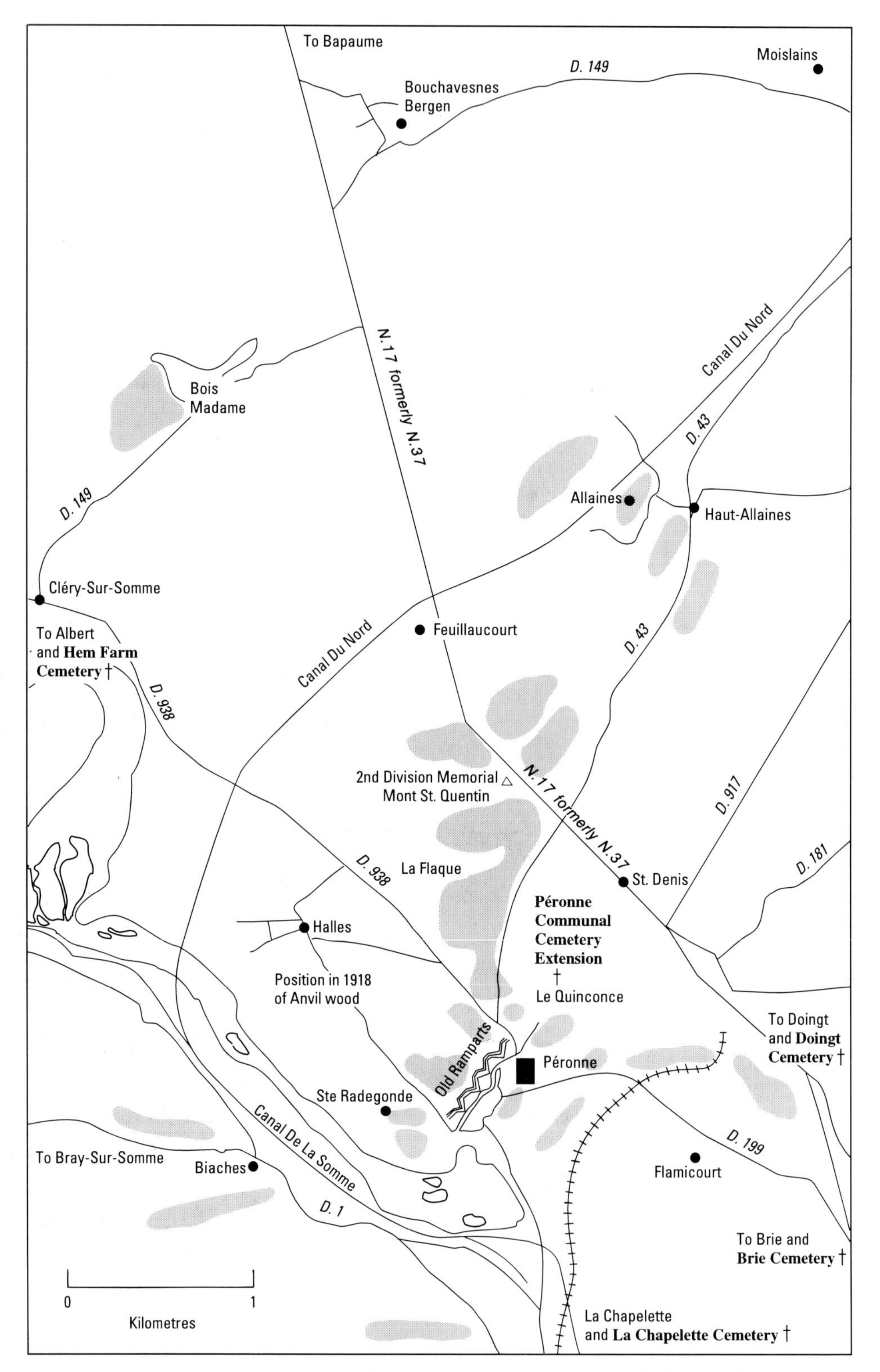

Map 12. Mont St Quentin and Peronne Battle Areas (Shaded) and Cemeteries

'exceedingly heavy fire' enfilading the companies from the south-west edge of the wood. Private George Cartwright stood up in this withering fire and advanced by himself, firing his rifle from the shoulder. He killed three of the enemy gun-team, then rushed forward and threw a bomb into the post. As it exploded, he charged to capture the gun and take prisoner the eight Germans who survived his attack. An amazing scene then occurred. The whole battalion stood up, wildly cheered Cartwright and then, inspired by his example, returned to the attack.

Directions

From Peronne, having visited Mont St Quentin, continue along the N37 to Bouchavesnes. The main part of the village is 200 metres east of the road. The Diggers were active in the valleys and on the slopes east and south-east of the settlement towards Moislains to the east and Allaines to the south-east. The 3rd Division's front ran from Bouchavesnes to Allaines.

George Cartwright's VC exploit

Stop your car on the southern edge of the N37 at the southern edge of Bouchavesnes. Walk down the farm road to the left — actually along the Vallée Malamin — 1 kilometre to Bois Madame. At the end of the wood, turn left along its southern edge to the next corner of the wood. It was here that Cartwright made his attack. The walk can be made only in summer. (Some maps show N37 as N17.)

Mont St Quentin

The 2nd Division's assault began at 5 a.m. on 29 August when its artillery opened on the mount. The 5th Brigade — the 17th, 18th, 19th and 20th Battalions — opened the infantry attack. The troops numbered only seventy officers and 1250 other ranks, scarcely one third of a brigade's normal strength. On the right, the 17th Battalion started along the Clery-Peronne road and quickly demoralised the Germans. The 20th came up from the flats to make a bayonet charge and capture Gottleib trench. General Rawlinson had not begun breakfast when he heard that the Australians had captured Mont St Quentin. He called it 'the finest feat of the war'. The AIF's reputation since the Battle of Hamel had preceded it and had terrified even the Prussian Guards, but the feat was not yet complete.

The 5th Brigade had fought its way to the summit but after a fierce struggle, the Germans, in overwhelming numbers, forced the Australians back across the trench-scored crest and through the wire to a point half-way down the slope. Here they held their ground. That night the 6th Brigade relieved the

The battle honours of the 2nd Division as shown on a bronze plaque on the memorial at Mont St Quentin, Peronne.

Above: 2nd Division gunners played a major part in supporting their infantry at Mont St Quentin. Their work was commemorated in bronze on the division's memorial.

Left: The 2nd Division Digger stands astride his plinth on Mont St Quentin. This town was captured by the AIF in a great feat of arms in September 1918. The Digger faces north-east, the direction of the AIF's attack at Mont St Quentin. This is one of the finest AIF memorials on the Western Front.

5th and at daylight renewed the attack and captured the village. The Germans counter-attacked and the Victorians were forced to pull back. At midday the Australian artillery opened a heavy bombardment and at the point of the bayonet the 6th Brigade again advanced, to gain a foothold on the crest. Next morning, the 7th Brigade took up the fight and finally drove the Germans from the vital height.

Three VCs were won at or near Mont St Quentin, by Sergeant Albert Lowerson, 21st Battalion, Private Robert Mactier, 23rd Battalion (posthumous award) and Lieutenant Edgar Towner, of the 2nd Machine-Gun Battalion, attached to the 24th Infantry Battalion.

Lowerson's battalion, with the 23rd and 24th, went into action on 1 September to take positions not attacked the previous day. Lowerson's company advanced through the right of Mont St Quentin village, where several strongpoints were dealt with. Troops on the left were stopped in front of a great crater where resolute Germans manned machine-guns and were throwing grenades. Lowerson arranged and led the charge to clear the position and capture twelve machine-guns and thirty prisoners.

Robert Mactier's VC exploit has been called a one-man offensive. The 23rd Battalion was attempting to move into position for an attack on positions at Mont St Quentin. The leading company, under Lieutenant F. J. Jenkins, was blocked in Florina Trench by a barbed-wire barricade and Jenkins sent Private Mactier to investigate. Mactier found that Corporal R. Finlay had started an assault but had been killed and the attack was stalled. Mactier, armed with a revolver and grenades, dashed through the leading Australians right to the barricade. Throwing a bomb, he climbed over the wire, killed the gun-crew and threw the weapon out of the trench. He captured the garrison of a second post and with barely a pause he attacked and killed the occupants of a third post. While attacking a fourth position he was riddled by machine-gun fire. His persistent courage enabled the battalion to reach its position.

The task of Edgar Towner, with his section of machine-guns was to help the 24th Battalion reach its main objective, the summit of the mount. During the early part of the advance Towner captured single-handedly an enemy machine-gun and by turning it on the enemy inflicted casualties. Skilfully handling his guns, he cut off and captured twenty-five enemy, and then gave the necessary support to the infantry assault. It was recognised that by his courage, energy, fortitude and tactical skill, he played a major part in the victory at Mont St Quentin.

After the war the 2nd Division erected its memorial by the roadside on Mont St Quentin to commemorate its great success. Atop a large marble plinth, a Digger symbolically bayoneted a German eagle. On the sides of the plinth are bronze plaques listing the division's battle honours and illustrating aspects of infantry and artillery in battle. The infantry scene depicts Australians storming an enemy trench.

Germans who occupied France during the Second World War were affronted by the Digger and his dying eagle and removed them. They have not been seen since. However, the Germans did not damage the plinth or the bronze plaques and in 1971 a new and splendid memorial was erected. It is an outsize bronze figure of a Digger in characteristic pose, feet apart, rifle slung over his shoulder, head bowed reflectively. It is one of the finest memorials on the Western Front.

Directions

Mont St Quentin can be reached by the N37 from Bapaume or the D938 from Albert. The 2nd Division's Digger memorial stands in lawns, in between houses, and a little back from the road. For the length of its passage through the village the road is called Avenue des Australiens. Behind the Digger is the Somme River, 2 kilometres distant, and between the river and the mount are the fields across which the 2nd Division's men advanced. Their forming up area was in front of the village of Halle, half-right from the memorial as you face it. In 1918 the N37 was a German trench, which the 5th Brigade captured. The main German trenches crossed the road and ran from north to south. The Digger faces north but the Australians were actually advancing eastwards. (Some maps show N37 as N17.)

Edgar Towner's VC exploits

About 100 metres on the Bapaume side of the 2nd Division memorial is a local road to the right, leading to the communal cemetery. Towner's area of activity was along this road and in the general vicinity. The crater where he captured the many machine-guns was to the right rear of the cemetery.

Robert Mactier's VC exploit

Florina Trench, from where the 23rd Battalion and Robert Mactier made their advance, crossed the N37 where the D43 Peronne — Haut-Allaines now crosses it. The Gendarmerie is near the corner. Mactier's single-handed fight took place in the field to the east of the crossroads.

Alby Lowerson's VC exploit

In effect, this was in conjunction with the actions of Edgar Towner. Lowerson and his company of the 21st Battalion were moving around the mount from the right while Towner was to the left. Both men were active at the quarry and crater near the cemetery.

Almost opposite the Australian memorial is a short street leading to a wood, the site of German positions in 1918. Shallow shell holes can easily be seen in the wood and I have found several Australian shell nosecaps and other relics of the battle here.

Peronne

In German hands, the town of Peronne was a fortress. To the west and south it had the natural defences of the Somme River and its swamps. To a large extent these water defences also covered the south-east. In addition, the ancient town was virtually surrounded by a moat and by stout ramparts, where the Germans had posted many machine-guns. Finally, belts of barbed wire protected the approaches to the town. Fortress Peronne had prevented General French from advancing in July–August 1916, although his troops reached Biaches, 1.5 kilometres west on the west bank of the Somme. In March 1917, before withdrawing to the Hindenburg Line, the Germans destroyed much of Peronne but a year later they regained the place and rebuilt its defences.

Parts of the 5th Division crossed the Somme Bridge at Brie, 3 kilometres south of Peronne. Some units of the 2nd Division crossed by a wooden bridge further north of Brie. Other troops crossed on light bridges of floats put together by the Australian Engineers.

The 14th Brigade's task on 1–2 September was to clear the area between Peronne and Mont St Quentin and capture Peronne if possible. The 54th Battalion, given the sector on the right, was to take the ground between the Somme and Peronne, which was liberally laced with barbed wire. While Australian Lewis gunners fought German machine-gunners other Diggers ran to the wire, wrenched out the pickets and crawled under the wire. At the second line of trenches, the battalion's advance was stopped by machine-gun posts. Corporal Alex Buckley and Corporal Arthur Hall, in separate actions, stalked then rushed the gunners. In this way they captured several small parties of prisoners and machine-guns and opened the way for the battalion. Because of Hall's bravery and then his courageous reconnaissance, large parts of the battalion made a comparatively easy crossing of the waterways and reached the centre of the town. Buckley was killed while rushing another enemy strongpoint.

The 53rd's task on the morning of 1 September was to clear a large area of ground skirting Anvil Wood and the village ramparts and then link with other battalions. The Germans strongly contested this advance and the 53rd sustained many casualties. The right portion of the unit entered Anvil Wood and came under fire from a 77 millimetre field-gun but Private William Currey rushed forward, killed the gun crew and captured it single-handedly. Later he rushed a machine-gun post and destroyed it. Finally, he volunteered to bring out an isolated 53rd Company which was in danger of being caught by Australian shellfire. Hall, Buckley and Currey each won the VC.

The 2nd Division had eighty-four officer casualties and 1286 others in the Battles of Mont St Quentin and Peronne. The 3rd Division suffered forty-three and 544; the 5th Division, forty-four and 1026 casualties. This was 20 per cent of the attacking force.

Directions

Peronne is now many times larger than it was in 1918 and most of the ground which Corporals Hall and Buckley crossed under fire is now a lake, the Etang du Can. The 54th had to cross the moat from the west of the present lake, at its centre. Anvil Wood has shrunk considerably, nevertheless it it possible to place the site of Currey's VC exploit as being near the rear of the communal cemetery. From the centre of Peronne, take the D43 signposted Mont St Quentin. After 0.5 kilometre, at the top of a hill, the cemetery is signposted right.

Soldiers of the 2nd, 3rd and 5th Divisions were all round Peronne in their persistent efforts to flush out the German defenders, especially in the suburbs of Flamicourt, Ste Radegond, le Quinconce, Doingt (2 kilometres east), and Brie (4 kilometres south).

The town of Peronne has built an 'Historial', a complex which depicts many aspects of war in France. It is a national centre of record and of education with much reference to the First World War.

In 1918 the Diggers gave the main street in Peronne the name Roo de Kanga. It meant nothing to the local people when they returned to their battered homes but Australians are regarded with affection in the town. They should be: many hundreds are buried in the military cemeteries of the town and district.

Allaines

After the capture of Mont St Quentin, fighting continued on 2 September with the Germans being pressed back steadily. Many of them took up positions in the twin villages of Allaines and Haut-Allaines which lie on the Canal du Nord, 2 kilometres south of Bouchavesnes and the same distance north-east of Mont St Quentin. The only unit of the 3rd Division then remaining in the line, the 43rd, was given the task of clearing a triangle of ground between the 2nd Division, advancing north-east, and a British division which was heading east.

The attack went well but as the Germans were driven back their fire became more concentrated until it was so heavy it stopped the 43rd's advance. Corporal Lawrence Weathers rushed in and bombed the Germans in two trenches, the garrison's leader being one of his victims. Returning for more bombs, Weather went out again, this time leading three mates in an attack under heavy fire. While Lance-Corporal H. H. Thompson, with a Lewis gun, kept enemy heads down, Weathers stood on the parapet and bombed them. He captured three machine-guns and 180 prisoners. On 28 September, when with his unit in the Beaurevoir Line, Weathers was seriously wounded and died the next day, before having learnt of the VC awarded for his gallantry on 2 September.

Directions

Lawrence Weathers' battalion was operating along the northern bank of the Canal du Nord. From the crossroads in Mont St Quentin, take the D43 to Haut-Allaines and in that village turn left and pass a small wood to a T-junction. Turn right and cross the bridge over the Canal du Nord. Scutari Trench, which Weathers attacked and captured, crossed the field to the left of this road and parallel to it. *Note:* the site cannot be reached by car from Allaines, only from Haut-Allaines.

Chapter 12

Cemeteries around Peronne - Mont St Quentin of Australian Interest

Brie British Cemetery

South of Peronne, the cemetery was begun by British and Australian units after the capture of the village during the fighting for Peronne in September 1918. Of the 442 graves, twenty-seven are Australians, all killed in September and October 1918. Among them is one of the most outstanding AIF NCOs of the war, Sergeant William Lehane DCM, MM, 4th Battalion Machine-Gun Corps. Lehane had shown great daring at Etinehem on 13 August. Scouting ahead of his two machine-gun posts, he saw some men in the moonlight and challenged them. When they fired at him he rushed them and they ran into a dugout. The sergeant stood over the entrance, with pistol on one hand and grenade in the other, and ordered the Germans to come out. He was amazed when sixty filed out as prisoners. Calling to two Australians to help him, Lehane marched the large party in. Aged 25, Lehane died on 18 September of wounds received in fighting east of Brie (Grave I.A.4). Close to Lehane's grave is that of Second Lieutenant Roland Machin, Australian Flying Corps, who also died of wounds on 18 September, received in air combat.

Directions

From Peronne, take the N17 to Villers-Carbonnel. At the crossroads in this village turn left on the N336, 1.5 kilometres across the Somme to Brie. Here turn right on the D88 for St Christ-Briost. After 1 kilometre the cemetery is on the left.

Doingt Communal Cemetery Extension

Doingt was captured by the 5th Division on 5 September 1918, the village being completely destroyed in the fighting. In the same month three CCSs based themselves in Doingt and remained until October. The cemetery was made in three plots. Plot I contained only British and Dominion burials, Plot II only American and Plot III the graves of both armies. The 115 American graves were removed by the American Graves Registration Service for concentration in purely American Cemeteries. Now there are 417 graves, sixty-seven of them Australian.

One Digger died in particularly tragic circumstances. Lieutenant John Simmonds, 12th Battalion, was in the advance against Templeux-le-Guérard when struck by short shooting from Australian guns. Seriously wounded, he was taken to a CCS at Doingt and died there (Grave I.C.13). Also in Doingt Cemetery is Lieutenant Cecil Jack McDonald MC, 3rd Battalion, who had been prominent in 'peaceful penetration' operations at Merris, French Flanders. At Hargicourt on 18 September, he was wounded by a machine-gun firing down the Bony-Hargicourt roads and died in a Doingt CCS the next day (Grave I.C.22). Company Sergeant-Major Bert Redding DCM, a distinguished soldier of the 54th Battalion, died of wounds on 2 October (Grave III.A.5). Sergeant George Fowden, 37th Battalion, one of the relatively few Australians to be awarded the Meritorious Service Medal, was killed in action 1 October (Grave III.C.14). Sergeant William Lorensini DCM, 10th Light Trench-Mortar Battery, is buried at Doingt (Grave I.C.31).

Directions

From Peronne take the D944 Tertry road for 2 kilometres to Doingt. Enter the town, which is just off the road, and follow the cemetery signs. The military extension is on the far side of the civil cemetery, next to farm fields.

Hem Farm Military Cemetery, Hem-Monacu

The commune of Hem-Monacu lies on the north bank of the Somme, west of Peronne. The cemetery, on the west side of a large farm, was begun by British units in March 1917 and used until the following March. Australian units buried 138 of their dead in it, all from the fighting in August and September 1918. Most of these Diggers were killed during the advance on Peronne and Mont St Quentin. The cemetery has another 663 graves, 205 of them unnamed. Private Robert Mactier, who was killed on 1 September 1918, while performing acts of gallantry which resulted in the award of the VC, is buried in this cemetery (Grave II.J.3). Another eighteen of Mactier's mates of the 23rd Battalion also lie here. The death of Lieutenant George Dutton, 38th Battalion, sets a sad note. He was scout officer of his unit, which fought and moved without respite from 26 August to 29 August and at last rested at Curlu. Having been without sleep for 72 hours, some officers collapsed asleep. George Dutton wanted a 'swim and a good feed' first. He barely had time for both before the battalion was on the move again and he was killed a few hours later, near Hem (Grave II.C.3).

Directions
From Peronne, take the D938, signposted Clery-sur-Somme. After Clery, the road is signposted Albert. Cross over the A1 motorway and within 300 metres turn left to Monacu, a minor crossroad. Turn right to Hem-Monacu. Pass through the village to the only T-Junction. Turn left and immediately right to the large farm and cemetery.

The grave of Private Bob Mactier, a VC winner at Mont St Quentin. He is buried at Hem Farm Cemetery, close to the Somme River.

La Chapelette British and Indian Cemeteries, Peronne

Various CCS's were situated close to this cemetery, south of Peronne, in 1917 and 1918. Forty-nine Australians are buried here, together with 203 British soldiers, thirty-one from India and one from new Zealand. With two exceptions, the Australians were killed during September 1918 in fighting east of Peronne. One was killed on 1 October and one in April 1918. This Digger, Corporal William Revaillion, had been wounded and captured many miles west of Peronne and died as a prisoner, to be buried by the Germans. No fewer than twenty-one AIF units are represented in this cemetery.

One burial, that of Captain Hayward Moffatt MC, 1st Battalion, carries a memory of the 1st Battalion's mutiny on 20 September 1918. The battalion was due to go into action at Hargicourt but the men of one company believed that the Australians were being asked to do more than their share and often had to make good British failures. Captain Moffatt had come up from the battalion's nucleus camp, to find that the mutinous company had just lost its two remaining officers in a shellburst. He ordered the company to join his own for the imminent battle but all except one man refused and walked to the rear. They were joined by others and in the end 119 men walked away. Lieutenant Colonel B. V. Stacey and his HQ went forward with ten officers and eighty-four men. In the consequent battle at Hargicourt, Captain Moffatt led his company through the German barrage but fell seriously wounded. He was evacuated to the CCS at La

Chapelette, more than 12 kilometres to the rear, where he died (Grave I.H.5).

Directions
From Peronne, take the N17 south, signposted Villers-Carbonnel. From the centre of Peronne the cemetery is only 2 kilometres away on the N17.

Peronne Communal Cemetery Extension

Peronne fell into German hands on 24 September 1914. In March 1917 British divisions entered the town and the Communal Cemetery Extension was begun at that time. It was used by the Germans in 1918 and resumed by Australian units in September 1918, after their capture of the town. Even so, at the Armistice it contained only 177 graves. It was then enlarged by the concentration of 1494 graves from battlefields north and east of Peronne and from some small cemeteries. It now contains 512 Australian graves out of 1804. Another four Australians who are believed to be buried in the cemetery are commemorated by special memorials.

For Australians, this is a VC cemetery since Corporal Alexander Buckley VC, 54th Battalion, is buried here (Grave II.C.32). Among the many other decorated Australians buried here is Major Cedric Brodziak DSO, 3rd Battalion Australian Machine-Gun Corps. A fine soldier, Brodziak had been in several battles since 1915 and was killed on 1 September at Bouchavesnes, north of Mont St Quentin, while referring to his map (Grave V.P.1).

On 2 September at Mont St Quentin the 27th Battalion had nine officers hit. Among them was Lieutenant Victor Lampard MC (Grave III.C.13). The most decorated digger at Peronne is Corporal Frederick Thurston, 33rd Battalion, who was three times awarded the MM. He was one of only eighteen Australian soldiers to be so decorated. His first MM was awarded during the 1916 Somme campaign, his second at Messines in June 1917 and his third on the Somme again in May 1918. He was killed by machine-gun fire on 30 August (Grave IV.P.6). Apart from Thurston, another twelve Australians at Peronne held the MM.

On 1 September, between Bouchavesnes and Mont St Quentin the 41st Battalion met the fiercest fire ever experienced by the battalion and lost five officers and more than 100 men. The results of the action can be seen at Peronne where the senior 41st

Corporal A. H. Buckley, a VC winner at Peronne in September 1918, is buried in that town's communal cemetery.

officer is Captain William Uren (Grave IV.J.16). Some soldiers died at Peronne even before the battle commenced. A fine scout, Sergeant Hugh Barber MM, 28th Battalion, was sent to reconnoitre the main road bridge across the Somme from the south and was standing on it, looking over the side, when an enemy sniper shot him dead.

On 2 September at Mont St Quentin, Major Augustus Woods MC, senior company commander of the 26th Battalion, was killed by a hail of bullets. Woods had had narrow escapes in the earlier years of the war. On 2 March 1917 at Loupart Wood, north of Warlencourt on the Somme, he had led his men so impetuously close to the protective Australian barrage that he had been hit on the thigh by an Australian shell shard and was put out of the fighting for three months (Grave III.E.2).

Directions
From Mont St Quentin, if approaching by the N37 from Bapaume, turn right into the D43, signposted Peronne at the Gendarmerie. After 1 kilometre, soon after an oval on the right, turn left past the communal cemetery to the military extension. If approaching from the main street in Peronne, take the D43 Haut-Allaines road up a hill for 0.5 kilometre and turn right where the sign on the left indicates *hôpital*.

Chapter 13

East of Peronne

The Diggers were not to know it, but after their great victory at Mont St Quentin and Peronne they had ahead of them only another five weeks of active service. For the second time in the war (though on a different sector from that in 1917) their service would take them eastwards into the Hindenburg Outpost Line and then the Hindenburg Line itself. However, even before the end of the Peronne fighting the Australians were approaching the end of their physical endurance and only their spirit was driving them. On 31 August Major-General J. J. Hobbs, of the 5th Division, warned Monash that his division was at the end of its tether. As it happened, the strain on the 2nd and 3rd Divisions was even greater and some battalions were going into fights only 150-strong, instead of with the ideal number of 800, or the 650 once considered the 'critical minimum'. Soldiers on leave in London told the Australian Prime Minister, W. M. Hughes: 'There will be no AIF if they don't rest us soon'.

General Lord Rawlinson, the Fifth Army commander, influenced by the Australians' magnificent performance since 8 August, ordered the Australian Corps forward. Monash, in obedience to this order, directed the 3rd and 5th Divisions to pursue the Germans vigorously, with the 1st and 4th Divisions to take over on 10 September. True veterans after their years of campaigning, the Diggers somehow threw off their physical and mental weariness and showed amazing skill, dash and initative in these final weeks. It was as if they had sensed that the end of the war was in sight and were determined to finish it in style. During the month they won another six VCs, which certainly proved that the German troops remained formidable. The Germans contested every position, they never failed to counter-attack after a reverse and they exacted a terrible toll of Australian and British life. Wooden crosses marking the grave of Allied dead were to be seen in the ruins of every hamlet and village and in the fields.

Passing out of the *département* of the Somme, the Australians entered the Aisne. Here they were campaigning in rolling country of farmland and woods, through which two tributaries of the Somme, the Cologne and the Omignon, flow down to the Somme marshes. The river valleys, the Cologne in the north and the Omignon in the south, roughly marked the Australian Corps' front, a distance of about 12 kilometres. The river valleys are wide and tree-covered, with villages dotted throughout their length.

Just 22 kilometres east of Peronne was the Hindenburg Line, though it was really a series of lines which incorporated three old British front lines from earlier in the war. The Germans had their Outpost Line and the Main Line; also integrated into their defences was the St Quentin Canal, a major bastion against attacking troops.

The Diggers' first action in the last phase of the war occurred on 6 September when the 3rd Pioneer Battalion, fighting as infantry, captured Buire Wood, on a hill north of Tincourt. Between that fight and the final battle at Montbrehain on 5 October, lay battles or lesser actions at Hancourt, Joncourt, Estrées, Jeancourt, Templeux-le-Guérard, Hargicourt, Bellicourt, Hindenburg Outpost Line, Roisel, Vendelles, Le Verguier, Bellenglise, Nauroy, Beaurevoir, Ste Emilie, Ronssoy and Epehy. In addition, there were many instances of 'peaceful penetration'.

Directions

The AIF's campaign area in the Aisne is best explored with Peronne as a base. The D6 to Roisel takes the visitor into the heart of the area. No two villages are more than 6 kilometres apart and from Roisel the most important villages and small towns — important, that is, to Australians — can be visited. They are Hargicourt, Bellicourt, Le Verguier and Montbrehain. Bellenglise is important only because of the AIF 4th Division memorial nearby.

As always, the presence of a particular military cemetery can make a village important for certain visitors. With Peronne as a base, the Australian arena can be adequately seen in half a day.

It should be noted that during 1918 the Australians were not fighting in shell torn quagmires and great areas of mud, as they had on the Somme in the autumn and winter of 1916–17 and in the Ypres Salient of July–November 1917. Only while the Divisions made their attack against the Hindenburg Line on 29 September was the ground massively chewed up by shellfire. As a fairly accurate guide, the ground was in this state east from Gillemont Farm on the Ronssoy-Bony road, east from Quennemont Farm on the Hargicourt-Bony road and east from Cologne Farm on the Hargicourt-Bellicourt road. The AIF captured all these massive fortified farms. Quennemont was never rebuilt but

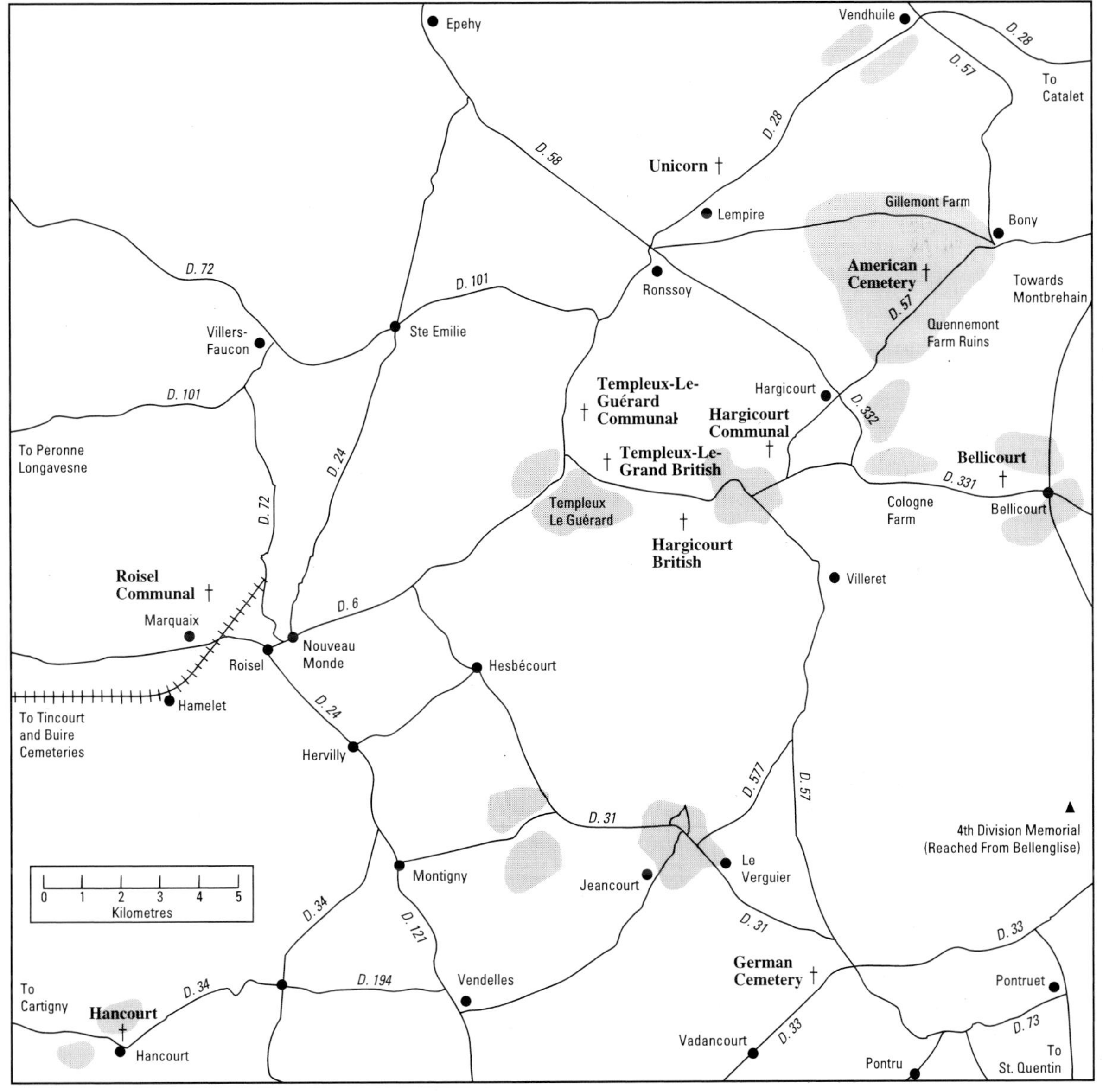

Map 13. East of Peronne: Battle Areas and Cemeteries.

Cologne and Gillemont are prominent today. Gillemont is 2 kilometres from Ronssoy and Cologne 1.5 kilometres from Hargicourt. They are the only farm buildings for several kilometres and stand out clearly.

Bellenglise

After the war, the 4th Division had several options for a site for its memorial and considered, among other places, Pozières, Passchendaele and Bullecourt. Its members decided on Bellenglise, lying on the St Quentin Canal east of Peronne. They decided to erect a characteristic AIF obelisk memorial on Les Chaudières, the dominant ridge above Bellenglise to the west. It was a good choice for here the 4th Division had fought its last fight of the war. Symbolically, it was the end of their campaign road which had begun at Pozières twenty-seven months earlier. While the selection was well made, the memorial is remote and isolated and apparently not visited by many Australian travellers. However, it is readily located.

The plaque of the 4th Division Memorial on the heights near Bellenglise and above the St Quentin Canal. The monument is the furthest east of all the AIF memorials.

Directions

From Peronne, take the N44 to Vermand. Without entering Vermand, turn left on to the D33 through Bihecourt and Vadancourt. 1 kilometre out of Vadancourt is a large German military cemetery: 2 kilometres further is the first settlement on this road, a farm and other buildings known as le Petit Arbre. Turn left on to a good farm road. After 1.2 kilometres turn right at the first crossroads which leads to a bridge over the motorway. The 4th Division's memorial is 0.5 kilometre on this road. Do not attempt to reach the memorial through the silos at Bellenglise; the track is rough even by Australian standards. Total distance from Peronne is 20 kilometres.

Bellicourt

Bellicourt is a village and commune between St Quentin and Cambrai. The St Quentin Canal passes under Bellicourt in a 5-kilometre tunnel. The Hindenburg Line ran west of the village and barges in the tunnel were used to shelter German reserves. About 5 kilometres south of Bellicourt, where the canal is open, is the village of Bellenglise, where another great tunnel or dugout was made by the Germans. The French-built St Quentin Canal Tunnel, captured on 29 September 1918, was first explored from the Bellicourt end by AIF 14th and 11th Field Companies, Australian Engineers, and some of the 5th Pioneer Battalion, who removed mines.

Estrées

On 3 October 1918 the 18th Battalion advanced on the enemy line at Estrées. An early casualty was the commander of the company whose second-in-command was Lieutenant Joe Maxwell. Taking command, Maxwell found his advance virtually stopped by machine-guns and rifle fire. Alone, he pushed through the enemy wire and captured the most dangerous gun after killing three and capturing four enemy.

Having led his company to its objective, Maxwell again went forward alone and silenced a machine-gun which had been blocking another company. A prisoner told him that the Germans in a nearby trench wanted to surrender but were afraid to give themselves up. With two men, Maxwell went to the trench but found himself surrounded by twenty men under an officer, who had no intention of surrender. Under his orders, the three Australians were grabbed and their weapons seized. In this crisis the enemy trench came under Australian shellfire, which caused confusion among the Germans. Maxwell kept an emergency revolver in his respirator case and, drawing it, he shot two Germans and escaped with his own men. Maxwell was the second most decorated Digger of the war after Harry Murray. (*See* **Gueudecourt, Pozières** and **Bullecourt**.) In the space of twelve months he won the DCM, the MC twice and, for his actions at Estrées, the VC.

Hargicourt

The 3rd Brigade of the 1st Division captured the village of Hargicourt in the major attack towards the Hindenburg Line on 18 September 1918. The Australian barrage was heavy and the German response no less intense. Captain Wally Hallahan was killed in this barrage and his men were distraught. Hallahan was an original member of the 11th Battalion and had been a machine-gunner. He had been in London on duty and was about to be married but put off his marriage when recalled to his battalion. Had he been married he would have qualified to join the 'Anzac leave' men then being shipped to Australia on home leave. Not far away from where Hallahan was killed, Captain E. W. Tulloch went ahead with two men and took on two enemy heavy machine-guns. In a 10-minute fight, Tulloch and his men killed or wounded the crews and captured the guns. Earlier in the year he might well have been recommended for the VC for this exploit, but such deeds had become common in the AIF. Nevertheless, he won the MC and before the war ended he became a Lieutenant-Colonel. At Hargicourt and in the area around it, the 1st Division captured all its objectives. Wally Hallahan is buried in Tincourt New British Cemetery.

Hindenburg Outpost Line Battle

This German line ran a mile west of the Hindenburg Main Line. The Australian Corps' front for the battle on 18 September 1918 was 6 kilometres long, between Templeux-le-Guérard on the left flank (north) and Bellenglise on the right. The 1st and 4th Divisions were the formations used for the attack. The battalions spent the night before the battle in whatever shelter they could find in the ruins of farms and old army huts from earlier years. In this battle the Australians captured many strongpoints, some of them being fortified farmhouses, as well as Le Verguier, Hargicourt and Villeret. In military terms, the taking of the various spurs and crests was just as important as capture of a French village. A total of 6800 Australian fighting men were involved. At a cost of 1200 casualties, they took 4300 prisoners and seventy-six guns.

Jeancourt

On 10–11 September 1918 the 2nd Battalion found this place empty of Germans but in the darkness a patrol heard a column of Germans approaching. The Australians quickly took up ambush positions and when the Germans appeared, marching in fours, they opened up with Lewis guns at close range. The Germans suffered very heavy losses, as their own regimental records state.

Hindenburg Line

For the Australians the attack on the Hindenburg Line, which began on 29 September 1918, was the major battle of the last stages of the war. The Hindenburg Line was the final great defence system the Germans had created in western France. They had used it as the base from which to conquer so much of France in 1914–17. They had withdrawn to it in March–April 1917 and in March–April 1918 they had again attacked from it. Now, in retreat in the autumn of 1918, they intended to make it impregnable.

The Hindenburg Line was several kilometres deep, a complex system of wide bands of barbed wire, trenches, strongpoints and fortified settlements. The Beaurevoir Line and the Le Catalet Line, both named after villages, were part of the Hindenburg

Line. On the Australian Corps' front the Hindenburg Line ran from Bony in the north to Bellicourt in the south. The 3rd and 5th Divisions were the formations involved and they were supported by the 30th American Division.

The Australian operations might be reviewed by following the actions of Major Blair Wark DSO, aged 24 and acting CO of the 32nd Battalion, 8th Brigade, 5th Division. The 32nd was on the right of the AIF advance and jumped off near Bellicourt at 9 a.m. Visibility was poor from fog and artillery smoke and enemy fire was heavy. Two machine-guns held up the 32nd so Wark commandeered a passing tank to deal with them. He then came upon 200 leaderless Americans, whom he attached to his own battalion. When he encountered another tank, Wark took it under his command and continued to Nauroy, which he captured after a brisk fight. Having captured more prisoners, machine-guns and artillery, he led his men beyond Nauroy to Etricourt, where he spotted a battery of 77-millimetre guns firing on his rear companies. Collecting a few men, Wark rushed the guns, capturing four of them and the enemy soldiers. Reaching Joncourt, he established a defensive flank at which later in the day he broke an attack by 400 Germans. Next day, after hours of fighting, Wark and his battalion took Joncourt itself. Wark's brigade commander said that the success of the operation was largely due to Wark's 'remarkable courage and leadership'. For this and equally forceful leadership and personal courage on 1 October he was awarded the VC.

On 30 September Private John Ryan of the 55th Battalion was alone responsible for breaking up a ferocious German counter-attack near Bellicourt. Taking charge of the men near him, he led them with bomb and bayonet against the Germans and drove them back. He was awarded the VC for 'determined bravery and initiative'.

For the AIF, the Battle of the Hindenburg Line was costly in men. Between 28 September and 2 October the 3rd Division lost sixty-three officers and 1006 other ranks killed or wounded; the 5th Division, seventy-seven officers and 1431 other ranks. The dead lie in a score of cemeteries in the Aisne *département*.

Le Verguier

The 4th Brigade was given the task of capturing one of the strongest points of German resistance, the hamlet of Le Verguier, during the British advance of 18 September 1918. In a well-coordinated approach, the 15th Battalion went around the north of the defences, the 13th circled to the south and the 16th tackled the defences the Germans had established in the ruins. The 13th followed its creeping barrage and captured several outposts, two of them falling to Sergeant Gerald Sexton DCM and his Lewis gun. As fog and smoke cleared, an officer spotted an enemy field-gun and a mortar on the bank directly ahead and pointed it out to Sexton. He made for it, firing his Lewis gun from the hip and calling for his section to follow. He shot the crew of the gun though under steady machine-gun fire, raced across a field and killed the mortar crew. Returning to the bank, Sexton fired into several dugout entrances and flushed out thirty prisoners. He had, in fact, captured the HQ of the German 58th Infantry Regiment. Throughout that day, as the 13th Battalion continued its advance, Sexton silenced other machine-gun posts. Sexton, whose real name was Buckley, was awarded the VC for his extraordinary courage, initiative and cool behaviour under fire.

On the right wing of the Australian front at Le Verguier was the famous 48th Battalion, with the 46th on its left and the British 1st Division on its right. A patrol of only four Diggers, led by Private James Woods of the 48th, found that many Germans were strongly positioned on a ridge to the right and rear of the 12th Brigade. Its existence was dangerous and Woods sent a runner to get help for a strong attack. However, assessing the situation as critical, Woods led his two mates in an attack on the two trenches of the German position. In a first attack he killed one German and the rest, at least thirty of them, fled leaving six machine-guns. Reorganising, the Germans counter-attacked across the open and along the trenches. Woods countered this move by climbing on to the parapet and lying there, he threw bombs which his mates passed to him. He created such havoc that the 48th Battalion reinforcements who arrived to help him had comparatively little trouble in securing the position.

Montbrehain

This dominant ridge village was so vital to the German defence system that its defenders had been ordered to hold it at all costs, even if this meant dying to the last man. On 4 October 1918 the British 139th Brigade managed to enter the ruins, only to be driven out. The AIF 2nd Division had a few units which had not been recently used, or used only lightly: the 21st and 24th Battalions and the 2nd Pioneers. They were ordered to capture Montbrehain on 5 October. The Australians had to advance for 550 metres over rough ground protected by wire and trenches.

The attack started at 6.05 a.m. The 24th Battalion's B Company had the most dangerous route and that it made ground at all was due to Lieutenant George Ingram, who led a rush against a strongpoint, where he captured nine machine-guns and forty-two enemy. Following several other such exploits, Ingram organised and led a charge which captured a quarry defended by forty machine-guns and more than 100 men. While his men mopped up, Ingram went on alone and found a machine-gunner firing through a cellar ventilator. He shot this man, smashed his way into the back of the ruined house, ran down the stairs and captured thirty more Germans — and calmly waited for his men to arrive. He was awarded the VC. It was the last Australian VC of the war in the AIF's last battle of the war.

By such spirited actions the Australian infantrymen and pioneers captured Montbrehain and then held it against desperate German counter-attacks. They also captured 400 prisoners. However, the action cost thirty officers and 400 men. Some of the 6th Brigade's best officers were killed at Montbrehain or soon died of their wounds.

Lieutenant Wilkinson's exploit

Australians should know that one of the great unrewarded exploits of the war took place at Montbrehain. Lieutenant N. F. Wilkinson, 6th Machine-Gun Company, in command of two Vickers guns, was attached to the 2nd Pioneer Battalion in the attack. South of the village, the Pioneers were checked by enemy machine-gun fire and Wilkinson, with one man, scouted ahead to a railway cutting, crept along it and came to an embankment. To his astonishment, about 100 German machine-gunners were manning a line of guns in position on the embankment. Wilkinson sent his runner to bring up his gun teams. In the process of doing this, the Australian gunners crept up and captured two other German gun crews. Wilkinson and his men quietly set up their two guns and opened fire on the line of enemy guns. The enemy wilted under this sudden fire and Wilkinson found he had killed thirty Germans wounded another fifty and put the rest to flight. He captured fourteen machine-guns here and a little further on, another two. A captured German told Sergeant J. P. Adam, Wilkinson's highly trusted senior NCO, that had they known Australians were attacking they would not have fought at all at Montbrehain. Wilkinson was wounded in the leg later that day but recovered. He was the only casualty among his party of machine-gunners, though two other officers of 6th Machine-Gun Company were killed. Wilkinson was not decorated. Such a gross omission may have been the fault of the 2nd Pioneer Battalion in not making a recommendation.

Directions

The railway line no longer exists but the embankment does. Enter Montbrehain from Remicourt by the D713 and circle right, within 0.5 kilometre take the D283 signposted Fontaine-Uterte. Within 300 metres an unformed road turns to the right. The old railway and embankment are along this road.

Roisel

The 41st and 44th Battalions, following their own barrage, captured the town on 7 September and seized ten machine-guns, sixty wagons and two guns. However, the Germans fought a stubborn rearguard action and the two Australian battalions were forced to outflank one machine-gun post after another. That evening the 44th cleared Hervilly, 1 kilometre south-east of Roisel. As the 11th Battalion was marching through Roisel on the night of 23 September a German aeroplane dropped a bomb near its HQ staff and mortally wounded the CO, Major A. H. Darnell, and his adjutant, Lieutenant J. A. Archibald.

Templeux le Guérard

On the night of 11–12 September, the 4th Battalion captured Hill 140, 0.5 kilometre south-east of the village. The Germans laid down a heavy bombardment and counter-attacked, forcing the 4th Battalion to withdraw. It lost five officers and ninety-eight men, including ten captured.

Vendelles

A platoon of the 50th Battalion, under Lieutenant A. S. Hawker, had a brisk fight forward of Vendelles on the night of 12 September. Hawker was on patrol with his platoon just before a general battalion advance when the Australians ran into a German post. An enemy soldier called out to ask if the approaching men were from the 7th Company. Hawker, who understood German, answered 'Ja', and ordered his men to fire. He then found the real German relief party coming up behind him. Soon the Australians were fighting enemy on all sides but in the confusion they extricated themselves though with the loss of several men, some being killed. At dawn, the 50th captured its objectives.

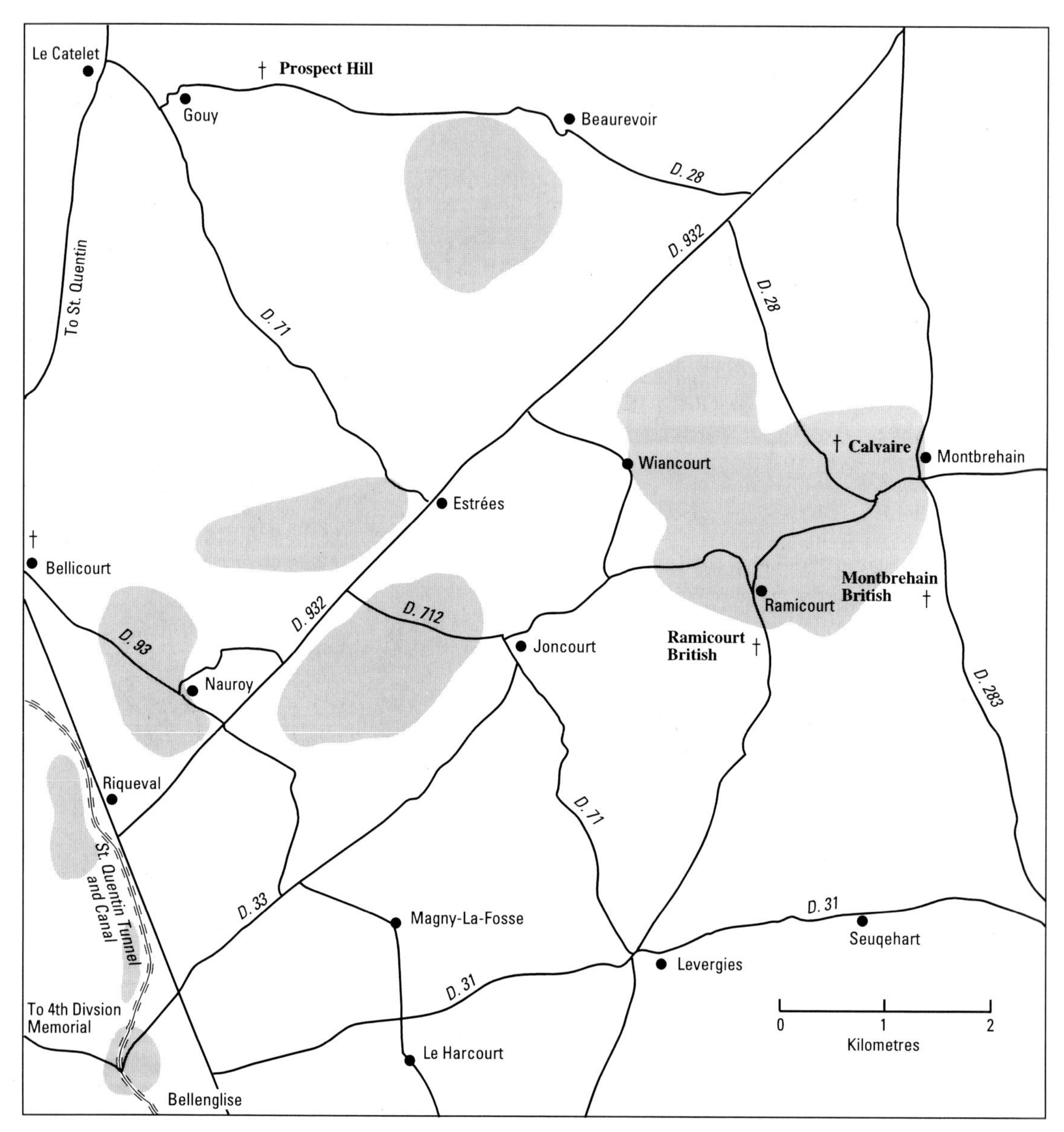

Map 14. Bellicourt to Montbrehain: Battlefields (Shaded) and Cemeteries

Chapter 14

Cemeteries East of Peronne of Australian Interest

Bellicourt British Cemetery

This is a major Australian cemetery with 305 Diggers, forty-six of them unknown; British graves number 869. The cemetery is on the west side of the village, on the Hindenburg Line itself. Fifteen of the Australians came from a burial ground no longer in existence, Melbourne Cemetery near Montbrehain. Thirteen of these men belonged to the 24th Battalion and fell at Montbrehain on 5 October 1918.

Among the Diggers is Sergeant Loftus Bauchop, one of the 14th Battalion's finest NCOs. He was killed on 20 September while leading the battalion bombers in one of several attacks on the Hindenburg Outpost Line. Had he lived he would have been decorated (Grave III.M.5). The youngest Australian in the cemetery is Private James Mackenzie, 44th Battalion. Aged 18, he was killed on 29 September (Grave II.K.1). The most decorated is 23-year-old Captain James Sullivan MC and Bar, MM, 21st Battalion. Sullivan, who had won his MM at Gallipoli, rose to command the 'Brewery' company of his battalion, so called because it had been billeted at Brewery Farm early in 1918. He led his company magnificently during the Battle of Ville-sur-Ancre in May, where he was wounded. At Herleville, on 18 August, his élite company was rushed forward to plug a gap. On 1 September Sullivan made a daring and valuable lone reconnaissance completely around Mont St Quentin. His luck ran out on 5 October at Montbrehain when a shell killed him, together with his signallers (Grave VI.S.7).

Directions
The cemetery is by the side of the D331 Bellicourt-Hargicourt road, on the edge of the village. A major part of the Hindenburg Line ran lengthwise through the cemetery. During the war American soldiers gave the name Buckshot Ravine to the hollow in which the cemetery lies.

Calvaire Cemetery, Montbrehain

Named from a crucifix standing near its south-west corner, Calvaire contains the graves of forty-eight Australians and British soldiers, as well as thirteen unidentified. Seven of these are known to be Australian. The cemetery stands on high ground with sweeping views to the north and north-east. Thirty-one of the Diggers from the 24th Battalion were killed on 5 October 1918 during the successful Battle of Montbrehain. Sergeant Reginald Davies DCM, French Medaille Militaire, of the 17th Battalion, was killed on 3 October and is buried here. The pioneers, rarely given enough credit for their service as frontline fighting solders, are well represented on this hill in Montbrehain, with five casualties from the 2nd Pioneer Battalion. They include Sergeant Eric Read MM and French Croix de Guerre.

Directions
Enter Montbrehain from Joncourt and Ramicourt by the D713. This was the direction taken by the Australians attacking on 5 October, the 24th to the the left of the village, 21st to the right. After reaching the village, take the second turn left and continue on at the crossroads to get to Calvaire Cemetery.

George Ingram's VC exploit
The fortified quarry which Ingram attacked was between the D713 as it enters Montbrehain and the inverted V it forms with a farm road to the right. Ingram's amazing progress took him right through the village to the northern edge near Calvaire Cemetery.

Hancourt British Cemetery

Ten kilometres east of Peronne, the village of Hancourt was captured by soldiers of the Australian

Corps in the middle of September 1918. The cemetery was made by Australian units and thirty-one Diggers are buried here, together with eighty-two British soldiers and one Canadian. Standing amid cultivated fields, the cemetery has long been simply a part of the remote and quiet village.

The cemetery is small but contains soldiers of six infantry battalions, and men from artillery, pioneer, machine-gun and field ambulance units. Two of the gunners and one infantryman were decorated. The cemetery also has examples of the foreign origins of some Diggers. For instance, Private Ferruccio Castoldi, 31st Battalion, though he came from Waverley, NSW, was a native of Milan, Italy. The home address of Gunner Charles Vuilleumier, who served under the name of Stormont, was Camden Road, London.

Directions
From Peronne, take the road south-east to Doignt, thence the D199 to Courcelles. Turn right into the D194 for Cartigny and Hancourt. The cemetery is signposted.

Hargicourt British Cemetery and Communal Cemetery Extension

This cemetery was begun in May 1917 and was used by fighting units until March 1918. Some further burials were made in September and October, all of them Australian. Fifteen Diggers lie in the cemetery of a total of 287 graves. In the fighting near Hargicourt the AIF suffered a particular loss when Lieutenant Thomas Keillor MC and Bar was killed. The Intelligence Officer of the 28th Battalion, Keillor was hit by machine-gun fire from a pillbox at Lormisset Farm (Grave I.L.4).

In the Hargicourt Communal Cemetery Extension, all the twelve Australians were killed on 29 September at Hargicourt.

Directions
The British Cemetery is at the south-west end of the village, 100 metres west of the road to Templeux-le-Guérard, the D331. The Communal Cemetery is on the north side of the village. Take the D572 towards Ronssoy.

Roisel Communal Cemetery Extension

The communal cemetery of this small manufacturing town was used by British units and field ambulances from April 1917 to March 1918, by German medical units in March and April 1918, and by British and Dominion units again in September and October 1918. During this period twenty-four Australians were buried here, among a total of 118 graves. After the war they were transferred to the cemetery extension and thirty-five other Diggers were brought in from Hesbécourt Communal Cemetery Extension, to make a total of 106 Australians in a total of 700 burials.

Australian Field Artillery casualties are noticeable here, including several gunners killed on 20 October, long after the Australian infantry had been withdrawn. On 3 October three officers of the 2nd Field Artillery brigade were killed by a single German shellburst. They were Captain Norman Hollis, Lieutenant Herbert Fisher and Captain Hugh Kirkland MC. Kirkland was the Brigade's Medical Officer (Grave I.M.3; I.M.2; I.K.9).

Directions
Roisel is 10 kilometres east of Peronne. From Roisel take the D72 signposted Villers-Faucon. The cemetery is on the edge of town.

Templeux-le-Guérard British Cemetery

A small cemetery until 1918, Templeux-le-Guérard was greatly increased after the Armistice by the concentration of 360 graves from battlefields surrounding the village. At this time twenty-two Australians were brought in from Ste Emilie British Cemetery at Villers-Faucon. Now, forty-five Diggers, one of whom is unknown, are buried here in a total of 757 graves.

Among the Australians is one of their chaplains, the popular Reverand Alfred Goller, 37th Battalion, who was killed on 29 September 1918. Goller, from Brighton Beach, Victoria, was killed while carrying out his usual duty of collecting the belongings of soldiers who had been killed; he was 35 years old (Grave II.F.29). In the same row is Captain Francis Fairweather, 38th Battalion, one of the AIF's most famous raiders. Fairweather had been conspicuous at Morlancourt, Proyart and throughout the advance after Peronne. This splendid officer was killed, with many of his company, on 29 September (Grave II.F.41). A battalion commander is buried close to Captain Fairweather. He is Lieutenant-Colonel Robert Henderson DSO, 39th Battalion, who had led his unit inspiringly at Mont St Quentin. He was killed at Gillemont Farm, north-west of Bony, on 29 September. Mortally wounded on the same dreadful day was Captain Stanley Neale MC, 59th Battalion (Grave II.F.43).

Australian visitors might like to spend a few minutes at the grave of Lieutenant Charles Callan, 38th Battalion. Just west of Gillemont Farm, on 29 September Callan had fought his way forward, finding shelter in one shell hole after another. In one such refuge he heard a wounded man calling for water from the next shell hole. His mates warned Callan that it was suicide to attempt to reach the stricken man but Callan tried. An enemy gunner shot him. Callan, who was 26, had married an English girl living in London and planned to take her back to Werribee (Grave II.F.42).

Templeux-le-Guérard Communal Cemetery

Twenty Australians are buried in this cemetery, together with ninety-eight from Britain. They include men who died of wounds received in the Battle of Montbrehain on 5 October. Among the diggers is Lance-Corporal Joseph Teal, 5th Field Ambulance, killed on 3 October. Had he lived, Teal would almost certainly have been decorated for his devotion to duty under fire.

Directions
Templeux-le-Guérard, a small village, is 13 kilometres east of Peronne. For the Communal Cemetery, in Templeux take the D6 signposted Ronssoy. On the edge of town, fork right on to a minor road. The cemetery is then in sight. For the British Cemetery, take the D6E Hargicourt road. The cemetery is on the left within 0.5 kilometre.

Tincourt New British Cemetery

Australia paid a high price in officers between 5 September and 5 October 1918 and this cemetery has the dubious distinction of more identified AIF officer burials than any other cemetery on the Western Front, although some cemeteries have a higher total of Australian burials.

Tincourt-Boucly is a commune in the *département* of the Somme, on the Cologne River. The villages were occupied by British troops in March 1917 during the German withdrawal to the Hindenburg Line. A year later the fresh German advance swallowed them up until they were recovered by the 3rd Australian Division on 6–7 September 1918. The price paid by the Australians at Tincourt and in this sector is evident in the cemetery, where 226 of them lie among another 1669 British and Dominion soldiers.

The 31 AIF officers buried here are: Lieutenant J.A. Archibald, 11th Battalion; Captain J. Bell, Australian Flying Corps; Lieutenant S. G. Bell, AFA; Lieutenant S. J. Bennie, 21st Battalion; Captain L. R. Blake MC, AFA; Second Lieutenant H. Boden MC, 40th Battalion; Lieutenant G. M. Browne, 42nd Battalion; Major A. H. Darnell DSO, 11th Battalion; Lieutenant A. J. Davidson, AFA; Captain F. S. Davidson, Engineers; Lieutenant G. S. Doods, 41st Battalion; Lieutenant D. M. Elliott, 11th Battalion; Lieutenant I. N. Gair, 31st Battalion; Captain W. R. Hallahan MC, MM, 11th Battalion; Lieutenant F. Halliday, AFA; Lieutenant J. T. Hampson MC, 11th Battalion; Lieutenant W. E. Hardwick MC and Bar, 21st Battalion; Lieutenant R. Hassell, 5th Pioneers; Captain C. A. Johnson MC, 53rd Battalion; Lieutenant F. R. Johnson, 1st Tunnelling Company; Lieutenant G. K. Herslake, Engineers; Lieutenant F. T. Petersen MC, Engineers; Major J. Ray DSO, AFA; Lieutenant G. E. Rennie, Machine-Gun Corps; Captain L. C. Roth MC, 2nd Pioneers; Lieutenant G. L. Scott, 18th Battalion; Lieutenant S. J. Sheen, 2nd Battalion; Lieutenant J. J. Thomson, 57th Battalion; Lieutenant F. G. Turner, 59th Battalion; Captain W. G. Wilson MC, 53rd Battalion; Second Lieut P. E. Ralph.

The army career of Second Lieutenant Percy Ralph, 53rd Battalion, shows how difficult it was to win a Victoria Cross and reveals how arbitrary decisions about awards could be. Ralph, from Bathurst and Nyngan, NSW, won the Military Medal at Polygon Wood. His citation reads: 'During the attack on Polygon Wood on 26 September 1917 Lance Sergeant Ralph showed great coolness and courage by single-handed attacking a troublesome machine-gun position and bayoneting the three gunners. During the consolidation he set a fine example to his men and displayed great courage in hanging on to a flank position under severe shell and machine gun fire until withdrawn. He unearthed a buried enemy machine gun and ammunition which he used effectively against enemy aircraft.'

Many citations for VC actions indicate less raw courage, less resourcefulness and no greater leadership than Ralph's actions at Polygon Wood. As if his exploits at Polygon Wood were not enough to win the supreme award, look at the report which referred to his actions a year later, when he was a Second Lieutenant: 'During the operations near Bellicourt between 30 September and 2 October 1918 this officer displayed the most conspicuous gallantry. Noticing an enemy strongpost on the left flank holding up the advance he charged forward accompanied by only 3 men and succeeded in mopping up the post, killing several Germans with bombs and capturing 2 officers and 31 men and taking 2 machine guns. When returning to the trench with his prisoners this very gallant officer was mortally wounded and died half an hour later.' This exploit ranks with the best of the AIF's recorded acts of gallantry, but Ralph was posthumously awarded only a Mention In Despatches. It must be said that at that time no award other than the VC or a 'Mention' could be made posthumously, so there was no chance of the dead young officer being awarded the MC.

Second Lieutenant Boden was hit twice at Anzac and three times in France, and had become the most trusted sergeant-major of the 11th Battalion. A boxing champion and a leader by example, Boden was vigorous and inspiring. Commissioned not long before the final campaign after Peronne, Boden performed his most courageous acts on 29 September near Gillemont Farm in the Macquincourt Valley. American troops were operating on the 40th Battalion's left but though willing, they were so inexperienced that they lost heavily. Becoming confused, they created difficulties for the Australians. Boden, going forward, found the Americans under attack. Single-handedly he drove the Germans back with bombs. Calling up his platoon, he reached the front American trench and organised the Americans for defence. While putting his men among the Americans to encourage and support them, Boden was mortally wounded by a machine-gun (Grave V.F.10).

Directions

From Peronne, leave by the D937, signposted Ham. After 1 kilometre from the centre of Peronne, turn left into Doingt. Pass through Doingt, Courcelles and Buire-Courcelles. After 1.2 kilometres, on the outskirts of Tincourt, the cemetery is on the left. In the communal cemetery of Buire, through which you pass en route to Tincourt, are six more Australians including yet another officer.

Unicorn Cemetery, Vendhuile

The German-held village of Vendhuile was on the extreme left of the Australian front in the push to the Hindenburg Line in September 1918. The 3rd Division was involved, with two American divisions on its left. The enemy positions were captured on 29–30 September and the Diggers who died were buried in Unicorn Cemetery. The rest of the cemetery was formed after the Armistice by the concentration of isolated graves. It contains seventy-eight Australians, 689 British servicemen, one Canadian and 218 unidentified soldiers. Of the AIF men, forty-three were killed in the furious fighting of 29 September, with machine-gunners and trench-mortar men particularly hard hit.

One of the casualties that day was Corporal Lawrence Weathers VC. Sadly, he did not know of his VC, awarded for extraordinary courage near Peronne. It was not gazetted until 24 December. (Grave III.C.5). Another outstanding soldier buried here is Lieutenant Henry Davis MC, 13th Battalion, who was a member of the 'Australian Mission', a group of handpicked officers and NCOs chosen to help the inexperienced American infantry. For instance, US infantry units were arriving in the front lines without water, rations, Lewis guns, ammunition and telephones. Lieutenant Davis was killed while reconnoitring for these Americans. (Grave I.D.19).

Directions

As for Hargicourt British Cemetery. Then take the D57 signposted Bony. 1 kilometre from Hargicourt, at the crossroads, turn left on to the D58 for Ronssoy. In this town turn right for Lempire and pass through it towards Vendhuile. Unicorn Cemetery is less than 1 kilometre from Lempire. Vendhuile, though the official site of the cemetery, is 2 kilometres further on. The valley across the road from this cemetery, Gillemont Valley, saw much Australian activity, as did Gillemont Farm, 1.2 kilometres distant.

Chapter 15

Other Cemeteries in Various Parts of France of Australian Interest

Australians are buried thoughout the length and breadth of France, sometimes in lone graves, often in considerable numbers. Many of these burial places are far distant from battlefields, some at ports of disembarkation, others in territory captured by the Germans and held by them for much of the war. In the ports of disembarkation the Australians buried there probably died of illness or from accidental causes. In the latter case, they died while prisoners of war and were buried by the Germans.

Large numbers of men died in rear area base hospitals, such as those which proliferated in the city of Rouen. Others died in the great training and staging camps, notably at Etaples on the coast of northern France. Single graves in locations where AIF units did not see action or were not in camp indicate administrative confusion or crisis. Sometimes the pressure on hospitals was so great, with wounded pouring in by train and ambulance, that some wounded were passed from one hospital to another before one was found that could accommodate them. In yet other cases, a detachment of specialist Diggers, such as signallers, engineers, and above all, artillery men, was posted to a front where their own units were not operating. If men from these detachments were killed or died of illness they were buried locally, often in a churchyard. All these burial places are important in Australian history and should be recorded here.

Busigny Communal Cemetery and Extension

Busigny is a small town 10 kilometres south-west of Le Cateau. When captured from the Germans on 9 October 1918 it became the site of CCSs. Eight AIF men lie in the communal cemetery and another twenty-four, among 723 burials in all, in the cemetery extension. The significance of the AIF burials is that they are of men killed very late in the war. Three members of the 1st Australian Tunnelling Company, who died on 29 October 1918, were among the last AIF men killed in action, though others died after this date from wounds or illness. They are Sapper Charles Bodinner, 43, from North Yelta, South Australia; Sapper Grehn, no details known; William Watson, aged 20, from Caulfield East, Victoria. The three are buried together in Plot II, Row A. The war ended eleven days after their deaths.

Several gunners died on 20 October and are buried here. Private Percy Duggan, 45th Battalion, died of accidental injuries on 30 November and Private Thomas Birch, 2nd Machine-Gun Company, of sickness on 2 December.

Etaples Military Cemetery

Etaples — 'Eat Apples' to the soldiers — is an ancient fishing port and lies at the mouth of the Canche, in the *département* of the *Pas-de-Calais*. The area around the cemetery held immense British reinforcement camps and hospitals. Here, on the famous (or infamous) Bullring soldiers were trained or retrained. In 1917 there were 100 000 troops camped among the sand dunes. In the immediate area were eleven General Hospitals, one Stationary Hospital, four Red Cross Hospitals and a Convalescent Depot. Collectively, they could deal with 22 000 wounded and sick at any one time.

Among the 11 000 burials at Etaples are 461 Australians. They died of wounds or disease in a proportion of 10 to 1. One man, Private Henry Mitchell, 25th Battalion, died from the effects of gas on 6 November 1917 (Grave XXX.K.10a). Major Clarence Taylor MC, 6th Battalion was brought all the way back to Etaples from Broodseinde on 4 October 1917 and clung to life for eight days before dying of his wounds (Grave XXVIII.A.1). Being away from the battlefield and its diseases did not save an airman, Albert Walker, 3rd Squadron Australian Flying Corps. He died of disease on 16 October 1918 (Grave LXVI.J.24).

Because of its many levels on a hillside, Etaples Cemetery is worth a visit and is easily reached as it is by the side of the main road from Boulogne to Paris and only 2 kilometres north of Etaples.

Le Rejet-de-Beaulieu Communal Cemetery

This cemetery is distinctive in AIF history since it contains the graves of almost certainly the last Diggers to be killed in action in the First World War. They are three members of the 1st Australian Tunnelling Company, all killed on 4 November 1918, just one week before the Armistice. Most Australian units, other than artillery batteries and 1st and 2nd Tunnelling Companies, had been withdrawn from the fighting after the Battle of Montbrehain on 5 October 1918. Many Australians died of wounds or illness after 4 November and there may have been others who were wounded after this date but survived. However, Sapper C. Barrett, Corporal A. Davey and Sapper Arthur Johnson probably have the sad distinction of being the last Diggers to be classified KIA.

Le Rejet-de-Beaulieu is a village and commune in the *département du Nord*, 10 kilometres south-east of Le Cateau. The cemetery, in which also lie forty-eight British soldiers and one South African airman, is easily seen at the eastern end of the small village. Precisely what operation the tunnellers were engaged upon is not now known but they appear to have been working with 409 Company Royal Engineers, some of whom were also killed on 4 November.

Maubeuge (Sous-le-Bois) Cemetery

This cemetery is, in effect, a postwar footnote to the history of the AIF on the Western Front since all forty-five Diggers buried here died after the end of the war. Except for two accidental deaths, all died of illness during the winter of 1918–19. This applies also to the sixty-four British soldiers buried at Maubeuge. These young and previously fit men, having survived the battlefields, were brought down by the influenza epidemic which swept Europe in 1918–19. The severe winter aggravated their illness. One of General Monash's favourite young staff officers is buried here. He is Major Throsby Morell MC, of 3rd Division HQ, who was only 23 when he died.

Maubeuge is an old fortified town and commune in the *département du Nord* and was captured by British troops only a few days before the Armistice. The soldiers who died here were received into the 5th CCS which buried them. The cemetery lies north-west of the Sous-le-Bois part of town.

Mazargues Cemetery Extension, Marseilles

Marseilles, a cathedral city, is a major port and the capital of the *département du Bouches-du-Rhône*. It was the base for Indian troops in France and throughout the war British and Dominion troops passed through the port. Nearly all Australians reaching France from Australia via Egypt, landed at Marseilles. In Mazargues cemetery lie fourteen Australians among 1239 British and Indian soldiers and sailors. These Diggers not only died far from home, they did so before they ever saw a Western Front battlefield. All died of illness or accidental injuries. Eight died of pneumonia, one of malaria, three from accidental injuries and one of 'sickness'. The cause of death of the other man is not recorded. The Diggers, from infantry, artillery and machine-gun units, died between March and September 1916. Mazargues Cemetery is on the south-east side of the city of Marseilles.

St Benin Communal Cemetery

East of St Benin, four Australian gunners, operating with British infantry, were caught by a single German shell on 22 October 1918. One was killed instantly, two others died later that day and the fourth died the following day. With six British soldiers, they lie in the communal cemetery of St

Benin, which is between Le Cateau and St Souplet in the *département du Nord*. Despite their heavy casualties throughout the war, the AIF artillery men were kept in action much longer than any other arm of the AIF, except for the tunnellers and men of the salvage units.

St Pol British Cemetery, St Pol-sur-Ternoise

This cemetery was begun in March 1918 when the extension to the communal cemetery was almost full. Twenty Australians lie among 243 British and Dominion servicemen, and one worker of Queen Mary's Army Auxiliary Corps. Of the Australian graves, seven are represented by special memorials; they were among sixteen men of the 58th Battalion killed by a shell at St Pol Station on 27 March 1918. The senior among them is Regimental Quartermaster-Sergeant Walter Osbourne (Grave II.A.11). Two members of the Australian Mining and Boring Company died of sickness, believed to be influenza, after the Armistice. They are Sapper John Pierce (II.D.1) and Sergeant Harris Quince (III.D.11). Surprisingly, the chaos at the station when the troop train was hit by a shell is still a topic of folk memory.

Directions
The cemetery is 1.6 kilometres south of the railway station, 30 metres east of the road to Frevent, the D916. In 1918 the 12th Stationary Hospital was just across the road from the cemetery.

St Pol Communal Cemetery Extension

The British and Dominion plot contains the graves of 226 servicemen. Only three are Australians but two of them make the cemetery distinctive for Australians. They are Lieutenant James Sandy and Sergeant Henry Hughes, both of the 69th Squadron Australian Flying Corps. The crew of a fighter plane, they were killed when shot down on 17 December 1917. Their plane crashed close to St Pol. They are buried close to each other, at H.8 and H.10. The other Australian is Lance-Corporal John Carey, 14th Battalion, who died of accidental injuries on 14 September 1917.

Directions
The cemetery is near the Rue d'Arras and alongside the Cimitiére Thuillier, the 500-year-old town cemetery. It stands on a hillside overlooking the town from the east.

St Sever Cemetery Extension, Rouen

After Tyne Cot, Lijssenthoek and Queant Road, this cemetery holds more Australians than any other, 783 of them in a total of 8293 British and Dominion burials. Rouen, an old cathedral city on the Seine River, was a great wartime base. British camps and hospitals were south of the river on the southern outskirts of the city. The hospitals at Rouen remained there in almost all cases for the whole of the war. They included eight general hospitals, five stationary, one British Red Cross, one native labour hospital and a convalescent depot. Many AIF men were treated in Rouen hospitals before returning to the front or going on leave to England.

The majority of men buried at St Sever died of wounds and the greater number of these after May 1918. However, fourteen died from the effects of gas. The variety of diseases from which the Australians at St Sever died gives some idea of the hazards of active service. They include pneumonia, influenza, bronchitis, appendicitis, meningitis, tenanus, pyaemia, uremia, pleurisy and nephritis. Many soldiers are recorded as having died of 'sickness' and one, Private George Smith, 2nd Battalion, was 'accidentally drowned'. Being a member of a non-fighting unit did not confer immunity from risk of disease. Sergeant Percy Bergman, 1st Field Bakery, died of pneumonia on 29 March 1917.

One of the AIF's most remarkable soldiers is buried at St Sever. He is Lieutenant Norman Dalgleish DSO, 58th Battalion. At the age of 22 he had won the DSO, a high distinction for a junior officer, but he most distinguished himself in the Battle of the Hindenburg Line. On 29 September 1918 he was wounded in the head while his battalion was pressing the fight east of the St Quentin Tunnel mound. However, with most other 58th officers either killed or wounded, Dalgleish held on and controlled a critical situation. The next day, despite the wounds from which he was suffering, he twice led patrols to test the strength of the German garrison of a fortified farm. On 1 October 1918 he made a spirited patrol in enemy territory to the north. The 58th Battalion formed a line in a dangerous position where it was heavily shelled. It lost nearly all its remaining officers including Dalgleish, who was seriously wounded and carried off the field. He died of his wounds at Rouen hospital on 9 October. He deserved a VC but received only a mention in despatches. At that time and for another forty years the only decoration which could be awarded posthumously was the VC. Had he survived, Dalgleish would at the least have received a second DSO (Grave S.III.Y.6). Lieutenant Dalgleish had been a fibrous plasterer on enlistment and his home address was 312 Flinders Street, Melbourne.

The large St Sever Cemetery has an extra grave location classification. Lieutenant Dalgleish's grave is S.III.Y.6 — that is Block S, Plot III, Row Y, Grave 6.

Two Australian women who served with the AIF are buried in St Sever Cemetery. They are Sister Hilda Mary Knox of the Australian Army Nursing Service and Louisa Riggall of the Australian Red Cross Society. Sister Knox, the daughter of James and Isabella Knox of Benalla, Victoria, was 33 years of age when she died on 17 February 1917 from an unspecified disease, possibly influenza. Louisa, also a Victorian, died of a haemorrhage, probably cerebral, on 31 August 1918. Australian women died while on service in military hospitals in Britain, but I have not found any others in France or Belgium. Sister Knox's grave is B.4.10, while that of Louise Riggall is close by in B.3.1. It would be interesting to know if any family members have ever paid these graves a visit.

Directions

St Sever Cemetery and Extension is five kilometres from Rouen city centre. Rouen is a large city and to locate the cemetery it is best to ask first for Rive Gauche (Left Bank) railway station. It is close to the south side of the Seine River. The road in front of the station runs dead-straight for nearly four kilometres south to the cemetery.

Terlicthun British Cemetery, Wimille

In the spring of 1918 it became clear that the burials from the British hospitals at Boulogne and Wimereux would more than fill the available space in the French cemeteries of those towns. A site for a British cemetery was therefore chosen near the hamlet of Terlicthun. The first burials were carried out on 16 June 1918 and the last in July 1920. The 2nd Australian General Hospital was one of the fifteen hospitals and four convalescent depots in the immediate vicinity.

The cemetery is a large one, with 3327 graves including eighty-eight Australians. All died either of wounds received during the period July–September 1918 or of illness, mainly influenza and pneumonia, after that month. Terlicthun is an 'open' cemetery for the interment of the remains of soldiers which are still being found on the old battlefields.

Directions

The cemetery is only 2 kilometres north of Boulogne, just off the Calais road, from where it is visible.

Chapter 16

Diggers in Odd Corners

Many an Australian soldier who died in France is buried in remote village or communal graveyard, some of them far removed from fighting areas or army camps. Several Australians, wounded in action, died as prisoners of war and were buried by their German captors, generally in French cemeteries. Others died of sickness while in captivity and were similarly buried. These are some of the Diggers in odd corners.

Auvers-sur-Oise Communal Cemetery, near Paris
Private Harry Cosson, 59th Battalion lies here. He died of accidental injuries on 1 July 1916.

Caucade Communal Cemetery, Nice, Riviera
This cemetery is situated opposite the British Cemetery. Staff Sergeant Thomas Mason, 1st Australian Tunnelling Company is buried here. He died of sickness on 15 December 1918.

City of Paris (Bagneux) Cemetery
Buried here is Lance-Corporal Thomas Oliver, 3rd Battalion, killed on 5 August 1918. The puzzle of Oliver's burial, so far from the battlefield, was solved by a reader, Tony Cable. Oliver was killed by long-range gunfire. I found that he was a victim of 'Big Bertha', the monster howitzer which shelled Paris from a range of 70 miles. Corporal Oliver, on leave, was caught in one of its occasional firings.

City of Paris (Pantin) Cemetery
Eleven Australians and eighty-two other soldiers are buried here. Most died of illness in hospitals in Paris. The Australians include Lieutenant Frederick Markham-Mills, 2nd Squadron Australian Flying Corps, who died on 18 December 1918. Another Australian, Private George Victor, 24th Battalion, drowned on 5 August 1919. Obviously Victor was on leave — he would not otherwise be in Paris — but how he came to be drowned is a mystery.

Denain Communal Cemetery
Situated between Valenciennes and Cambrai, this cemetery has the grave of Private Frederick Bell, 16th Battalion. He died while a prisoner of war, on 8 September 1917.

Highland Cemetery, Le Cateau
Gunner John Ellis MM, 11th Brigade, Australian Field Artillery, killed in action 3 November 1918 is buried here. Ellis is another very late AIF casualty and I have found no other artilleryman killed in action so late in the war. Highland Cemetery is south of Le Cateau, on the west side of the road to Wassigny. Here, Gunner Ellis is the only Australian among 633 British soldiers.

Janval Cemetery, Dieppe
Dieppe was a minor British base and the site of 'A' Section of No. 5 Stationary Hospital. Here 218 British soldiers died and were buried at Janval. Among them is one Australian, Driver Frederick Larter, 2nd Field Company Australian Engineers, who died of sickness on 27 November 1918.

La Motte - Brebière Communal Cemetery
Close to Amiens, this communal cemetery has nine military burials, including four Australians, all machine-gunners. They include Lance-Corporal John Andrew MM of the 3rd Battalion Australian Machine-Gun Corps.

Landrecies Communal Cemetery
Private C. C. Phister, 47th Battalion lies here. He died on 9 October 1918 while a prisoner of war. The Germans buried Phister among French civilians although there was already a plot here for the British dead from 1914.

Les Pejoces Cemetery, Dijon
The burial place of Sapper Edward Dunn, 2nd

Australian Tunnelling Company. Died of pneumonia 29 December 1918.

Luxeuil-les-Bains, Haute Saone; west of Belfort
Flight Sub-Lieutenant Alfred Mann, serving with No. 3 Wing, Royal Naval Air Service, died on 29 November 1916 and was buried here. Mann came from Philip Street, Sydney.

Morlancourt British Cemetery No. 2
Located at Ville-sur-Ancre, 6 kilometres south of Albert on the D120, this cemetery has only one Australian grave among fifty-four burials. The soldier is Sergeant Vernon Drake of the 30th Battalion, killed on 22 June 1918.

Naours Churchyard
Close to Amiens, Naours has only three military burials, one of them Australian. He is Driver S. Franks of the 4th Division Train, Australian Army Service Corps.

Salmaise Communal Cemetery, Côte d'Or
Private Harold Meston, 9th Battalion is buried here. He is recorded as having been 'killed on the railway' on 4 April 1916. No other details are given.

Solre-le-Château Communal Cemetery
Here lies Lieutenant-Colonel Leslie Mather DSO, 5th Division Engineers, died 23 January 1919. Mather, who was aged 30, had married a French girl, Marcelle Elizabeth, of 17 Rue de Rivoli, Nui, France. As chief of 5th Division Engineers, Colonel Mather was an important officer, with the DSO and three times Mentioned in Despatches. A 5th Division report, numbered 14/11/32 and dated 23 January 1919, states: 'LtCol L.F.S. Mather DSO CRE 5th Aust Div was found dead in his bed this morning, shot through the heart'. The next day a Court of Enquiry was held on the death of the CRE and a military funeral was held at Solre-le-Château cemetery. (Report 14/11/32, 24 Jan 1919.) The suspicion is that Colonel Mather committed suicide. The cemetery register gives no cause of death. It would have been easier to see the results of the court enquiry in 1919 than it is now. His epitaph reads: 'I am the resurrection and the life'.

St Germain-au-Mont d'Or Communal Cemetery Extension
The cemetery overlooks the Saone Valley and was used by a small British hospital and rest camp between October 1917 and November 1919. AB David Goff, RAN, of *HMAS Encounter* died on 4 May 1918 and is buried here. What this 22-year-old sailor was doing in the middle of France is a mystery. With him are Private T. B. Galbraith, 15th Battalion, and Private Michael Mackay, 2nd Australian Stationary Hospital.

Vaire-sous-Corbie Communal Cemetery
This is the burial place of four Digger gunners, killed by the one enemy shell on 8 August 1918, the first day of the great Allied counter-offensive. They are Gunner George Bayliff, Driver L. Chandler, Gunner Sydney Dutton and Driver William Morrissey. The village of Vaire-sous- Corbie is on the south side of the Somme, across from Vaux-sur-Somme.

Chapter 17

Diggers' Epitaphs

Soon after the war, when the Imperial (later Commonwealth) War Graves Commission was establishing the military cemeteries which now proliferate on the Western Front and the regions behind it, next-of-kin were given the opportunity to have an inscription or epitaph on the grave headstones of fallen servicemen. The maximum number of letters allowed was sixty-six and the charge was 3½ pence (2 cents) a letter but the charge was not enforced.

The New Zealand Government did not permit its soldiers to have headstone inscriptions and only one NZ grave on the whole of the Western Front is known to carry one. Many Australian families did not take advantage of the opportunity but the majority did. For those who found it difficult to express their grief, pride or other feelings the CWGC suggested some wordings, usually with a religious element. However, most Australian next-of-kin produced inscriptions of their own and they make interesting reading. They can only be read in the cemeteries on the headstones.

No official consolidated list was kept and the documents requesting inscriptions have not survived. My wife and I have collected many headstone inscriptions. Some still have the power to move us to tears; a few irritate us. Hazelle always indignantly rejects the commonly found 'Thy will be done'. She asks, 'Do people really believe that this is what God wanted?'

Collectively, these inscriptions reveal nothing less than Australia itself. Here are the attitudes of the people to the war and to the sacrifice they had made. The 'last words' variously show pride, love, bitterness, anger, sadness — desperate sadness and sense of loss — patriotism, resignation, hopelessness, despair, hope and religious belief. Occasionally, there is dry humour. Some wordings are terse and direct, others eloquent and some poetic. Occasionally we find a Latin tag, and some epitaphs quote a passage from literature. A common theme in Australian inscriptions is the regret, disappointment and sometimes the despair of relatives in not being able to visit the loved one's grave, because of the vast distance. One of the purposes of this book is to help bridge that distance.

From the thousands of epitaphs we have collected I have assembled a representative sample under certain classifications. All information given on a soldier's headstone is engraved in capital letters and often without punctuation. In some of the examples of epitaphs I have supplied punctuation to make the message clear. Some headstones do not give the age of the soldier. The next-of-kin may have failed to ask for its inclusion, or requested that it be not included.

Directions to all the cemeteries mentioned are given elsewhere in the book (see index). For each epitaph I give the soldier's name, unit, date of death and age.

Australia's Sons

Many epitaph writers brought the word Australia or Anzac into the inscription they requested for their soldier's grave. Even if they did not actually mention these words they implied them, as in 'the land of the wattle'. One next-of-kin refers to the dead soldier as 'One of a type of our chivalry' and I am convinced that by this is meant Australian chivalry. These widows and parents had no doubt that Australian soldiers were heroes and 'among God's bravest and best' and it is good to see this sentiment unashamedly expressed.

Private W. F. J. Sellen, 43rd Battalion 19.7.1918 (29)

He was just
An Australian soldier
one of God's bravest and best

Sergeant F. L. Partridge DCM, 58th Battalion 26.4.1918 (26)

A soldier and a man
one of Australia's best

Private A. C. Powe, 26th Battalion 28.6.1918 (35)

In answer to the call
he fought and helped to show
Australia's might

Private G. Brown, 28th Battalion 9.7.1918 (35)

For the homeland
he was fighting
in honour's name he fell

Lance-Corporal N. G. Piper, 43rd Battalion 22.4.1917 (25)

Behold France
Thou holdest one of Australia's
bravest and best

Lance-Corporal A. Clark, 29th Battalion 27.11.1917 (24)

An Australian soldier's noble end

Private F. C. Davies, 8th Battalion 14.4.1918 (26)

Our Anzac
Lovingly remembered
till we meet again

Private G. E. Smith, 8th Battalion 14.4.1918 (21)

Our hero, Australia's best

Gunner H. R. Mayers, Field Artillery 23.4.1917 (21)

One of many who perished
not in vain
as a type of our chivalry

Private P. F. Ware, 26th Battalion 22.4.1917 (24)

An Australian soldier's
noble end

Private E.A. Newton, 50th Battalion 2.4.1917 (21)

He died for Australia
his native land.
Gone but not forgotten

Sergeant T. Weber, 20th Battalion 3.5.1917 (20)

An Anzac

Private E. J. Wensor, 55th Battalion 26.9.1917 (19)

Australia mourns
her hero's fate

Private Alan O'Shannassy, 58th Battalion 15.7.1916 (21)

Beloved only son
of P. & S. O'Shannassy
of Hastings
An Anzac

Private A. J. Wootton, 58th Battalion 15.7.1916

He died an Australian hero
'Tis the grandest death of all

Private Nathaniel Smith, 18th Battalion 25.2.1917 (34)

Our hero
A beautiful memory
left behind in Australia

Corporal A. C. Lewis, 16th Battalion 1.9.1916 (26)

He died a soldier brave
to keep Australia free

Private H. Warwicker, 11th Battalion 27.2.1917 (30)

He was
Just an Australian soldier
one of God's bravest and best

Private I. D. Hart, 60th Battalion 27.11.1916 (30)

I gave my son
he gave his all his life
for Australia and empire

Private C. West, 6th Battalion 16.8.1916 (22)

He gave his young life
to keep Australia free

Lieutenant I. G. Thompson, 58th Battalion 4.7.1918 (21)

He fought for peace
liberty freedom and honour
of Australia

Sergeant H. Jarman MM, 2nd Pioneer Battalion 16.4.1918 (28)

An Anzac
at rest

Private A. Q. Savage, 23rd Battalion 10.6.1918 (31)

He died
the helpless to defend
an Australian soldier's
noble end

Private V. Mann, Machine-Gun Corps 5.4.1918

He died
an Australian hero

Private W. Gar, 4th Battalion 30.11.1916 (25)

He died for Australia

Private W. G. M. Forsyth, 3rd Battalion 11.8.1918 (31)

Far away
from the land of the wattle
he lies in a hero's grave

Private F. W. Thornton, 11th Battalion 25.2.1917 (23)

Fond memories cling
to our loved one
true son of Australia

The Simple Truth

Some next-of-kin took the opportunity that epitaph-writing gave them to be descriptive about their soldier and in so doing many addressed him personally. 'Dear Birt, we miss you', wrote the parents of Private A. V. Ross, 33rd Battalion. He was killed on 9 March 1917 and is buried at Trois Arbres, on the French-Belgian border. This form of epitaph is more resigned, less bitter, more matter-of-fact, less consciously striving for expression. It is easy to see the writers of an epitaph of this nature sitting at a table in Australia and saying 'Well, nothing we can say will bring Ned back. What will we say about him?'

Private O. B. Price, 42nd Battalion 8.8.1918

Faithful son
and faithful friend
soldier faithful to the end

Corporal E. Slater, 17th Battalion 14.5.1918

A loving son
noble and true
ended his life
as he lived it through

Private V. S. Burns, 57th Battalion 17.8.1918 (23)

In fond memory
of my hero laddie

Sergeant J. E. Smeeton, 22nd Battalion 14.5.1918 (23)

Our dear Jack
in the dawn
of splendid manhood

Private J. J. Cundill, 45th Battalion 19.9.1918 (25)

To the sacred memory
of our dear son

Private T. R. Wallace, 5th Battalion 23.9.1918 (21)

One who never
turned his back
but marched breast forward
Mother

Lance-Corporal S. J. A. Sawyers, 52nd Battalion 7.9.1916 (21)

Bright intelligent lad
was respected and loved by
all his regiment

(Corporal Sawyers' next-of-kin were quoting from a letter received from his battalion after his death.)

Private T. H. Burrows, 7th Battalion 24.8.1918 (24)

Dear Tom
you gave your life for us
that we may be free
Peace

Lieutenant G. Simpson, 6th Battalion 23.8.1918 (26)

Yours for ever
in utter surety of love
Mother, Father and Jack

Private J. S. Reid, Army Medical Corps 31.8.1916 (26)

It's jist oor Jeems
but he'll never be forgotten

Private J. Kirkby, 3rd Battalion 3.5.1917 (26)

Sleep on dear boy
and take
Your much needed rest
Mum, Dad, Brothers

Gunner W. H. Ratcliff, Field Artillery 10.2.1918 (19)

The sun has set
my beloved
I await the dawn
and thee

Lance-Corporal G. D. Wilson, 8th Battalion 29.6.1916 (19)

In memory of our
beloved soldier
He died that we might live

Private E. Palk, 9th Battalion 19.7.1918 (25)

Goodbye and God rest you
dear Ern and Sid
Till we meet again

Private L. J. Knight, 30th Battalion 4.10.1917 (31)

A brave and noble soldier
A better husband never could be

Corporal S. B. Murphy, 37th Battalion 5.10.1917 (41)

A man who in all things
gave his best

Corporal G. W. Reilly, 26th Battalion 8.8.1918 (33)

Sleep son beneath
The soldier's ragged cross
your duty nobly done

Private W. Tyson, 41st Battalion 4.4.1918 (34)

He was born a soldier
to meet his death
as a brave soldier

Captain H. E. S. Armitage, 50th Battalion 3.4.1917 (22)

A loving son
a devoted officer
a soldier and a man

Private C. E. Kirkness, 6th Battalion 17.4.1917 (27)

Dear Charlie
though lost to sight
to memory ever dear
Mother

Private E. H. Leake, 3rd Pioneer Battalion 7.7.1917 (48)

A gentleman at rest,
best of fathers
and best of friends

Private T. A. Byrnes, 47th Battalion 7.7.1917 (27)

The whitest of them all
my son

Private W. H. Coulter, 56th Battalion 20.7.1916 (23)

We are thinking of you
today dear Wal,
we are thinking of the past

Private G. E. Mitchell, 7th Battalion 4.10.1917 (19)

The bravest lad
God ever made
Deeply mourned
our hero

Corporal H. G. Spencer, Machine-Gun Corps 6.10.1917 (21)

Our hero Herb
loved in life
honoured in death
treasured in memory

Lieutenant T. B. Keillor MC & Bar, 28th Battalion 3.10.1918 (29)

Remembered
by those who knew him
for his unselfishness
and integrity

Private W. H. Moore, 39th Battalion 10.9.1918 (25)

Deeply loved deeply mourned
Youngest of
Four soldier brothers

Sergeant A. F. Bath, 22nd Battalion 5.8.1916 (25)

Tall, eager
a face to remember
a spirit
that brightened our home

Private A. Walker, 45th Battalion 29.9.1917 (24)

He never spoke
of what he did
but kept it to himself
R.I.P.

Private J. Boyd, 26th Battalion 14.11.1916 (24)

He forgot himself
whenever he could be
of use to others

Corporal A. H. Buckley VC, 54th Battalion 1.9.1918 (27)

Dearly loved and sadly missed
by his parents
sister and brothers

Private Robert Mactier VC, 23rd Battalion 1.9.1918 (28)

His memory
will always live
in the hearts of
those who knew him best

Lieutenant S. Rosenthal, 58th Battalion 25.9.1917 (35)

In loving memory
of my darling daddy
who died for us
Jean

Gunner L. M. Hayes, Field Artillery 3.11.1916 (27)

One of the best,
loving husband of Florrie
and daddie of little Edna

King and Country, Sacrifice, Duty, Honour and Patriotism

At the time of the Great War the concept of loyalty to king and country, to the point of dying for either or both, was very strong. At the end of the 20th century, in a more cynical, materialistic age, many people might see such an attitude as a mere pose. In fact, it was strongly held. Honour and duty required many a man to go to war and risk his life for the flag and what it represented. The official recruiters knew all about the emotions of duty and honour and they exploited both in their often unscrupulous efforts to induce young men to join the colours. Many Australian soldiers of that era were more conscious of fighting for Britain and the empire than for Australia. Nevertheless, I was startled when I first came across the grave of Private E. G. Raybould, 28th Battalion, who was killed on the Somme on 4 August 1916. A Pozières casualty, he is buried in Serre Road No. 2 cemetery and his epitaph reads:

There is a spot
forever England's

His family were quoting from Rupert Brooke's famous poem and England, sacrificially at least, meant more to them than Australia did.

Private C. F. Barnard, 18th Battalion 1.8.1918 (20)

Father and brothers
are proud of you dear Charlie
doing your duty

Lieutenant W. F. Clarke MC, 55th Battalion 17.4.1918 (26)

He chose the path of duty
which led to glory

Sergeant L. W. McNamara MM, Engineers 18.9.1918 (31)

He died as he had lived
faithful to duty
and true to his ideals

Private L. V. R. Womersley, 7th Battalion 23.8.1918 (21)

He never shunned
his country's call
but gladly gave his life

Sergeant C. S. Garland, 30th Battalion 19.7.1916 (30)

There was his duty
to be done
and he did it

Bombardier F. McDonnell, Field Artillery 19.4.1917 (34)

Honour the fallen brave
flag, flower and tree

Private A. N. Moore, 49th Battalion 12.4.1917 (22)

Proud of thee dear son
for answering
Your king and country's call

Lance-Corporal A. Burch, 55th Battalion 15.5.1917 (37)

Noble and grand he fell
for Britain and her allies
God rest his soul

Private G. W. Buckridge, 17th Battalion 15.4.1917 (21)

He served
that we might safely stay
and dying was his fee

Private H. V. Dogral, 24th Battalion 27.7.1916 (27)

Fighting
for home and country
he like a hero fell

Sapper S. L. Bruth, Engineers 29.6.1916 (23)

I gave my life
for my God
my king and country
farewell loved ones

Private V. A. Camps, 30th Battalion 20.7.1916 (26)

He heard the call
he gave it heed
and now he sleeps
in Flanders

Private F. S. Pearce, 32nd Battalion 19.7.1916 (26)

His country called
and honour bade him go

Lance-Corporal A. S. Boyd, 34th Battalion 7.5.1918

We should not weep,
for such as he
will live in Britain's memory

Private C. T. Comben, 44th Battalion 4.7.1918 (29)

May we prove worthy
of his noble sacrifice

Private P. J. Gore, 50th Battalion 25.4.1918 (24)

His brave young life he gave
that Britons still might live

Private B. Clapham, 34th Battalion 21.7.1917 (22)

He shouldered his gun
in honour's cause
and in the battle died
Thy will be done

Private J. M. O'Brien, Machine-Gun Corps 20.9.1917 (47)

Honour with duty done
may God grant you
eternal happiness dear

Sapper J. Mackinnon, Australian Engineers 20.9.1917 (40)

Died for his country

Private Cleve Milne, Machine-Gun Corps 17.10.1917 (20)

For faith for liberty
for truth
he offered up
his stalwart youth

Lance-Corporal E. A. Hallow, Army Medical Corps 8.8.1918 (24)

In memory
of our dearly beloved son
who died for England's sake

Private C. O'Rourke, 31st Battalion 9.9.1918 (19)

In proud and loving memory
of our dauntless one
who fell to defend us

Private E. E. Leonard, 49th Battalion 5.4.1918

'A Hero'
He answered
his country's call
fighting to save us all

CSM A. Harvey, 49th Battalion 4.9.1916 (32)

He fell for
the honour of his race
and those he loved

Lance-Corporal F. F. Bevan, 43rd Battalion 31.6.1917 (20)

A great sacrifice
has my son made.
He gave his life
our flag to save

Sergeant S. R. Green, 5th Battalion 31.10.1916 (19)

Ready to do whatever
my God and the king
shall appoint

Private F. Whiston, 50th Battalion 21.7.1916 (26)

Neath a storm
of shot and shell
fighting for the flag
he fell

(Private Whiston died of wounds received at Fromelles, where there was certainly a storm of shot and shell.)

Lieutenant E. M. Hillman, 2nd Battalion 18.9.1918 (22)

He gave his life
that you might live

The Purely Eloquent

Some next-of-kin show in their epitaphs that they had a feeling for language. They express themselves with rich though not extravagant sentiment and sometimes they are poetic, though in a uniquely personal way. In this category I place one of my favourite epitaphs. It is for Sergeant K. W. Vear, 37th Battalion, who was killed on 3 October 1917 at the age of 25. He is buried in White House Cemetery, Ypres

Good old Ken,
a man's man

No apparent mourning here, just an understanding of Ken and how he would like to be remembered. In the conventional sense it is not poetic and yet the sentiment has the temper of poetry. It is magnificently Australian, magnificently Digger. I know of no similar epitaph to this one, which was written by Ken's parents, Frederick and Gertrude of Healesville, Victoria. I wish I had known them — and Ken.

Other epitaphs in this section are more eloquent and more moving. I think that all would be appreciated by the soldier for whom they were written.

Sergeant J. P. Perry, 18th Battalion 19.5.1918 (23)

Gone west in all the glory
of the setting sun
Thy will be done

Private D. R. W. Porton, 46th Battalion 17.9.1918 (34)

In loving memory
To a beautiful life
came a peaceful end

Gunner A. G. Pratt, Heavy Artillery 10.11.1916 (32)

The last post has sounded
you have laid aside your gun.
Called home

Private N. R. McLeod, 3rd Battalion 11.11.1916 (34)

We shall know
each other better
when the mists
have rolled away

Private C. R. Stevenson MM, Army Medical Corps 10.7.1918 (24)

Peace came and shut
the door for evermore
against pain and sorrow

Lance-Corporal G. E. Pape, 54th Battalion 25.7.1918

Beyond earth's
farthest hills he fares
song-crowned immortal

Driver G. H. Pickett, Engineers 20.12.1916 (33)

My first pride my first joy
my darling soldier boy.
Mother

Private F. Hampton, 43rd Battalion 3.7.1917 (32)

The hours I've spent
with thee dear heart
are as a string of
pearls to me

(This lovely message came from Hampton's wife Eleanor, of Carnegie Library, Milland Junction, WA.)

Gunner F. M. Juster, Field Artillery 16.7.1917

He did but do his duty
simply bravely
and in the doing died

Lieutenant E. Cruickshank, 10th Battalion 25.12.1917 (23)

His manhood faultless
his honour clean

Private C. H. Howell, 23rd Battalion 23.4.1918 (23)

His life's short journey o'er
given for freedom and home
Gran's boy

Private E. T. Farris, 28th Battalion 19.5.1918 (20)

The dedication of a man's life
and mind to a cause —
there's heroism.

Private J. A. P. Scott (served as W. Jamieson), 54th Battalion 24.7.1918

He sleeps with
the noble dead
who signed the charter
of our freedom

Private W. C. Durrant, 25th Battalion 17.7.1918 (40)

He heard the distant cooee
of his mates across the sea

Private A. E. Lane, Machine-Gun Corps 11.8.1918 (26)

A mate
in good times and bad

Private A. S. Plummer 51st Battalion 14.10.1917 (20)

On the banks of West Tamar
we parted
In heaven we hope
to meet again

Seeking Solace

Next-of-kin were not required to write epitaphs for their soldier's headstones until the early 1920s, when the enormous task of changing the rough battlefield crosses for marble markers was in progress. They had had two or three years, at least, to come to terms with their loss and in this time many had found a form of solace, some reflection or outlook which enabled them to see their soldier's death in the perspective which comes with the passing of time. If they felt any anger or bitterness these people did not express it. A supremely simple form of rationalisation is shown in the epitaph provided by the family of Gunner W. J. Dalton, Australian Heavy Artillery, killed on the Somme on 1 January 1917 at the age of 22.

Finished his work
and gained his glory

Lance-Corporal J. W. Moyle, 44th Battalion 5.7.1918 (31)

Our loss
but his eternal gain

Private R. C. McKeon, 56th Battalion 8.4.1918 (25)

Sunshine passes, shadows fall
loving remembrance
outlasts all
RIP

Private P. R. Pakes, 3rd Battalion 18.9.1918 (19)

Farewell my dear Reg
we are only parted
for a little while
Mum and you

Private A. E. Gore, 13th Battalion 19.9.1918 (31)

Happy he lies and at rest
after duty nobly done

Private H. R. Andrew, 16th Battalion 19.9.1918 (29)

It is enough
earth's struggle
soon shall cease
then perfect peace

Captain W. G. Boys, 25th Battalion 5.8.1916 (26)

One less at home
one more in heaven
his duty nobly done

Lance-Corporal H. A. G. Kent, 14th Battalion 31.5.1918

'Till the roll
is called in heaven lad
you may well take your rest

Private K. D. Hyam, 18th Battalion 17.8.1916, a Jewish soldier

Take comfort
ye who mourn a loved one
lost upon the battlefield

Driver I. E. Ferrier, Machine-Gun Corps 22.3.1918 (24)

He fought a good fight
he ran a straight race
he earned his reward

Private R. Bennett, 23rd Battalion 5.10.1917 (23)

The sweetest flowers
are gathered first.
Loving wife and mother

Private J. T. Holroyd, 22nd Battalion 16.9.1917 (37)

Too far away
thy grave to see
but not too far
to think of thee

(This inscription is so frequently found that it may have been one of the standard epitaphs suggested by CWGC.)

Private A. J. Hart, 13th Battalion 8.6.1917 (27)

Honour defied death
love despised it
memory venerates it

Gunner C.A. Coombes, Field Artillery 13.5.1917 (24)

He is just away
he has wandered
into an unknown land

Sergeant E. T. Foord, 19th Battalion 15.4.1917 (20)

Out of the stress
of the doing
Into the peace of the done

Private A. R. Trevena, 46th Battalion 8.7.1916

His message
God makes no mistakes
I am willing to abide
His will

Private A. J. Healey, 50th Battalion 4.7.1918 (25)

'Lost'!
How can such lives be lost.
Just gathered up
jewels rare of cost!

Private D. N. Peters, 43rd Battalion 26.8.1918 (27)

He died a hero brave
his resting place a soldier's grave
Gone but not forgotten

Private G. A. Connor, 39th Battalion 26.4.1918 (29)

In the soldier's home
in glory
there remains a land of rest

A Few Well-Chosen Words

More Australians chose brief epitaphs for their Digger son then any other type. Perhaps this says something about Australian directness or an individual belief that in the face of such enormity of loss a few words can mean more than several sentences. It could be — though I do not want to believe it — that some families could not afford the cost of 3½ pence for each engraved letter of their last message.

It is very likely that some widows and parents could not bear the anguish of writing epitaph after epitaph until they found one that satisfied them and so settled for the few words which expressed everything. What more would Private J. G. Forgie of Australian Trench-Mortar Battery expect than 'My beloved', especially in the beautiful cemetery at Etaples, France, overlooking the English Channel.

Private H. J. Gibb, 14th Battalion 7.6.1918 (45)

Peace after strife

Private J. G. Jacob, 50th Battalion 7.7.1918 (22)

Also in memory of his brother
Private G. W. Jacob, 50th Battalion 25.9.1917

Gunner J. L Lawrence, Field Artillery 7.10.1918 (43)

He served his fellow man

Sergeant Percival Blick, 44th Battalion 29.9.1918 (25)

It is well

Lieutenant F. W. Appleton, 14th Battalion 8.8.1918 (36)

He gave for us

Private A. G. Ray, 14th Battalion 31.5.1918 (29)

Evening shadows fall

Private S. E. Beverley, 14th Battalion 31.5.1918

Faithful to God
to duty and to love

Second Lieutenant H. V. Swain, 47th Battalion 7.8.1916 (21)

Life is service

Second Lieutenant M. E. Kozminsky, 7th Battalion 19.8.1916

A soldier and a gentleman

Private S. N. Kingham, 34th Battalion 24.2.1917 (19)

A Christian soldier

Sergeant S. Atkinson, 26th Battalion 7.10.1917 (30)

A hero

Private H. Nock, 40th Battalion 7.6.1917 (18)

He died a man

Gunner G. S. Smith, Field Artillery 31.3.1917 (20)

Only a youth
with a loyal heart

Private L. Edgar, 50th Battalion 2.4.1917 (24)

Tired of war and fell asleep

Sergeant G. Kirkpatrick MM, 17th Battalion 15.4.1917 (24)

He did what he could

Private E. Tootell, Trench-Mortar Battery 24.4.1918 (21)

My darling Ned

Brigadier-General D. J. Glasfurd, 12th Infantry Brigade 12.11.1916 (43)

A brave man
and a gallant soldier

Private H. L. Lander, 56th Battalion 5.12.1916 (22)

He gave his life for another
a brave stretcher bearer

Private J. G. Trezise, 28th Battalion 1.1.1918

One of
the deathless army

Private W. R. Jackway, 21st Battalion 15.6.1918 (21)

Deeply regretted

Corporal E. Gladstone, 58th Battalion 2.9.1918 (20)

Upright brave unselfish

Private J. R. Purcell, 22nd Battalion 3.5.1917 (20)

Sweet rest after victory

Private F. G. King, 59th Battalion 27.3.1917 (18)

Though so young
he did his best

Private A. S. Thom, 47th Battalion 12.10.1917 (33)

The piper's played
the gathering of the clans

Corporal J. R. Bishop, 30th Battalion 30.9.1917 (24)

My beloved son

Private A. J. Lane, 60th Battalion 25.4.1918 (21)

Boys ye fought
as heroes fight
and died as men

Corporal J. R. Allan DCM, 19th Battalion 3.10.1918 (41)

Fought bravely
died honourably

CSM G. C. Brodie MM, Australian Engineers 26.8.1918 (25)

A son a soldier a man

Private J. M. Gregory, 57th Battalion 13.4.1918

Beautifully sleeping

Gunner W. H. Brown, Field Artillery 20.4.1918 (19)

Go forward

Private N. Kay, 45th Battalion 5.4.1918

His last post

Private C. R. Quelch, Machine-Gun Corps 18.9.1918 (23)

His life for ones he loved

Profound Despair

Those epitaphs which express deep despair and sense of loss are perhaps the most poignant of all. The soldier's widow or parents have, understandably, not sought to conceal their grief or their terrible apprehension that life will never again be worth living. The epitaphs of most bachelor Diggers appear to have been written by mothers, as some of these examples show. A few were written by the children of a dead soldier.

Sergeant H. Woodnoth, 21st Battalion 1.8.1918 (29)

Gone
and the light
of all our life
gone with him

Private D. E. Arnold, 55th Battalion 16.4.1918 (20)

The ships came back
with honoured brave
but none came back
with our Dave

Sergeant R. W. Wigger, 22nd Battalion 5.8.1918 (30)

Also in memory
of Reg and Charles
killed on Gallipoli
My all. Mother

(Sergeant Wigger, who died of wounds and his brothers Reg and Charles, were the sons of Charles and Eliza Wigger, of Fitzroy, Victoria.)

Private H. Foster, 5th Pioneer Battalion 29.9.1918 (28)

In the midst of life
we were parted
RIP

Gunner T. Pentney, Field Artillery 12.9.1918 (39)

Only those
who have loved and lost
can understand
war's bitter cost

Private W. T. Menzies, 25th Battalion 1.9.1916 (36)

I thought not
when I cradled thee
in battle you'd fall
far from me

Private W. H. Hicks, 53rd Battalion 8.12.1916

My only child dies
the empire lives
a lonely mother mourns

Private E. G. Jeffries, 50th Battalion 2.4.1917 (28)

To love and then to part
is the saddest story
of the human heart

Private W. Lewis, 7th Battalion 25.3.1917

Somewhere in France
he is sleeping
the son I love so well

Private F. L. Sexton, 51st Battalion 2.4.1917 (23)

Oh why are we dead
we youth
all ye that pass by
forget not

Private W. R. Doughan, 55th Battalion 26.9.1917 (23)

A mother's part
is a broken heart
and a burden of
lonely years

Lance-Corporal Charles J. Mestrez, 1st Australian Tunnellers 25.9.1917 (35)

My joy-bringer gone
over the sun
a black cloud came
I am left alone

Lance-Corporal T. Stevenson, 30th Battalion 20.11.1917 (38)

He was the loved of all
yet none
o'er his grave may weep

Private W. R. Scott, 35th Battalion 27.7.1917 (25)

The midnight stars
are gleaming
on a grave I cannot see

Private H. Murdie, 18th Battalion 18.4.1917 (23)

No loved ones
stood around him
to bid him a last farewell

Lance-Corporal J. Gavin, 31st Battalion 19.7.1916 (30)

Though nothing
can the loss replace
a dear one
taken from our side

Private Nelson Sing, 26th Battalion 3.10.1918 (21)

Could I have just
raised his head
or said a fond farewell

Private W. J. Armstrong, 58th Battalion 15.10.1917

Oh memories
that bless and turn
oh barren gain
and bitter loss

Sergeant A. J. Skowronner, 19th Battalion 1.8.1916 (32)

Wondering if we
shall meet again
Lord Jesus pity me

Private H. W. Brown, 59th Battalion 6.3.1917 (23)

Dad's and Mum's darling
at rest

Private D. C. Thompson, 32nd Battalion 4.12.1916 (21)

The weed and the wild flower
creepeth around a lone
and silent bed

Gunner M. M. Isaacs (served as C. M. Jackson), Field Artillery 2.7.1918

When days are dark
and friends are few
my dear son
how I long for you

(This inscription has additional poignancy as the Issacs family were Jewish. Jews have always felt that they had few friends.)

Private J. W. Hendry, 20th Battalion 31.8.1918 (20)

A widow's only son
he was the loved of all

Private W. E. Redford, 28th Battalion 1.6.1918 (23)

In memory of
our only boy's
noble sacrifice

Gunner I. N. Flower, Field Artillery 20.9.1917 (27)

Would God
that I had died
for thee
my son, my son

Private J. Fagan, 29th Battalion 29.7.1918 (25)

Darling Jack
how I miss you
nobody knows but me
Mother

Private D. C. Thomas, 10th Battalion 20.8.1916 (32)

He carefully did his duty
what more could
our dear father do

Private H. T. Hammond, 48th Battalion 6.8.1916 (39)

A painful shock
a blow severe
to part with one
we loved so dear

By God's will and in His hands

A large number of epitaphs invoke God's name, either to explain the soldier's death on the ground that God's mysterious will has been done, or to express belief in a peaceful after life in 'God's home port'. Clearly, many families at home in Australia, after the great shock of hearing of their soldier's death, found some solace in their religious beliefs. *Thy will be done* is the most common of this type of epitaph.

Private R. Moyle, 44th Battalion 4.7.1918 (23)

His short race
On earth is run.
We weep but say
God's will be done

Lieutenant R. G. Henderson MC, 18th Battalion 9.4.1918 (25)

Ronald, born 5 July 1892,
pure and beautiful
God be thy portion, beloved

Private M.P. Higham, 51st Battalion 24.4.1918 (21)

Because I live
ye shall also live
John XIV. 19

Lance-Corporal D. J. Ferguson, 14th Battalion 15.5.1918 (22)

His trials and his griefs
are past
a blessed end is his at last

Lieutenant F. R. Johnson, 58th Battalion 29.9.1918 (35)

Shall not the Lord
of all the world do right

Private A. Prout, 42nd Battalion 26.8.1918 (22)

Then the gods pitied him
and took him to their midst

Private D. P. Arrow, 22nd Battalion 14.5.1918 (37)

Father remember him
when You sit on Your throne

Sergeant E. D. Davison, 32nd Battalion 29.9.1918 (26)

A loving and lovable
boy and man
now safe
with the God he served

Private N. McLeod, 14th Battalion 31.5.1918

Nothing in my hand
I bring
simply to the cross
I cling

Private Edward Covey, 3rd Battalion 2.7.1916

Dead did you say:
Nay, only heaven sped
Just safe in God's home port

Private F. W. Walker, 2nd Pioneer Battalion 29.10.1917 (29)

Thy purpose Lord we
cannot see
But all is well
that's done by thee

Private H. W. Pettit, 24th Battalion 6.10.1917 (32)

One of the best
that God could send
beloved by all

Private F. W. Olsen, 47th Battalion 12.10.1917 (31)

He rests
for our freedom and liberty
in God's hands,
a Christian hero

Lance-Corporal F. W. Mawson, Engineers 9.11.1917

Till He come

Private D. McDougall, 18th Battalion 5.11.1917 (23)

It was hard to give thee
up but Thy will O God be done

Private A. L. Weddon, 9th Battalion 7.5.1917 (31)

With Christ,
which is far better

Private J. T. R. Easton, 14th Battalion 4.7.1916 (25)

Our Roy
approved unto God
a workman that needeth not
to be ashamed

Private F. Beardsley, 35th Battalion 7.4.1918 (20)

Thy will be done

(Private Beardsley's headstone carries no engraved Christian cross, indicating that on his enlistment papers he claimed no religious affiliation. His next-of-kin either did not know of this or invoked the Deity on his own behalf.)

Private W. Davis, 26th Battalion 29.8.1916 (20)

I hope to see my pilot
face to face
when I have crossed the bar.
Resurgam

Lance-Corporal W. Hartley, 17th Battalion 6.11.1916 (21)

In loving memory
of only son of W. E. Hartley
God knows best

Emphasising Identity

A surprising number of next-of-kin put their own names on the headstone, indirectly stressing the family relationship and bond. They may have been considering posterity and wanting people to know more about the dead soldier as they pass the grave in the centuries ahead.

Private M. A. Betts, 37th Battalion 12.10.1917 (22)

In memory
of the beloved son
of T & M Betts
Wallaroo Mines

The brothers W. A. Clayton, 42, and E.C. Clayton, 29, both of the 52nd Battalion, were killed on 12 April and are buried side by side. Each headstone carries the same inscription:

Beloved son
of Mr & Mrs J. Clayton senr.
of Dover, Tasmania

Private C. Keenan, 16th Battalion 11.4.1917 (19)

Sacred to memory.
Second son of the late
Dr Alfred Keenan of Sydney

Second Lieutenant F. P. Callinan, Field Artillery 6.5.1917 (22)

Dear brother of
Captain Laurence Hurley Callinan
buried at Rouen

Private H. W. Wilson, 32nd Battalion 2.12.1916 (20)

Beloved son
of Geo and A Wilson
Williamstown, S Australia
Duty done

Literature and language

Some next-of-kin found themselves better able to express themselves in Latin or some other language or in quotations from literature. They may have been saying something about their soldier's standard of education — or their own. Or they may have found everyday English inadequate to meet their emotional or intellectual needs. It is difficult to imagine a more appropriate epitaph than that for Captain Clarence Smith Jeffries VC, aged 23. From the 34th Battalion, Captain Jeffries was killed on 12 October 1917 and is buried in Tyne Cot Cemetery, Ypres Salient.

On fame's eternal camping ground
their silent tents are spread

Fame he had won with the award of the Victoria Cross, the camping ground military metaphor is fitting and the 'tents' of Jeffries and his AIF mates are certainly silent. The thinking behind other quotations is much less obvious, except perhaps for that on the grave of Lieutenant A. R. Allan, 40th Battalion, in Bailleul Communal Cemetery Extension, French Flanders:

Dulce et decorum est pro patria mori.

Allan was a member of the 40th Battalion and was killed on 10 January 1917 at the age of 22. Wilfred Owen, the finest of war poets, called 'Dulce et decorum est pro patrie mori' (How sweet it is to die for your country) 'the old lie.'

Gunner M.D'E. Brady, Field Artillery 15.8.1917 (19)

Beloved son of F. L. Brady
West Australia
Munere perfunctus

Sapper G. M. Berry, Engineers 4.10.1917 (22)

He was a veray
parfit gentil knight

Private A. McCrimmon, 1st Battalion 16.9.1917 (46)

Cha till e gu brath
gu la na cruinne

Captain B. H. Mack, Army Medical Corps 10.4.1917 (24)

Ante diem per iit
sed miles sed pro patria

Lance-Corporal G. M. Wyeth, 22nd Battalion 23.6.1916

Mizpah

Private C. H. Winter, 32nd Battalion 19.7.1916 (28)

When could a man die better
than facing fearful odds

Lance-Corporal F. H. Dealy, 43rd Battalion 26.8.1918 (23)

Quant je puis

Private C. G. Salmon, 40th Battalion 28.3.1918 (29)

'I shall go to him
but he shall not return
to me.' II Sam 12.23

Driver R. B. Cochrane, Field Artillery 3.8.1916 (26)

Agnus dei
out tollis peccata mundi
dona fis requiem

Gunner A. A. Munro, Field Artillery 14.9.1918 (37)

'That man to man —
Wad brithers be far a' that'

Private Carl Sundowist, 40th Battalion 31.8.1918 (31)

'Frid vare med dig'

Captain J. H. Tillett, Army Medical Corps 2.10.1917 (23)

Aioih Sciebat

Captain H. Burke MC, 5th Battalion 23.8.1918 (23)

Soldat sans peur
et sans reproche
tombe sur le champ d'honneur

(The French inscription is appropriate since Captain Burke is buried in a French military cemetery at Cerisy-Gailly, Somme).

Private C. L. Fuller, 57th Battalion 1.10.1918 (36)

Theirs not to make reply
theirs but to do and die.

Travellers will find many appealing and interesting inscriptions for themselves. Never miss an opportunity to visit a military cemetery.

Chapter 18

Further Significant Cemeteries where Australians are Buried

Namps-au-Val British Cemetery

When the German offensive in Picardy began at the end of March 1918, various Casualty Clearing Stations were set up to the rear of Amiens, the city which was one of the main targets of the enemy advance. The small village of Namps-au-Val is beside the railway line, which made it convenient for the wounded to be delivered to the CCS. Those buried at Namps-au-Val also included men who had not passed through a CCS. One of these was Private Charles Lawson McLellan, aged 28, of the 50th Battalion.

Charles McLellan, from Goodwood, South Australia, is shown in the cemetery register as having 'died of accidental injuries'. This is only technically true. The diary of Private H.J. Moody has this cryptic entry for 11 April 1918: 'Charlie McLellan shot by MPs in Corbie'. The comment by Moody, who was Charlie's mate, might lead some people to suppose that he had been executed following a court martial.

I believe that a party of Diggers, carrying their rifles, had a few too many drinks in the town, and that when they became rowdy a patrol of MPs cautioned them. The Diggers always reacted badly to British MPs or 'Jacks' and on this occasion one of the Diggers made a move with his rifle which an MP regarded as threatening. He aimed his pistol at the Australian and fired, accidentally hitting and killing Charlie McLellan. My supposition is that Charlie himself was sober and in control of himself, but I cannot verify this because under the rules of the Central Army Records Office, a soldier's records can only be released to next-of-kin. Whatever the details of the accident, Charlie was unlucky and I think his story should be told.

Whenever I travel between Amiens and Rouen I visit his grave and I suggest to other Australians that they might do so. Among the other fifty-six Diggers in the cemetery is Lieut-Colonel David McFie, CMG, DSO, who was CO of the 55th Battalion and killed on 29 March 1918.

Directions
The cemetery is easily found near the railway station of Namps-Quevaufillers, 0.5 kilometre south-west of Amiens on the Rouen road.

Cite Bonjean Military Cemetery

In an industrial suburb of the city of Armentières, Cite Bonjean was begun by the British Army in October 1914. On the edge of lowland Flanders where much fighting took place, it was used by many units. It has 2 131 war graves and of these 473 are Australian and 453 from New Zealand. Nearly all the Australians in Cite Bonjean fell in the winter of 1916–17 and almost without exception were from the Third Division.

The Third was the last of the AIF's divisions to reach the front and during that winter its battalions were trained in 'the Nursery', where the other divisions had been trained before them, mostly in raiding activity. The Third's machine-gunners, pioneers and gunners are also all too well represented.

The most striking feature of Cite Bonjean is the large number of Australian casualties aged 19 and 20—scores of them. I know of no other cemetery with such a large proportion of very young men. For that reason alone it is worth visiting.

Two burials of not so young soldiers are noteworthy. One is Lieut Colonel James Simpson MC, CO of the 36th Battalion, killed in action on 21 January 1917, at the age of 33 (Grave IV.D.47). The other is Major Andrew Honman, 9th Field Ambulance, a highly regarded surgeon (Grave VI.A.26).

This cemetery has a New Zealand memorial bearing the names of 48 officers and men lost in the Armentières sector who have no known grave. Three other soldiers buried without a name are known to be Australian.

On 11 April 1918 the Germans, in their overwhelming advance, swept over Armentières, and with it, the Cite Bonjean cemetery, and held it until the Allies recovered it on 3 October.

Directions

Armentières is a large place and is signposted as far away as Ieper (Ypres), Lille and at several exits on the Dunkirk-Lille-Paris motorway. Head for the railway station, which is also well signposted (La Gare). Cite Bonjean cemetery is 0.5 kilometre west on the north of the railway line and in sight of it.

Vignacourt British Cemetery

The burials in this cemetery reflect the fierce, almost desperate, fighting of the AIF on the Amiens front following the German advance in March–April 1918. Of the 581 graves, 423 are Australians. They were buried mainly by the 20th and 61st CCS. The cemetery garden contains a French monument unveiled in August 1921. It shows a French soldier on a base which bears the words: 'Frères d'armes de l'Armée Britannique, tombés au Champ d'Honneur, dormez en paix. Nous veillons sur vous.' ('Brothers in arms of the British Army, fallen on the field of honor, sleep in peace; we are watching over you.')

Certainly the cemetery does contain 146 British soldiers, but the inscription should also mention the Australian Army. That it does not do so is an indication of how, at that time, the armies from the dominions and colonies were considered to be integral parts of the British Army. We might be exasperated by this attitude today but the French meant no offence.

The best known AIF soldier in Vignacourt cemetery is Captain George Meysey Hammond MC, MM, of the 28th Battalion, who had been born in Britain. Hammond, though only 25 at the time of his death, had the manner and authority of a much older man. He had risen from the ranks and been decorated with the MM and the MC, and his courage commanded respect. His left arm had been paralysed by a wound received at Flers in November 1916 and he carried it permanently in a sling. His superiors considered him important enough to allow him to take part in the battle of Broodseinde in 1917. Seriously wounded at Morlancourt on 10 June, he was carried out of the action. As the stretcher bearers took him past battalion HQ, Hammond said to his colonel, 'Keep the old flag flying sir.' He died of wounds on 14 June, not 20 May as shown in the cemetery register (Grave III.C.17).

Vignacourt was a major HQ for the RFC/RFA and the Royal Australian Flying Corps in 1918 and the military cemetery became the burial place of probably more Australian fliers than any other cemetery on the Western Front. Seven of them are buried here. They are: Lieut George Best, Lieut William Buckland, Lieut Sydney Jones, Lieut Stanley Loram, Captain Henry Ralfe, Lieut Albert Taylor and Lieut Arthur Brook, all of No 3 Squadron, and all killed in the spring or summer of 1918.

Many of the AIF men in this cemetery were decorated veterans, including a score of officers. The grave of Corporal Ernest Bailey of the Australian Salvage Corps is a reminder that this little known but busy unit faced serious dangers without actually fighting the enemy on the front line. Bailey, aged 32, died of accidental injuries on 17 May 1918, possibly when a fired but unexploded enemy shell blew up as he was salvaging it (Grave II.D.15).

Directions

Vignacourt cemetery is easily reached from the Amiens–Flesselles road. It is just south of Vignacourt railway station, close to the railway line and the road to Flesselles.

Frechencourt Communal Cemetery

The military section of Frechencourt village cemetery is one of many that I wish could have been given an appropriate name of its own. That name would be 'Australian Gunners Cemetery'. Of the 57 graves, 49 are Australian and of those all but one are artillery-men. Most fell near where they now lie, for the village is on a wooded hill at one end of the settlement. From this vantage point various AIF batteries were in action towards the south and east and were in turn targeted by German counter-battery fire. Ten of the gunners were killed on 5 April 1918 and almost as many on 24 April, when they were supporting AIF infantry fighting at Villers Bretonneux.

Captain Archibald Martin of 11th Bde AFA was one of those killed on 5 April. The lone infantryman is Lieut Herbert McBean, 40th Battalion, of Scottsdale, Tasmania. He was killed on 9 May 1918 and just why he was not buried closer to the front where his battalion was serving is puzzling.

Directions

Frechencourt, a pretty one-street village, is nestled in the valley of the Hallue River and is only 3 kilometres north of Querrieu on the main Amiens-Albert road. The cemetery is considered too small to have a register and visitors' book of its own. A few older villagers have fond memories of Australians. It is easy to find the old people to talk to because they frequently tend graves in the communal part of the cemetery.

Crouy-sur-Somme British Cemetery

This is another 'died of wounds' cemetery established close behind the lines on the Amiens front. Of the 739 British and Dominion burials, 275 are Australian and nearly all of them fell mortally wounded between April and August 1918. The 5th and 47th CCS, like so many other CCSs, were posted along the railway from Amiens to Abbeville and it was they who used Crouy cemetery.

Two captains are the senior officers, Joseph Gard of 11th Brigade HQ (Grave IV.D.1) and Albert Mitchell MC, 4th Bn Machine Gun Corps. Notable among the NCOs is CQMS Alfred Taylor MSM, of the 44th Battalion. At the age of 38, Taylor is also one of the oldest men in the cemetery. A lone Light Horseman, Trooper John Whitehead of 13 ALH Regiment, rests in this cemetery (Grave III.A.10). Mortally wounded on 3 June 1918, Whitehead had been scouting for the infantry.

Directions

The village of Crouy lies between the Amiens-Abbeville main road and railway, both of which follow the course of the Somme River. The cemetery is on the road to Cavillon, 0.6 kilometre south of Cavillon itself.

Ebblinghem Military Cemetery

This cemetery is an interesting example of one 'taken over' by a single division, in this case the 1st Division AIF. When the German Army broke through the Allied lines in Flanders in April 1918, the 1st Division was thrown into the breach as a last attempt to block the offensive. The Australians succeeded. The graves at Ebblinghem, together with 266 of British servicemen, three from the Channel Islands and one from South Africa, are the result. Most of these soldiers died of wounds in the 2nd and 15th Casualty Clearing Stations. Of course, 1st Division men are also buried in many other cemeteries in the region.

One of the youngest AIF men killed on the Western Front lies in the Ebblinghem cemetery. He is Private Gerald Heavey, 1st Battalion, who was 17 when he died of wounds on 17 April 1918. He was the son of Andrew and Teresa Heavey of Minnahaha Road, Katoomba, NSW, who stressed his Irish lineage in the epitaph they supplied for his headstone. It reads: 'Great grand-nephew to Michael Dwyer, the famous Wicklow chieftain' (Grave I.C.19).

Another formidable Australian warrior with an Irish background was Regimental Sergeant Major William Edgar, DCM. Edgar, who had the army number of 10, was 43 years of age when he died of wounds on 28 May 1918. AIF unofficial history claims RSM Edgar as one of the finest RSMs of the AIF (Grave II.C.31).

The most senior Digger is Major Herbert Gould of 1st Division Engineers, who died of wounds on 8 May at the age of 31. Major Gould had been reconnoitring Lys River crossings when hit (Grave I.E.31). An 18-year-old, Private Turner Turner, 4th Battalion, lies in II.C.37. There are three 19-year-olds: Private Victor Needham, 4th Battalion, of Redfern, NSW, died of wounds on 10 June; Private Leonard Riches, 10th Battalion, of Peake Post Office, South Australia, died of wounds 25 April; and Private Harry Sinclair, 1st Battalion Machine Gun Corps, of Numerkah, Victoria, died of wounds on 12 June. The graves, respectively, are II.D.23, I.B.26 and II.D.24.

Directions

Ebblinghem is easily reached from either St Omer or Hazebrouck and is on the main road linking them, the N42. The cemetery is in an isolated position, 0.5 kilometre east of the village, on a plateau at the edge of a small wood.

Chapter 19

75th Anniversary Commemorations

In 1993 numerous events took place on the Western Front to coincide with the 75th anniversary of the end of the war. The Australian commemorative activities further established the Australian presence on the front.

One year earlier an Australian national memorial had been erected at Bullecourt. Built by the Department of Veterans Affairs, it was dedicated on Anzac Day 1992. On 24 April 1993—25 April, Anzac Day, would have clashed with French commemorations—a Digger figure was placed atop the base that had been erected the previous year. The sculptor, Peter Corlett, modelled his creation on his father, who had served at Bullecourt in 1917.

More casual in appearance than the Mont St Quentin Digger, Digger Corlett captures the cockiness of the AIF warrior. He looks carefree, as if he is going on leave rather than towards battle. Standing in the middle of the battlefield, on the edge of the sunken road that was so much a feature of the fighting, Digger Corlett is a fine mate for the Mont St Quentin soldier. He was unveiled by the Ambassador to France, Kim Hughes.

Commemorative Plaques

In August 1993 an Australian Commemorative Mission arrived in France to celebrate the 75th anniversary of the end of Australian war service there. It consisted of 13 veterans of the 1st AIF, a group of war widows, two junior Legatees, the Governor-General, Bill Hayden, the Minister for Veterans Affairs, Senator John Faulkner, Chief of the General Staff, Lieutenant General John Grey and numerous other dignitaries.

The mission's activities between 29 August and 3 September were organised around the unveiling of ten battlefield plaques, all of them sculpted by a Melbourne dentist, Dr Ross Bastiaan. Dr Bastiaan, aged 42 in 1993, had gained great admiration for the AIF through his friendship with Lawrence McCarthy VC. Two generations older than Ross, McCarthy encouraged the youth's interest in the AIF and lent him books about its many distant battlefields. 'McCarthy was my hero and inspiration', Ross told me. 'Without his memory the plaques would never have taken shape.' Before his great commitment to the Western Front, Bastiaan had braved bureaucratic entanglements to create and erect plaques to commemorate Australian service in Gallipoli, South East Asia and Papua New Guinea.

His Western Front plaques have a common central graphic representation of the entire area of conflict. Around this is an account of the operations on each battlefield. Presented in English and French (in France) and in English and Flemish (in Belgian Flanders), the texts are written for the layperson without military knowledge. Each plaque has been sponsored by a well-known company or organisation. Ross Bastiaan's attitude to his work is summed up by what he told me on the Somme battlefield: 'The plaques are a tribute to Australia and not to any division, battlefield or person. The value of the plaques can only be measured by those who take the time to read them. I hope that Australians will read and reflect; if so, my work is worthwhile.'

Sites of the plaques

Ypres (Ieper) On the ramparts above Menin Gate.

Passchendaele (Passendale) Outside the church in the town square.

Villers-Bretonneux In the town square near the Town Hall.

Villers-Bretonneux Australian National Memorial To the left of the flagpole.

Pozières Two plaques. At the windmill site on the Albert-Bapaume road and at the 1st Division's memorial.

Fromelles Close to VC Corner Australian Cemetery.

The Pozières windmill site plaque gives the visitor a remarkable amount of information. The sculpted relief map shows the area bounded by Arras to the north, St Quentin to the east and Amiens to the west.

The Bastiaan plaque at Bullecourt, with Digger Corlett in the background. The photograph was taken from the sunken road which runs across the battlefield.

Pirenne Laffin studies the plaque at Mont St Quentin, near Peronne. Her grandfather took part in the 20th Battalion's capture of this position.

Dr Ross Bastiaan with his personal tribute to Lieut Lawrence McCarthy VC. The plaque is displayed at Vermandovillers, east of Villers Bretonneux.

Bullecourt In the sunken road by the entrance to the Digger memorial.
Mont St Quentin To the rear of the 2nd Division's Digger, which is by the side of the N17 (shown on many maps as N37).
Peronne Near the Town Hall.
Messines This plaque, the eleventh, was unveiled in November 1993.

Ross Bastiaan presented a 'private' memorial plaque to the Mayor of Vermandovillers to commemorate Lawrence McCarthy's remarkable VC exploit near the settlement. It graces a wall in the hamlet.

Note: Some of the heavy concrete bases on which the plaques rest were misoriented, through some mishap, when set in the ground, so that the north arrow on the plaque does not actually point north. Be sure when visiting the plaques that you know where north really is. Do not blame the sculptor for the error.

Memorials to Come

A third Digger memorial in the general style of those at Mont St Quentin and Bullecourt will be erected at Fromelles during 1994–95. It will reflect the nature of the battle at Fromelles, which was a victory of the spirit rather than a victory of arms. The Fromelles Digger is likely to be placed close to VC Corner Australian Cemetery.

This leaves just one more important memorial—some form of AIF presence to be established at Le Hamel (or 'Hamel' as it is known in Australian military annals). For historical justice and for the sake of future generations the Hamel memorial needs to be a battlefield park or 'an acre of France', as Colonel Kevin O'Brien, former chief of the Australian Army's Training Command, calls it. For many years I have drawn attention to the need for an Australian battlefield memorial park of the kind that the Canadians are so proud of at Vimy Ridge, the South Africans at Delville Wood and the Newfoundlanders at Beaumont Hamel.

After World War I the Canadians, whose service on the Western Front was comparable to that of the Australians in achievement and sacrifice, obtained 240 acres on Vimy Ridge, where they erected their great memorial. They preserved a score of large mine craters, thousands of shell holes, lengths of trenches and several kilometres of tunnels. The Battlefield Memorial Park that resulted is one of the great attractions for the many visitors to the Western Front. It is managed by a resident warden who, in summer, directs up to 100 Canadian multilingual students who act as guides for visitors. Being a guide is considered a great honor and many students compete for the privilege.

The South Africans 'own' Delville Wood, where the South African Brigade was virtually wiped out in July 1916. In this great wood they not only have a fine memorial, built in the style of a Cape castle, but a modern museum. The resident warden is available to help visitors and the memorial is open throughout the year for the sale of books, souvenirs and refreshments.

Newfoundland, then a small but independent dominion, had so few men it could give only one regiment to the war effort. After the war its government secured as a memorial park the battlefield of Beaumont Hamel, where the Newfies made a desperate attack and were slaughtered almost to a man. A giant caribou atop a mound looks across the preserved trenches.

Australia has nothing comparable to these evocative and interesting parks. A number of interested people, including retired Major General Whitelaw and still-serving Colonel O'Brien urge the acquisition of an Australian 'acre of France'. The Prime Minister, Paul Keating, has approved the idea in principle and I hope that positive action will follow.

Le Hamel is the obvious place for these main reasons:

- Under General Monash, the AIF achieved one of the only two decisive British and Empire victories before August 1918.
- Hamel was the AIF's first battle on the Western Front fought totally under Australian planning and leadership.
- From the enemy positions captured here, the great offensive of 8 August 1918 began.
- I believe that trenches that I have found at Hamel are the only ones occupied by Australians that still exist on the Western Front.
- Hamel is ideally situated, being only 5 kilometres from Villers Bretonneux and the Australian National Memorial.
- The battle of Hamel set the pattern for the subsequent battles of 1918 that were to lead to the Allied victory.

A walking circuit of the battle of Hamel could begin in the hamlet (population 500) itself and take visitors, via a series of prominent markers with explanatory texts, from one battle feature to the next. Many of them are mentioned in my book—Pear Trench and Vaire Wood, for instance. The acre of France is available; the mayor of Hamel and the citizens are agreeable. The Australian Battlefield Memorial Park, under this or some similar name, will certainly be ready for visitors by 1995.

My mother, who was Sister Nellie Pike of the Australian Army Nursing Service before she changed her name by marrying my soldier father, Lieut. Charles Laffin, often spoke angrily about the AIF's massive casualties as the 'wicked waste of good men'. This book is my way of ensuring that other generations can follow in the steps of those good men and learn about their experience of war on the Western Front and the Australian spirit which sustained them.

John Laffin

Index